Inspire English International

Year 7 Student Book

David Grant

Overview contents

Detailed contents

Unit 1: Survival

Unit 2: Danger!

Detailed contents

Detailed contents

About the Student Book

Welcome to Inspire English International! We hope you will find this book useful (and inspiring!) as you develop your skill and knowledge in written English. Through explicitly addressing the areas needed to excel in this subject, you should gain mastery of the subject and make excellent progress.

This Student Book provides a clear structure to your learning. Each unit is based around a theme and uses a range of engaging texts to help you focus on the mastery of key skills. These skills are set out at the start of each unit, along with a clear explanation of what you will be able to do by the end of that unit.

Within each unit, the theme is broken down into sections designed to help you master those key skills in a clear learning progression. Activities and Boosts (covering skills, grammar, spelling and punctuation) all build towards your learning.

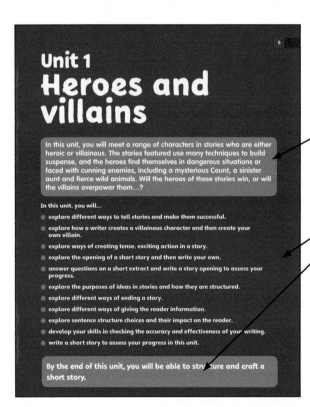

Each unit is based around a theme – at the start you will find a description of this theme and an idea of some of the texts you will explore.

Learning objectives are listed here, as well as a clear outcome – so that you understand what you will learn by following the unit.

Each section begins with an engaging text on the unit's theme.

Activities throughout each unit focus on key skills and help structure your learning.

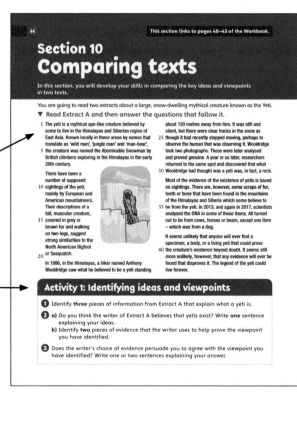

About the Student Book

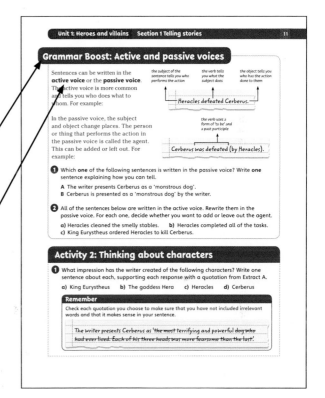

Section 11
Assessment

In this section, you will answer questions on two extracts to assess your progress in this unit.

Extract A is about a mythical water creature believed to live in Great Britain.

▼ Read Extract A and then answer the questions that follow it.

The History of the Loch Ness Monster

1 The Great Glen in the Scottish Highlands contains three famous lochs. The most famous of these is Loch Ness because of the monster said to 'lurk' in its deep waters. It is deeper than the North Sea and is
5 very long and very, very narrow, and has never been known to freeze.

There have been numerous sightings of the monster, affectionately known as 'Nessie'. The first recorded account is of an eyeball to eyeball confrontation with
10 the Irish saint Saint Columba in the 6th century. Saint Columba, so the story goes, ordered one of his monks to swim across the loch and fetch a boat. Halfway across, the monster appeared and rushed at the swimmer, roaring in a most frightening way! Columba
15 cried out to the monster, "Go no further, nor touch the man! Go back!" The monster is said to have fled!

1933 was the year when the first photograph was taken of the monster, or what is said to be the monster. It showed something with a long neck
20 arched over a thick body. This photograph, taken by a London surgeon, caused a sensation when first published in the Daily Mail.

The circus owner Bertram Mills offered a £20,000
25 reward (the equivalent of £2 million today) to anyone who could capture the monster for his circus, but so far no one has claimed the reward.

In 1951, Lachlan Stuart, a forestry worker who lived beside the loch, also managed to photograph the
30 monster, if that is indeed what it was. He saw three humps in the water appear in line and ran back to his house to get his camera. After taking one photograph his camera shutter jammed, but his photograph got wide publicity as further proof of the existence of Nessie.

35 Interest in Nessie became intense and over the years several scientific investigations have taken place. In 1961, the Loch Ness Phenomena Investigation Bureau was formed and even two submarines have been brought into the search, with sonar experts on board! When
40 the submarine Pisces was diving off Castle Urquhart, where the water is 950 feet (290 metres) deep, a vast underwater cavern was found. Was this Nessie's home?

Nessie provides us with an enduring mystery, and in the 21st century, where there is an explanation for
45 everything, it is pleasing to think that there are still mysteries like the Loch Ness Monster.

Activity 1: Reading Extract A

1 What do you think is the writer's opinion about Nessie's existence? Write **two or three** sentences explaining your answer.

2 a) What impression does the writer create of the sightings of the Loch Ness Monster?
   b) Make brief notes explaining how this impression is created. Consider the writer's choice of ideas, vocabulary and sentence structure.

> Assessment units help take the stress out of testing by giving you tools and structure and by walking you through the steps needed to produce outstanding answers every time.

Grammar Boost: Active and passive voices

Sentences can be written in the **active voice** or the **passive voice**. The active voice is more common and tells you who does what to whom. For example:

the subject of the sentence tells you who performs the action   *the verb tells you what the subject does*   *the object tells you who has the action done to them*

Heracles defeated Cerberus.

In the passive voice, the subject and object change places. The person or thing that performs the action in the passive voice is called the agent. This can be added or left out. For example:

the verb uses a form of 'to be' and a past participle

Cerberus was defeated (by Heracles).

1 Which **one** of the following sentences is written in the passive voice? Write **one** sentence explaining how you can tell.
   A The writer presents Cerberus as a 'monstrous dog'.
   B Cerberus is presented as a 'monstrous dog' by the writer.

2 All of the sentences below are written in the active voice. Rewrite them in the passive voice. For each one, decide whether you want to add or leave out the agent.
   a) Heracles cleaned the smelly stables.   b) Heracles completed all of the tasks.
   c) King Eurystheus ordered Heracles to kill Cerberus.

Activity 2: Thinking about characters

1 What impression has the writer created of the following characters? Write one sentence about each, supporting each response with a quotation from Extract A.
   a) King Eurystheus   b) The goddess Hera   c) Heracles   d) Cerberus

Remember
Check each quotation you choose to make sure that you have not included irrelevant words and that it makes sense in your sentence.

The writer presents Cerberus as 'the most terrifying and powerful dog who
had ever lived. Each of his three heads was more fearsome than the last'.

> Boost boxes will develop your key skills further to help support you.

> Key technical terms are in blue. You will find the definitions of these terms in the complete glossary at the end of the book.

GLOSSARY

abbreviation - shortened **word** or **phrase** (e.g. Doctor becomes Dr; Susan becomes Sue; telephone becomes phone)

abstract noun - **noun** that names ideas you cannot see, hear, smell, taste or touch (e.g. 'happiness'; 'idea')

account - telling or retelling of factual or fictional events (e.g. an account of the football match, or an account of an adventure)

active voice - form in which the thing that is performing the action of a **verb** is the grammatical **subject** of a **sentence**

adjective - **word** that adds information to a **noun**

adverb - single-word **adverbial**

adverbial - **words** (adverbs), **phrases** or **clauses** that add information to a **verb**, **adjective** or other adverbial

alliteration - use of one sound to begin two or more **words**

character - fictional person in a **story**, play or film

chronological - in a manner showing the order in which events happen or happened

clause - group of more than one **word**, including a **verb**

cliché - **phrase** or idea that is overused and so has lost its impact

climax (in a story) - moment of greatest **conflict**

comma splice - incorrect use of a comma to link two **main clauses**

comparison - looking at similarities and differences between two or more things

conclusion (of a text) - last part, often a result or summary

concrete noun - **noun** that names a physical thing you can see, hear, smell, taste or touch (e.g. 'cat'; 'tree')

conflict (in a story) - challenge or opposition

determiner - **word** (such as 'the' and 'a') that begins a **noun** or **noun phrase**, indicating whether the noun names something general or specific, and **plural** or **singular**

diagram - simple picture used to illustrate a point or idea, usually in **non-fiction**

dialogue - speech between people or fictional **characters**

direct address - method of speaking directly to the reader or listener

direct speech - **words** exactly as they are spoken, usually given within **speech marks** and with an **identifier**

embedded quotation - **quotation** positioned inside a **sentence** and that functions as a part of the sentence

emotive language - **words** and **phrases** that stir readers' emotions

emphasis - forcefulness of expression that suggests importance

---

> The glossary at the end of the book contains the key terms identified across all years of the course, along with clear definitions.

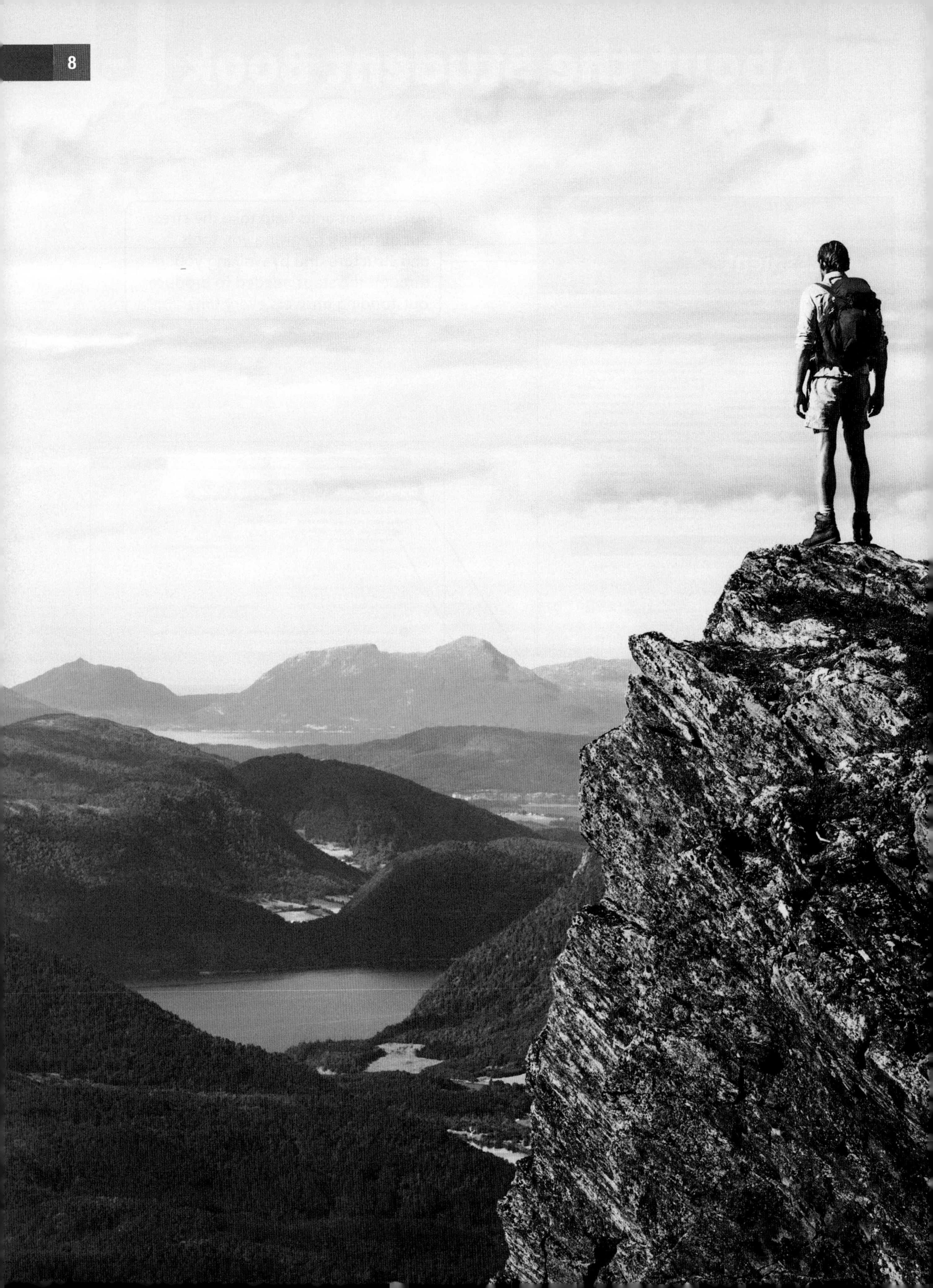

Unit 1
Survival

In this unit you will discover a range of stories exploring the theme of survival in the face of adversity. The characters and people featured in this unit find themselves in dangerous and often life-threatening situations including being caught in an avalanche and trapped in a confined space. They will require enormous courage and determination to survive…

In this unit you will…

- explore key ideas and vocabulary choices the writer has used to create an engaging description.

- identify and summarise key points, and explore how the writer has structured them.

- consider the writer's intention and your response, supporting it with evidence from the extract.

- explore how writers use sentence length to express their ideas and to help them to achieve their intention.

- answer questions on a short extract and write a short, narrative text to assess your progress in the unit so far.

- explore how a writer expresses a point of view to influence the reader's opinions.

- explore how writers structure news articles and choose vocabulary to engage the reader's attention.

- explore two magazine articles. You will identify key points in both articles, and compare similarities or differences in the experiences described.

- explore the conventions of letters. You will then use these to write your own letter about an experience you've had.

- develop your skills in checking the accuracy and effectiveness of your writing, and revising it to make improvements.

- answer questions on a short extract and write a short, narrative text to assess your progress in this unit.

By the end of this unit, you will be familiar with the skills you will develop over this course.

This section links to pages 6–9 of the Workbook.

Section 1
Description

In this section, you will explore key ideas and vocabulary choices the writer has used to create an engaging description.

In this **extract** from a short **story**, the **narrator** is skiing with her mother in the Rocky Mountains when she is caught up in an avalanche.

▼ Read the extract and then answer the questions that follow it.

1 The noise was deafening – I was skiing through a huge cloud of snow which blocked out all light. I choked as it covered my face and goggles. In an instant, the intense cold sucked the heat from my body.

A faint cry came from Mum far, far away: "Avalanche!"

Ramming in my poles, I pushed myself blindly on, harder, faster down the steepening slope in a desperate attempt
5 to escape. Suddenly the air was knocked from my lungs. My skis were off, and I was tumbling helplessly forwards into the snow. My terror grew in a flash as I remembered the huge drop that lay nearby. Would I be hurled into a **chasm**[1]? Or would I be buried under metres of snow and suffocate? Which was worse?

Desperately, I pulled in my arms and cupped my freezing hands over my mouth. The advice on the safety leaflet we'd been given was to create an **air**
10 **pocket**[2] around your mouth. This would give me extra air and time if I was buried in an avalanche. But what if there was no time at all? What if I were pushed over the edge into that chasm? My arms were out again, snatching for anything to hold onto.

Then the force of the snow began to weaken. A moment of relief. But I'd been
15 foolish. I'd panicked. I'd taken my hands away from my mouth in an attempt to grab on to something to save me.

The deafening roar stopped, but I was still sliding across the hard, icy ground. Next a thud, and an excruciating pain in my knee. I'd been thrown against a rock. I screamed, "Mum!" but my call was muffled by the snow on my face.

20 Gasping, I used all my strength to push some of the snow away so I could breathe. I listened in the thick, ice-cold darkness. An **ominous**[3] silence. Then I heard a distant shout. Or was it the bark of a dog? My Mum and a rescue team perhaps? I waited. I knew there was only a short window of time before I would suffocate. My mind was already getting foggy. **Hypothermia**[4] was setting in. What would Mum tell me to do? I must preserve oxygen. Keep focused, keep breathing slowly, I thought. Mum will save me. I was sure of it.

Key vocabulary

chasm[1]: a deep hole
air pocket[2]: a space filled with air to breathe
ominous[3]: suggesting that something bad will happen
hypothermia[4]: a dangerous drop in a body's temperature

Remember

When you have finished reading an extract, ask yourself:

• What is the extract about?

• How do I feel about the **characters**, places or ideas in the extract?

If you cannot answer both of these questions, you should read the extract again.

Activity 1: Making sure you understand the extract

When you first read an extract, make sure you understand all the different events or ideas the writer has included. When you are sure that you understand the extract, you are ready to start thinking about how and why the writer has written it.

1 Look at all the different events and ideas below.

   a) Which event has the writer not included in the extract on page 10?

   b) In what order does the writer include the other events and ideas? Put the letters in the correct order.

A	B	C
The narrator tries to save some air to breathe.	The narrator is sure her Mum will find her.	The narrator hears a loud noise.

D	E	F
The narrator tries to grab hold of something.	The narrator loses her skis.	The narrator listens in the darkness.

G	H	I
The narrator tries to keep calm.	The narrator clings to the edge of a huge drop.	The narrator is thrown against a rock.

Activity 2: Inferring ideas

Writers do not always state clearly what they mean. Sometimes writers suggest meaning, and you have to use the skill of **inference** to work out what they are suggesting.

1 The writer clearly states the narrator's feelings twice in the extract on page 10, describing her terror and that she feels foolish .

   a) Write down the line numbers on which these **words** appear in the extract.

   b) For each feeling, write a **sentence** explaining what causes the narrator to experience it.

   c) Use your skills of inference to work out **three** other feelings the narrator experiences in the extract. You could choose from the suggestions below or use your own ideas.

helpless | desperate | hopeful | panicky | scared | relief | determined | optimistic

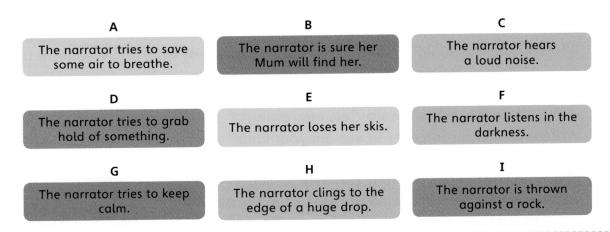

The narrator feels

   d) For each feeling you have identified in the extract, write a sentence explaining what causes the narrator to experience it.

Activity 3: Thinking about the writer's vocabulary choices

Writers can create powerful **descriptions** by choosing their **vocabulary** very carefully.

1 Reread the following sentences from the extract on page 10. The **adjectives** and the **adverb** in the sentences have been highlighted.

> My skis were off, and I was tumbling helplessly forwards into the snow.

> I listened in the thick, ice-cold darkness. An ominous silence.

What difference would it make if the highlighted words were removed from the extract? Ask yourself:
- Would it change the meaning of the sentences?
- Would it make the sentences less interesting?

Write one or two sentences to explain your ideas.

2 Choosing vocabulary carefully can help to add impact to writing. Look at the following **phrases** from the extract, focusing on the highlighted words.

> the intense cold sucked the heat from my body

> Then I heard a distant shout.

The writer could have used many words other than the **verb** 'sucked' and the **noun** 'shout'. Look at the different options below.

Other words for 'sucked'	Other words for 'shout'
pulled	cry
took	yell
stole	call
moved	roar

Look again at the phrases and the vocabulary above. Are the words 'sucked' and 'shout' the best choices to describe the narrator's situation, or would one of the others have been a better choice? Write one or two sentences to explain your ideas.

Remember

Word Classes

A **noun** describes a person, place, object or idea: *Huge <u>clouds</u> filled the blue <u>sky</u>.*

An **adjective** adds information to a noun: *<u>Huge</u> clouds filled the <u>blue</u> sky.*

A **verb** describes an action, event or state: *Nish <u>ran</u> home quickly.*

An **adverb** adds information to a verb or adjective: *Nish ran home <u>quickly</u>.*

Punctuation Boost: Sentence punctuation

A sentence must begin with a **capital letter** and end with a **punctuation** mark.

Remember

A statement ends with a **full stop**: *She walked down the stairs.*

A question ends with a **question mark**: *Why did she walk down the stairs?*

An exclamation ends with an **exclamation mark**: *Get down those stairs now!*

An exclamation expresses a strong emotion or shows someone is speaking loudly.

.   ?   !

1 Rewrite these sentences, adding the correct punctuation:
   a) have you ever acted in a play
   b) i was in our school play last year
   c) i played the part of an elderly lady
   d) it was great fun but absolutely terrifying

Activity 4: Writing descriptions

Imagine

Imagine a dangerous situation in which you might find yourself. You could be:
- lost in a strange or dangerous place
- facing a dangerous person or a dangerous animal
- stuck or lost somewhere else.

Identifying ideas

1 Think about what you can see, smell and hear in the situation you have imagined.

2 Choose **three** feelings you might experience in that situation. For example:

   fear | despair | determination | hope | anger | disappointment

Vocabulary choices

3 Think about the danger you are facing.
   a) Using precise vocabulary, name **two** things you can see. For example: *a river and a boulder*
   b) Add descriptions to create a clear picture. For example: *a deep, fast river and a heavy boulder*

4 Think about how you try to survive.
   a) Using precise vocabulary, name **two** actions you take. For example: *I gasp and flee.*
   b) Add descriptions of the manner in which you will do these things. For example: *I gasp loudly and immediately flee.*

Writing

5 Using your ideas and the vocabulary you have gathered, write **one or two paragraphs** describing the dangerous situation you have imagined.

Section 2
Information

In this section, you will identify and summarise key points, and explore how the writer has structured them.

▼ **Read the webpage and then answer the questions that follow it.**

● ● ● Search…

Getting lost in the desert

1 There are many interesting and surprising stories of how people, both young and old, have got lost in the desert and survived. What would you do in a similar situation? If you ever find yourself lost in the desert, you will certainly need to make some important decisions to stay alive. Your decisions will, of course, depend on your exact situation, but there are three key things to remember that can help you to survive in many situations.

Keep covered

5 One of the biggest dangers of being lost in the desert is **exposure**[1] – to the sun during the day and to the cold during the night. So, your number one priority is to look for ways to reduce your exposure as much as possible. Start by covering your head to protect yourself from direct sun (if you do not have a hat, then use another piece of clothing to wrap your head in). Next
10 look for any shade – depending on your location, there might be shade from shrubs, cacti, or shelter under rocks. Finally, remember that when the sun goes down, so does the temperature, so you will need to think of ways to keep yourself warm. If you have the equipment you can light a fire, or use all the clothing you have to keep yourself as warm as possible at night.

Drink water

15 The desert heat will make you very thirsty and it might be tempting to drink all your water at once. Try to take smaller sips to prevent yourself from getting **dehydrated**[2]. If you start to feel dizzy, which is a sign of dehydration, then drink more water immediately. If you have food, eat only a little at a time as the more you eat, the thirstier you will become. Try to eat just enough to stop yourself from feeling hungry.

Get help

An important decision to consider is whether you stay in one spot or move on. If you have head cover, shelter
20 and water, it's probably best to stay where you are and wait for help. Remember, if you do decide to move, only do this at night so you don't get over-heated. If you have packed the correct equipment, you can signal for help. Make a signal by building a fire or use a signal mirror to reflect light at distant cars or passing aircraft.

Key vocabulary

exposure[1]: not having protection from harmful things
dehydrated[2]: harmful lack of water and fluids in the body

Remember

The title and the first few sentences of a text usually give the reader a clear idea of what it will be about.

Activity 1: Picking out key points

In any text, some ideas or pieces of information are more important than others. These are called its **key points**.

1 Look at all the points in the first paragraph of the webpage on page 14:

   A We can read many interesting stories of how people have survived in the desert.
   B You will need to make important decisions to survive.
   C There are three key things that can help you to survive in many situations.

   a) Which is the most important point?
   b) Which is the least important point?

2 Reread the second paragraph of the webpage: 'Keep covered'.
   a) Write down **four** pieces of information given in this section of the **article**.
   b) Which **one** of the four pieces of information is the most important? Tick it.

Activity 2: Summarising a text

When you summarise a text, you need to use only the most important information, and rewrite it in your own words.

> **Remember**
>
> A **summary** should:
> • contain all the key points from the text
> • be brief and clear
> • be written in your own words.

1 Look at these three summaries of the third paragraph of the webpage on page 14: 'Drink water'.

> The heat will make you thirsty and so you should drink more water.

> It's important to drink enough water to prevent dehydration and remember that eating will make you thirstier.

> Take sips of water and only eat a little food in one go.

   a) Which is the best summary?
   b) Why is it more effective than the other two? Write one or two sentences to explain your ideas.

2 Reread the fourth paragraph of the webpage: 'Get help'.
   a) Write down **three** pieces of information given in this paragraph of the article.
   b) Write a summary of this paragraph of the article.

Activity 3: Thinking about structure

Look again at the webpage on page 14.

The article uses the following **structure**:

- a **heading** **Getting lost in the desert**

- an **introduction**   There are many interesting and surprising stories of how people, both young and old, have got lost in the desert and survived. What would you do in a similar situation?

- three **subheadings**   **Keep covered**   **Drink water**   **Get help**

- a section of text under each subheading   One of the biggest dangers…

  The desert heat will make you very thirsty…

  An important decision to consider…

1 Each of these structural features helps to guide the reader through the information given in the webpage. For each of these structural features, write a sentence explaining the job that it does. You could use some of the words and phrases in the **Vocabulary Bank**.

Vocabulary Bank

- tell
- introduce
- explain
- summary
- guide
- reader
- information

2 Why do you think the writer has chosen to put the three following sections of the webpage in this order?

Keep covered   **Drink water**   **Get help**

Grammar Boost: Adverbials of time

Adverbials of time can be positioned at the beginnings of sentences to link and **sequence** ideas. For example:

Firstly… | Next… | Then… | Later… | Finally…

1 Write **three** sentences summarising the three key things you should do if you find yourself lost in the desert. Sequence them in order of importance, using an adverbial of time at the beginning of each sentence.

Activity 4: Structuring an information text

How would you structure a short **information text** intended to inform readers about the three key things that would help them when starting at a new school?

Identifying ideas

1 Choose the **three** most important things to think about when starting a new school.

You could choose:
- friends
- teachers
- lessons
- homework
- equipment
- rules
- uniform
- anything else

Planning the structure of your text

2 What ideas or information will you include in your introduction? Look again at the introduction to the article on page 14 to give you some ideas.

3 Look again at the three key ideas you chose in question 1. In what order will you sequence these ideas?

Writing

4 Write your information text, including:
- a heading
- an introduction
- three subheadings
- a sentence or two of helpful information under each subheading.

Remember

Every part of a text has a job to do. Look again at your answers to Activity 3, and make sure each part of your text is doing its job.

This section links to pages 14–17 of the Workbook.

Section 3
Intention and response

In this section, you will consider the writer's intention and your response, supporting your ideas with evidence from the extract.

This is an extract from a short story. Thirteen-year-old Esteban and four men are the only survivors of a ship that sank in a terrible storm.

▼ Read the extract and then answer the questions that follow it.

1 Mr Gomez was rowing. He groaned and winced with every stroke. Esteban glanced around the sunburnt faces of the other three men, their shoulders hunched in misery and hunger and thirst.

5 "Your turn, boy," panted Mr Gomez gruffly, staring at him.

Esteban stood and swapped seats with Mr Gomez, taking the oars in his blistered hands. He could barely grip them. The boat bobbed helplessly in the waves.

10 "You're useless, boy," growled Mr Gomez. "Cal?" he barked. "Take the oars."

"What's the point?" muttered Cal, stumbling forward and taking the oars from Esteban. "We might as well give up and die quietly."

15 Esteban staggered back to his seat and trailed his sore hands in the cool water, staring miserably to the horizon. He noticed something bobbing in the water just a few feet away.

"Look!" he cried, pointing. "What is it?"

20 "It's a coconut!" said Mr Gomez. "Well done, boy! Cal! Row for it. Lean out and grab it, boy!"

Esteban got up on his knees, his desperate fingers outstretched.

"Got it!" he cried. The men cheered. "How do we eat
25 it?" he asked.

"We have to open it," said Mr Gomez snatching it from him. "We need something heavy." He grabbed one of the oars from Cal and hit the coconut as hard as he could, again and again.

30 Their mouths watered, and their eyes burned hungrily, willing the coconut to break open. None of them noticed the approaching storm: the rising wind, the darkening sky. They yelled in terrified surprise as the boat sharply lurched and reared up
35 on a massive wave. Sudden rain battered them, waves crashed down on them and the little wooden boat reared and dropped and reared again and they clung to it for dear life.

Minutes later, when the storm vanished as quickly as
40 it had arrived, the men and their tiny little boat had survived. But its oars and the coconut were gone, lost to the waves. For the rest of the day the boat drifted and bobbed and they sat in dejected silence, hunger gnawing at their insides.

45 "Land!" cried Cal as the sun was sinking, raising himself up and pointing a shaking finger into the distance. "Land! We're saved!"

Remember

Try to summarise the extract in one or two sentences. This is a good way to check if you have understood what it is about.

Activity 1: Exploring the writer's intention

When you read a text, you should aim to think about the writer's **intention**. Ask yourself: Why did the writer write the text in this way?

1 Make a **list** of everything that goes wrong in the extract on page 18. Think about:
  - the weather
  - the boat
  - the men

2 Now think about the writer's intention.
  a) Why do you think the writer decided to focus in such detail on what goes wrong? Choose one or more answers from these suggestions, or use your own ideas.

> to build up a feeling of drama and tension

> to make the reader feel sympathy for the characters

> to show how difficult the lives of these characters are

> to warn the reader that the sea is dangerous

  b) Write one or two sentences to explain your ideas.

Activity 2: Responding to the text

As well as thinking about the effect the writer **wanted** a text to have on you, you need to think about the effect it **actually** had on you: what was your **response**?

1 Think about the effect that the extract on page 18 had on you.
  a) How would you feel if you were on the boat? Write a sentence explaining your answer.
  b) How did you feel as you read the extract? Choose one or more of the words below.

excited | worried | entertained | amused | sad | upset

2 When you write about a text, you should always support your ideas with **evidence**. The evidence will often be a **quotation** from the text: a phrase or a key word. You should write this inside punctuation called **speech marks** or **quotation marks**. For example:

'their eyes burned hungrily'
—— speech marks ——

Look again at your answer to question 1b.
  a) Which paragraph in the extract made you feel this way most strongly?
  b) Which sentence in that paragraph made you feel this way most strongly?
  c) Which word or phrase in that sentence made you feel this way most strongly?
  d) Write one or two sentences to explain **why** you think it made you respond in this way.

Grammar Boost: Paragraphs

1 How many paragraphs might you need to use if you were asked to write each of the following texts? Look at the **Remember** box for support.

a) An entertaining article entitled 'The People Living in My House'.

b) A story extract in which three students shout out different answers to a teacher's question.

c) A diary entry about what you did yesterday.

> **Remember**
>
> You should start a new paragraph in your writing when there is:
> - a change of topic
> - a change of **setting**
> - a change of time
> - a change of speaker.

Activity 3: Thinking about structure

1 Look at the sequence of events in the extract on page 18: How might the reader respond at each of these points in the story?

A Esteban and the men are hungry, thirsty and exhausted.

B Esteban spots a coconut and grabs it from the water.

C There is a terrible storm.

D Esteban and the men survive the storm.

E The coconut and the boat's oars are lost in the storm.

F One of the men sees an island.

a) Write a short response to each event, following the examples given in A and B. You could choose from the suggestions below, or use your own ideas.

b) Look at all the responses you have written. Label the positive responses with a smiley face (☺) and the negative responses with a worried face (☹).

c) Can you see a pattern in the way the structure of the extract controls the reader's response?

Activity 4: Writing to achieve your intention

You are going to write an extract from a story in which you aim to guide the reader's response.

Imagining

1 Imagine going on a long journey all by yourself. You could be:
- travelling by train
- riding on a bicycle
- walking.

Note down where you are going and how you will travel.

Identifying ideas

2 Think of **two or three** dangers you could face on your long journey. For example:
- you could get lost
- you could hurt yourself
- your train or bike could break down.

Structuring your ideas

3 In what order will you sequence the dangers you have chosen? You could:
- alternate between safety and danger
- build up tension from the least dangerous situation to the most dangerous
- end at the most dangerous point.

Writing

4 Using the ideas you have gathered and the structure you have planned, write **two or three** paragraphs of your story extract. Aim to:
- write in paragraphs
- think about how you want the reader to respond
- end your story extract at an exciting point.

This section links to pages 18–21 of the Workbook.

Section 4
Sentence structure for effect

In this section, you will explore how writers use sentence length to express their ideas and to help them to achieve their intention.

In this extract, Mira has just arrived at a campsite in the middle of a forest, with her mother and father. They are on a family holiday in Canada.

▼ Read the extract and then answer the questions that follow it.

1 It had been a long drive deep into the forest and Mira's parents had gone to bed early. For Mira though, it was the first time she'd been allowed to come on one of their camping trips and she was far too excited to sleep. She lay on her side, on her sleeping mat, breathing slowly and evenly and listening. Soon she heard her father's familiar snore rumble through the canvas between them. She moved her head closer to the edge of the tent because she was

5 trying to listen to the sounds of the forest insects and birds outside. Some people her age might have been worried, but not Mira. She thought the whole trip, from the drive through the dark forest, to the mysterious sounds outside now were all one big adventure.

Just then, Mira heard another noise. A muffled scraping, maybe a snuffling as well … just outside. Intrigued, Mira slowly reached for her rucksack to pull out her torch and realised she'd left it out by the campfire. As quietly as she

10 could, she rolled onto her knees, unzipped the tent and stepped out into the darkness. Searching for her bag, she suddenly heard a rustling, and an aggressive, high-pitched growl that echoed around the camp. Mira span to face the noise and stared open-mouthed.

"Don't move!" Her mum's voice was clear and strong, "Back away slowly … slowly … it's a grizzly bear. It'll

15 attack if we scare it."

Mira forced herself to obey, unable to take her gaze away from the creature in front of her. Staring at Mira now, it rose up on its back legs, towering over them all and roared.

"Back slowly, move back. Concentrate Mira," urged

20 her mum.

Her dad spoke now, "Listen to your mother, Mira. Slowly. Move slowly away."

Tears began to stream down her face, but Mira stepped back now. Slowly. One step, then two, then three. She

25 tried to make herself feel brave. She forced herself not to cry out.

The bear dropped back down onto all four paws. It stared at her without moving until it finally seemed to make a decision. It turned its huge body back into the

30 forest and lumbered back into the night.

Remember

Think about your response to the events described in this extract. What were you thinking and feeling as you read it?

Activity 1: Thinking about the writer's intention

1 Complete these sentences to check your understanding of the extract on page 22. You could use some of the words in the **Vocabulary Bank** to help you.

a) At the start of the extract, Mira is…
b) Outside, Mira hears…
c) When the bear rises up on its back legs, Mira's mother…
d) Mira…
e) The bear…

Vocabulary Bank

• in	• listens	• forces	• nearby	• tent	• noise	• urges	• moves
• cries	• steps	• growls	• turns	• muffled	• slowly	• goes	• drops

2 What **impression** is the writer trying to create of Mira? Write down **two or three** words or phrases that describe this character.

3 What impression is the writer trying to create of the grizzly bear? Write down **two or three** words or phrases that describe this character.

Activity 2: Exploring sentence structures

1 Look again at the first two paragraphs of the extract on page 22.
a) Are the sentences in the first two paragraphs mostly long or short?
b) How would you summarise the events described in the first two paragraphs? You could choose some of the ideas below or use your own.

worrying | frightening | fast-moving | tense | dramatic

relaxed | calm | descriptive | hopeful | positive

2 Look again at the last two paragraphs of the extract.
a) Are the sentences in the two paragraphs mostly longer or shorter than the sentences in the first two paragraphs?
b) How would you summarise the events in the last two paragraphs? You could choose some of the ideas above or use your own.

3 Why do you think writers might use some longer sentences and some shorter ones? Write one or two sentences explaining your ideas.

Grammar Boost: Conjunctions

You can link two or more pieces of information in one sentence using **conjunctions**.

1 Use a conjunction from the **Conjunction Bank** to link these pairs of sentences in order to create one longer sentence. Try not to use any of the conjunctions more than once.

a) I walked home from school. It was raining.

b) I put on some dry clothes. I stopped shivering.

c) I tried to do my homework. It was time for dinner.

Conjunction Bank

and	but	when	as
before	after	until	so
because	although	if	

Activity 3: Building sentences

1 Look at these sentences from the extract on page 22:

A   Just then, Mira heard another noise.

B   Mira span to face the noise and stared open-mouthed.

C   She moved her head closer to the edge of the tent because she wanted to listen to the sounds of the forest insects and birds outside.

Sentence A is made up of one **clause** containing one verb. It describes one action or event.

a) How many actions or events does sentence B describe?

b) How many actions or events does sentence C describe?

c) How has the writer linked the actions or events in sentence B and sentence C together? And why?

Remember

Verbs describe an action, an event or state:

The bear dropped back down onto all four paws.

A **clause** is a part of a sentence containing a verb and the other words linked to that verb.

Activity 4: Writing sentences

1 Read the story opening below. Each sentence in the story contains one clause.

> I am in an old, dark house. I walk through the house. I see a door. I open the door. I see stairs going down into a deep, dark cellar. I start to walk down the stairs. I hear the door slamming shut behind me. I hurry back up the stairs. I try to open the door. It will not open. I am trapped.

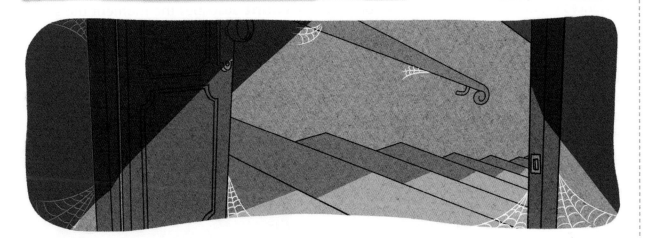

Rewrite this story opening, using a variety of different sentence lengths. You could:
- join two or three sentences together using conjunctions
- leave some sentences as short **single-clause sentences**.

2 Prepare to continue the story, thinking carefully about the length and structure of your sentences.

a) Think about what might happen next in the story. How would you escape from this difficult situation? Would you:
- see if you already have anything that would help you escape?
- call for help?
- look for something in the dark cellar that could help you escape?
- try something else?

Note down **two or three** ideas about what might happen next.

b) How would you feel in this situation? What thoughts would be running through your mind? Note down **two or three** ideas about your thoughts and feelings as you try to escape from the cellar.

c) Write the next **one or two** paragraphs of the story. Aim to:
- write at least **eight** sentences
- use some longer sentences and some shorter sentences
- use a variety of conjunctions to link the clauses in your longer sentences.

This section links to pages 22–23 of the Workbook.

Section 5
Assessment

In this section, you will answer questions on a short extract and write a short narrative text to assess your progress in the unit so far.

When the *Titanic* was launched, it was the largest passenger ship in the world. On its first voyage in 1912, on its way from Southampton in the UK to New York in the US, the *Titanic* hit an iceberg and sank. More than 1,500 people died. In this diary extract, the writer describes his experiences on board the *Titanic*. This part of his **account** describes the moment the ship hit the iceberg.

▼ Read the extract and then answer the questions that follow it.

1 We were steaming along at 22 or 23 knots, not reducing speed at all, in spite of the many warnings of the presence of ice, which had come in from other ships during the afternoon and evening.

5 We were out for a record run.

I had called 'Good night' to my Father and Mother in the next room. In order to get plenty of air, I had half opened the **port**[1], and the breeze was coming through with a quiet humming whistle.

10 There was the steady rhythmic pulsation of the engines and screws, the feel and heaving of which becomes second nature to one, after a few hours at sea. It was a fine night for sleeping, and with the day's air and exercise, I was sleepy.

15 I wound my watch – it was 11:45 pm – and was just about to step into bed when I seemed to sway slightly. I immediately realised that the ship had **veered to port**[2] as though she had been gently pushed. If I had had a brimful glass of water in my hand, not a drop would have been spilled, the shock was so slight.

Almost instantaneously, the engines stopped. The sudden quiet was startling and disturbing. Like the subdued quiet in a **sleeping car**[3], at a stop, after a continuous run. Not a sound except the breeze whistling through
20 the half-open port. Then there was the distant noise of running feet and muffled voices, as several people hurried through the passageway. Very shortly the engines started up again – slowly – not with the bright vibration to which we were accustomed, but as though they were tired. After very few revolutions they again stopped.

I hurried into my heavy overcoat and drew
25 on my slippers. All excited, but not thinking anything serious had occurred, I called in to my Father and Mother that I was 'going up on deck to see the fun.' Father said he would put on his clothes and come right up and join me. It was
30 bitterly cold.

Key vocabulary

port[1]: port-hole; a round window in a ship's cabin
veered to port[2]: suddenly turned to the left
sleeping car[3]: a train carriage with beds, for long, overnight journeys

Activity 1: Reading

1 Look carefully at the first paragraph of the extract on page 26. Was the ship travelling quickly or slowly? Write down one word or phrase that supports your answer.

2 On line 1, the writer says there had been 'many warnings of the presence of ice'. Why do you think the writer begins his account with this information?

3 Look carefully at lines 15–19.
  a) Write down **two** things from these lines that suggest something wrong with the ship.
  b) Which words in this part of the extract show this most effectively? Write one or two sentences explaining your ideas.

4 Look carefully at lines 20–22. At this point, the writer did not realise that the ship had hit an iceberg.
  a) How does the writer show he did not realise this? Write down **one** piece of evidence.
  b) How do you, as a reader, respond to this part of the account? Why do you respond in this way? Write one or two sentences explaining your ideas.

5 Look at the final sentence of the extract.
  a) What kind of sentence is this?
  b) Why do you think the writer decided to structure this sentence in this way?

Activity 2: Writing

Imagine that you are on a ship, travelling over the ocean. You are woken in the middle of the night. You can hear voices. You quickly realise that the ship is sinking.

1 Write an account describing your experiences.

Before you start writing

• Plan your writing by gathering all the ideas you could include.
• Think carefully about how you will structure your writing. How will you begin your account? How will you end it?

As you write

• Use a variety of sentence lengths and conjunctions.
• Choose your vocabulary carefully.

When you have finished writing

• Check the accuracy of your punctuation, especially full stops.
• Check the accuracy of your paragraphing.

This section links to pages 24–27 of the Workbook.

Section 6
Argument

In this section, you will explore how a writer expresses a point of view to influence the reader's opinions.

This article was written by Bear Grylls, a British survival expert.

▼ **Read the article and then answer the questions that follow it.**

The lessons children should be learning at school

1 If I had to write the education curriculum for every child in this country, they wouldn't learn French and maths. They'd learn how to light a fire, tie a knot, use a penknife, build a raft, get on with people, eat healthily, keep fit, be part of a team and practise leadership.

You've got to be prepared to take a few risks if you're going to achieve anything in life. There is risk everywhere,
5 even when you go out on the street. You empower kids by teaching them how to do something dangerous, but how to do it safely. Kids respond to that sort of thing.

I say to budding adventurers, "Listen, a blunt penknife is a dangerous knife. Make sure it's really sharp." (It's true: with a blunt knife, you'll get frustrated and often cut yourself.)
10 The kids' faces light up. Like all kids, they want a sharp penknife – which is great, but you need to teach them to respect it and use it properly.

The thing is, sometimes in life we will get cut. My six-year-old recently cut himself on a knife, and came in with blood
15 pouring everywhere, but he's not cut himself again. He has learnt how to handle a knife. I had my first penknife at six, but 200 years ago I doubt there was a six-year-old in Britain who couldn't start a fire with a knife and a flint. Kids were taught to be resourceful and practical.

20 I think it's important to say, "Don't jump off there without knowing if there are rocks underneath," or "Don't play with fire without me," because you love and care for your kids, and you don't want pain or hurt to come to them, of course – but, on the other hand, you've got to let kids have the odd adventure.

Let's have fun again. Let's get muddy; let's live a bit more freely. Perhaps then we will also discover what it takes to
25 survive.

Remember

When you read a text in which the writer expresses their **point of view**, look carefully at:
• the **title**
• the final paragraph or **conclusion**.
They usually sum up the writer's point of view.

Activity 1: Identifying key points

1 Each paragraph in an **argument text** may make two or more points, but there will be one key point.

a) Which **two** of the following points does the writer make in the first paragraph of the article on page 28?

A Schools should teach children some important survival skills.

B The writer wants to go back to school to learn French and maths.

C French and maths are not as useful as survival skills.

D Being able to build a raft is more important than learning to be a leader.

b) Look again at your answer to question 1a. Which **one** is the key point in the first paragraph?

2 Look at the key point below that the writer makes in the article. In which paragraph or paragraphs does this point appear?

Children should be taught to do dangerous things as safely as possible.

3 The writer makes **all** of the following points in the fourth, fifth and sixth paragraphs.

A Children must learn that they can hurt themselves.

B Children can learn from their mistakes.

C We should keep children safe but we should not stop them having adventures.

D Children should have enough freedom to learn to look after themselves.

a) Which **one** is the key point in the fourth paragraph?
b) Which **one** is the key point in the fifth paragraph?
c) Which **one** is the key point in the sixth paragraph?

Activity 2: Linking key points

1 To answer each question below, you will need to find at least **two** pieces of information from different parts of the article on page 28.

a) In the writer's **opinion**, what dangerous things should children be taught to use?
b) In the writer's opinion, who should help children to learn useful survival skills?

2 Look again at all your answers to Activities 1 and 2 on this page. Write **one** sentence linking all the writer's points to sum up his point of view.

Activity 3: Using emotive language

In an argument text, the writer expresses a point of view and tries to influence the reader's opinion. A powerful way to influence the reader is by using **emotive language**: words and phrases that stir the reader's emotions.

1 Look at the following section from the article on page 28.

> You've got to be prepared to take a few risks if you're going to achieve anything in life. There is risk everywhere, even when you go out on the street. You empower kids by teaching them how to do something dangerous, but how to do it safely.

    a) Which of the highlighted words has the writer chosen to shock the reader with surprising views?

    b) Which of the highlighted words has the writer chosen to appeal to the reader, showing the benefits of letting children take risks?

2 Look at the following sentence from the article.

> My six-year-old recently cut himself on a knife, and came in with blood pouring everywhere, but he's not cut himself again.

Which words or phrases in this sentence has the writer chosen to shock the reader?

3 Why do you think the writer has chosen to shock and to appeal to the reader? Write one or two sentences to explain your ideas.

Activity 4: Using rhetorical devices

Rhetorical devices are language techniques that writers and speakers often use to present their ideas persuasively.

1 Look at the final paragraph of the article on page 28:

> Let's have fun again. Let's get muddy; let's live a bit more freely. Perhaps then we will also discover what it takes to survive.

The writer has used two rhetorical devices to make his **argument** more powerful:
- a **triple structure** – the writer presents a persuasive pattern of three ideas
- **direct address** – the writer is directly addressing the reader.

    a) Which word or phrase has the writer repeated three times?

    b) Which words or phrases show the writer is talking directly to the reader?

Grammar Boost: Standard English – subject-verb agreement

When you write in **Standard English** it is important to choose the correct form of all the key words in a sentence so that they 'agree'.

1 Correct the errors in the following sentence, rewriting it using Standard English.

> Some child walk to school.

2 Look at the words in the table below. They have not been made to agree. Write **four** sentences in Standard English, using one adverbial, one **determiner**, one **subject** noun, one verb and one **object** noun in each sentence.

Adverbials	Determiners	Subject nouns	Verbs	Object nouns
Last night,	a	people	watch	a film.
Every night,	an	boys	watches	television.
Tomorrow,	the	girl	watched	the football match.
Sometimes,	some	adult	will watch	cartoons.

Activity 5: Writing an argument text

You are going to write a paragraph arguing your point of view.

Select your ideas

1 Do you agree or disagree with the writer of the article on page 28? Choose **one** key point from the ideas below.

I agree:	I disagree:
• Having some freedom helps prepare children for adult life.	• Children are not old enough or wise enough to make their own decisions.
• Children need the opportunity to learn by making mistakes.	• Children do not have to be put at risk to learn about what is dangerous.

Write

2 Write a paragraph that explains your chosen point. Aim to write four or five sentences. You could:
- begin the paragraph by stating the point
- support your point with a real or imaginary **example**
- explain how your chosen example supports your opinion.

Review your writing

3 **Review** the choices you have made in your writing and try to make your argument as powerful as you can.
- Could you choose more emotive language?
- Could you use a triple structure or direct address?

Section 7
Newspaper report

In this section, you will explore how writers structure news articles and choose vocabulary to engage the reader's attention.

▼ Read the newspaper article and then answer the questions that follow it.

'I WAS CERTAIN I WOULD DIE,' SAYS SURFER, RESCUED AFTER 32 HOURS AT SEA

1 Just moments before he was rescued by a helicopter
crew, a surfer lost at sea believed he was certain to die.

Speaking from his hospital bed in Belfast as he recovers
from hypothermia, Matthew Bryce has vowed he will
5 never surf again.

He was reported missing by family when he failed to
return from a Sunday-morning surf off the Argyll coast
in north-west Scotland.

He was eventually spotted, after 32 hours at sea, by
10 the search-and-rescue helicopter at about 7:30 pm on
Monday. At this time he was drifting in the Irish Sea,
13 miles from Northern Ireland and 16 miles from
Scottish shores.

As the sun began to set on a second day at sea, Bryce
15 thought he had just hours to live and had 'made peace'
with himself.

The 22-year-old, from Airdrie in North Lanarkshire,
fought back tears as he told the BBC: 'I knew I had maybe
three hours, and I was pretty certain I was going to die
20 with that sunset – so I was watching the sunset and I'd
pretty much made peace with it all, and then a helicopter
flew right over.

'I jumped off the board and I lifted the board up, and I
started waving it from the water and they flew right over.
25 I thought they'd missed me. Then they turned around...
and then they saved my life. I can't thank them enough.'

Fear really set in as night fell on Sunday. He added: 'It
was incredibly lonely and quiet, because there was just
nothing – just waves. I hadn't seen any helicopters. I was
30 thinking I was going to die – I was almost convinced. I
didn't think I would see sunrise.'

An RNLI lifeboat has since recovered his surfboard, but
the 22-year-old has no plans to take it back to sea. Asked
if he was finished with surfing, Bryce said: 'I think so – I
35 couldn't do that again.'

Based on: 'Missing surfer found alive after 32 hours off
Argyll coast', *Guardian Online*, 2 May 2017 <https://www.
theguardian.com/uk-news/2017/may/02/missing-surfer-
found-alive-matthew-bryce-32-hours-argyll-coast>
[accessed 25 January 2019]

Remember

The headline and the first paragraph of a news article usually summarise the whole story.

Activity 1: Looking at structure

Narrative stories are usually written using a **chronological** structure: they tell the reader about a series of events in the order they happened. News articles, however, are usually written using a non-chronological structure.

1 Copy and complete the table below, noting key events from the article on page 32 and putting them into chronological order.

Day 1: Sunday morning	Matthew Bryce went surfing.
Day 1: Sunday night	
Day 2: Sunset on Monday	

2 Look again at your answers to question 1.
   a) What are the key points in this story? Underline **three** of them.
   b) Which of these key points does the writer include in the headline?
   c) Which of these key points does the writer include in the first paragraph of the article?
   d) What do the other paragraphs add to the article?
   e) Why do you think journalists structure news articles in this way?

3 Look at the different paragraphs from a news article below. In what order would you sequence them?

A   Javid Gilani, 37, went out to work one morning, leaving his wife at home. He didn't return. Despite an extensive police search, no trace of Mr Gilani was found.

B   A man who disappeared more than five years ago has been found, alive and well and living in Poland.

C   Years afterwards, in an extraordinary twist of events, his wife, Sara Gilani, made a startling discovery.

D   Mr Gilani has no memory of his former life. He has learned to speak Polish, but says he now wants to learn English again so he can start to rebuild a relationship with his wife.

E   Mrs Gilani, said: 'I was looking at a magazine five years later, and read a story about a man who had been found in Poland. He had no identification papers and could not speak or write. I recognised his photo immediately.'

Activity 2: Exploring vocabulary choices

Journalists often choose dramatic language to make news stories sound as exciting as possible.

1 Look again at the article on page 32. Compare these sentences from the article with far less dramatic sentences that the writer could have written:

> Just moments before he was rescued by a helicopter crew, a surfer lost at sea believed he was certain to die.

> For a while before he was rescued by a helicopter crew, a surfer lost at sea believed he was probably in difficulties.

> Matthew Bryce has vowed he will never surf again.

> Matthew Bryce has said he will probably not surf again.

For each difference you can find between the two versions, write a sentence explaining why you think the writer of the article chose the language used.

2 Look at the writer's vocabulary choices in the news article extract below. Using the words given around the article, rewrite the extract, making the highlighted vocabulary choices more dramatic.

disappeared | vanished | was lost

A boy who went missing during a game of hide-and-seek has been found.

Bill and Brenda Jones and their three children had gone out for a day's walking in the mountains near their home in Wales. After eating their picnic lunch, the family decided to play hide-and-seek. Some time later, they

more than an hour | a long time | 63 minutes

became worried that they did not know where their son, Ryan, was hiding.

anxious | concerned | alarmed

were unsure | had no idea | were unclear

Mr Jones phoned the Mountain Rescue service, who quickly came to the scene.

urgently | immediately | instantly

rushed | hurried | raced

Grammar Boost: Writing in the past and present

News articles are usually written mainly in the **past tense**. However, headlines are often written in the **present tense**.

1 Copy and complete the table below with details from three imaginary news articles, adding:
- a headline in the present **tense** for article B
- opening sentences in the past tense for articles A and C.

	Headlines	Opening sentences
A	100-year-old woman wins lottery!	
B		A letter posted in 1967 has finally been delivered more than half a century late.
C	Teenager has to land plane when pilot faints	

Activity 3: Writing an article

You are going to write a news article about a dramatic rescue.

Imagine

1 Think of a situation in which someone needs to be rescued – perhaps they are lost, trapped or hurt.
You could borrow ideas from one of the stories you have read over the course of this unit.

Plan

2 a) Note down the following key points for your article.
- **Who** was rescued?
- **When** did it happen?
- **Why** and **how** did it happen?
- **What** happened?
- **Where** did it happen?

b) Think about the structural and **presentational features** common to news articles, and sketch how you could lay out your news story.

Write

3 Write the headline and the first **two or three** paragraphs of your article. Aim to:
- write a clear, attention-grabbing headline
- include all the key points of the story in the first paragraph
- add detail in the second and third paragraphs
- make your vocabulary choices as dramatic as possible
- use presentational features to structure your article in an appropriate and interesting way, perhaps considering any images you would like it to include.

This section links to pages 32–35 of the Workbook.

Section 8
Comparing texts

In this section, you will explore two magazine articles. You will identify key points in both articles, and compare similarities or differences in the experiences described.

In Extract A, which is taken from a magazine article, a scientist researching climate change in the Himalayas describes a terrifying experience.

▼ **Read Extract A and then answer the questions that follow it.**

I fell 70ft into a crevasse

1 The next day, I left my tent to collect snow samples. It should have been only a short stroll. Suddenly, the snow gave way beneath me and I was plunged into darkness. I was inside the **glacier**[1], tumbling into a **crevasse**[2]. My face smashed against ice as I **ricocheted**[3] between the frozen walls. I felt
5 bones snap and my arm was pulled clean out of its socket.

Apart from my legs, every part of me hurt. With just one working arm, I knew I couldn't climb up the way I'd fallen, but nor could I survive a night there as the temperature plunged. I spat blood and wondered if I was bleeding internally. If I was to stand any chance of making it out alive, I had to start at
10 once.

I reached across my body with my left arm to whack in one ice axe, and then stretched back for the other and repeated that, resting at each ledge. I made slow progress, and at times the challenge seemed overwhelming. It was the thought of my mother never learning what had become of me that helped
15 me push through the pain and fear.

At the top, the crevasse was a narrow crack covered with foot-deep snow, thick enough to have obscured it from above. Now I had to dig my way out of my own grave. That took the last of my strength; free at last, I found I couldn't stand and had to crawl back to my tent. It had been six
20 hours since I'd fallen and it took two more to cover the 100 yards to the tent, where I called for help on the satellite phone.

Key vocabulary

glacier[1]: large mass of ice
crevasse[2]: deep, open crack
ricocheted[3]: violently bounced off

Activity 1: Gathering key points

1 Using the **Key Points Checklist** to help you, note down the key points about information and approach in Extract A.

Key Points Checklist

- Where was the writer?
- Why was he there?
- What happened to him?
- How long did it last?
- How was he rescued?
- Did his attitude change?

In Extract B, which is also from a magazine article, a 13-year-old boy describes what happened when he and his cousins took a football to their local park.

▼ **Read Extract B and then answer the questions that follow it.**

I was trapped in a sewer for 12 hours

1   After kicking the ball around for a bit, we found an abandoned building on the edge of the park, so we climbed over the fence and started playing tag. I wasn't looking where I was going when I felt a piece of wood underneath me break, and I fell 25 foot into a pipe.

I landed in water, and it was running pretty quickly. It felt like being
5   on a waterslide, but the water smelled nasty, like a toilet. It was dark, so I grabbed my phone from my pocket to use as a torch – but the water knocked it out of my hand and I lost it. In those first few moments, I panicked. I thought I was going to die.

I shouted for help but I could just hear my own voice echoing back to
10 me, and the sound of rushing water. I started crying a little because I was so scared. I was in the dark, alone, thinking, 'Where am I?' and 'Will I ever get to see my family again?'

I thought about walking through the pipe to find a way out, but it looked scary so I decided it was better to stay put and hope that
15 someone would find me.

Not too long after that, I heard helicopters and I knew people were looking for me. But when nobody came after what felt like hours, I went back to thinking I was going to die. Over 12 hours after I'd first fallen in, I saw a light above me and I heard someone shout, "Here's
20 the kid!" I started calling for help, and a rope got lowered down, so I just held on and they pulled me out.

Activity 2: Comparing key points

1 Note down the key points of Extract B, again using the **Key Points Checklist** on page 36 to help you.

2 Compare the key points of information you have found in the two extracts. Copy and complete the table below, adding as many similarities and differences as you can.

Similarities	Differences
Both writers found themselves trapped in a difficult situation.	The writer of Extract 1 was collecting snow samples in the mountains. The writer of Extract 2 was playing tag.

Activity 3: Selecting evidence

Look at these points comparing Extract A on page 36 and Extract B on page 37.

Point 1

> The writer of Extract A was much more seriously hurt. For example, he tells the reader, 'I felt bones snap'. I do not think the writer of Extract B was hurt at all, because he does not say anything about being injured or in pain.

Point 2

> The writers of both extracts describe being frightened.

1 Point 1 is much more successful than Point 2 because it contains supporting evidence from the extracts.

a) To support Point 2, choose **one** quotation from Extract A and **one** quotation from Extract B that show each writer is frightened.

How do I do that?

Read through the whole extract carefully, looking for a sentence, phrase or word that supports the point being made. If you find more than one, choose the one that proves your point most strongly. Quotations should be:

- short – choose the fewest possible words to support your point
- exact – copy the words and the punctuation from the extract precisely
- inside speech marks – these show that the words are taken from the extract.

speech mark to mark the beginning of the quotation ⟶ 'I felt bones snap' ⟵ speech mark to mark the end of the quotation

---

b) Use your quotations to improve Point 2. To help you, look at the way Point 1 is structured.

> The writers of both extracts describe being frightened. For example, the writer of Extract A describes...

2 Write **two or three** sentences comparing how long the two different experiences lasted. Support your **comparison** with a quotation from each extract.

Grammar Boost: Adverbials for comparison

When you write a comparison, you can signal to the reader whether you are writing about a similarity or a difference.

Adverbials to signal a similarity	Adverbials to signal a difference
Similarly, | In the same way,	However, | In contrast, | On the other hand,

1 Rewrite the following sentences, adding adverbials to help guide the reader.

   a) The writer of Extract A was a scientist carrying out important research. The writer of Extract B was a boy playing a game in the park.

   b) The writer of Extract A fell down a crevasse and was trapped. The writer of Extract B fell into a sewer and was unable to escape.

   c) The writer of Extract A was determined to climb out of the crevasse. The writer of Extract B waited helplessly for someone else to rescue him.

Activity 4: Writing a comparison

You are going to write a comparison of the key points in the two extracts on pages 36 and 37. Your comparison should contain **two** paragraphs.

Selecting key ideas

1 Write down **two** key points of comparison between the two extracts. You could look back over your work during this section to help you.

```
        Plan
        1
        2
```

Selecting evidence

2 Choose a short, relevant quotation from each extract to support each point: **four** quotations in total. Remember to use speech marks to show where each quotation begins and ends.

Sequencing your ideas

3 How will you sequence your points of comparison? For example, you could start with the most important, or organise them in chronological order.

Write

4 Write your comparison. In each paragraph, aim to:
   • compare key information from Extract A **and** Extract B
   • support your points with evidence from **both** extracts
   • use an adverbial to signal whether you are writing about a similarity or a difference.

This section links to pages 36–39 of the Workbook.

Section 9
Letters

In this section, you will explore the conventions of letters. You will then use these to write your own letter about an experience you've had.

▼ **Read the letter and then answer the questions that follow it.**

1

Sea Cottage
Cliff Road
Coastmouth
CS7 9YF
3rd May 2020

5

Padma Sengupta
299/C Daksha Appt
Ankur Road
Ahmedatar 670925

10 Dear Padma,

Guess what! I've been on TV, and now I want to write and tell you all about it!

I've spent the last week visiting my grandma in her cottage by the sea. On the day I arrived, I felt a bit lonely because my brother was too ill to come with me. I didn't think it'd be much fun playing on the beach all by myself! There's a really nice girl called Ana living next door
15 now, though, and I met her only a couple of hours after I got here.

The next day, I went to the beach to meet Ana. Then, after we'd been there for about half an hour, we heard a strange sound. It seemed to be coming from the ocean itself! We couldn't see anything from where we were, so we climbed the steps up the cliff.

From up there, we spotted a man in a little boat, waving and calling out. He was caught in
20 the tide and couldn't get back to shore! Quickly, I rang the coastguard, and then we tried to wave to the man so he knew help was coming.

When I look back on it now, I can hardly believe I acted so calmly!

After only 15 minutes, we heard a deafening whirring sound and a seaplane whizzed overhead. It circled a couple of times and then it landed in the water. We could see the
25 man being pulled into the plane, and then it set off again. We hoped the man would be okay — but we didn't expect that he would turn up with a TV crew the very next day!

"These are the two extraordinary young ladies who saved my life," he told the camera. "If it hadn't been for them, I would never have made it back to dry land." We felt so proud.

30 I know you said you were going to visit family soon, too, and I'd love to hear all about that. I hope your sister and her baby are doing really well.

Love,
Penny

Activity 1: Understanding the text

1 The main purpose of a **letter** is to communicate information.

   a) In your own words, write **one** sentence that summarises the information in the letter.

   b) The **main body** of the letter contains eight paragraphs. Write **one** sentence for each paragraph, summarising the information it contains.

2 The reasons listed on the right for starting a new paragraph are used in the letter. Look at the letter, and note down the reason each new paragraph is started.

Remember

You should start a new paragraph in your writing when there is:
- a change of topic
- a change of time
- a change of setting
- a change of speaker.

Grammar Boost: First and third person

When you write a text, you need to think about the **viewpoint** from which you write:
- If you are writing about yourself, you should write in the **first person**, using the **pronouns** 'I' and 'we'.
- If you are writing about other people, you will write mainly in the **third person**, using the pronouns 'he', 'she', 'it' and 'they'.

1 Rewrite the following sentences using the first **person**.

> When he was only five years old, he went to the museum with his family. His parents and his sister were interested in seeing all kinds of things, but he was interested only in looking at the dinosaurs. As he stared up at the massive creatures' skeletons, he imagined himself living in the time of the dinosaurs.

Activity 2: Starting sentences

There are lots of ways in which you can start a sentence.
- You can begin a sentence with a **pronoun** (such as 'I', 'you', 'he', 'she', 'it', 'they'). For example: *I shouted for help.*
- You can begin a sentence with a **noun** (such as 'water' or 'night'). For example: *Water dripped on my head.*
- You can begin a sentence with a **noun phrase** (such as 'cold water'). For example: *Cold water dripped on my head.*

1 Write **five** short sentences describing a dangerous situation. Your sentences should:
- describe how it felt to be in the dangerous situation
- be written in the first person
- each start with a different word.

Activity 3: Features of letters

When you write a letter, there are some key features you need to include.

The top of a letter should include:
- the sender's address
- the recipient's address
- the date
- a salutation or greeting.

Look carefully at the start of this letter:

> 11 Wordsworth Avenue
> Wingston Regis
> Southshire
> SU23 4PQ
>
> Zhang Min Li
> 1462 Fleming Street   23rd June 2019
> Tai Mun
> Hong Kong
>
> Dear Ms Min,
> Thank you for offering to answer some questions for our school newspaper. Our class is very grateful.

At the end of a letter, the sender should sign their name.
- If you are writing an **informal** letter to a close friend or relation, you might sign off affectionately, for example, 'Lots of love' and your name.
- If you are writing a **formal** letter to someone you do not know very well, you should sign 'Yours sincerely,' and your full name.
- If you are writing a formal letter that begins 'Dear Sir or Madam', you should sign 'Yours faithfully,' and your full name.

1 Use the examples above to write a guide explaining where each key feature of a letter should be positioned on the page.

2 Look again at the letter on page 40, and at the examples above. Judging by the letter conventions she used, what kind of letter was Penny writing to Padma? How would you describe their relationship?

3 Using all the key layout features, write the opening and closing of letters to:
a) a family member
b) your headteacher
c) the manager of a local business that is advertising a job you would like.

Activity 4: Writing a letter

You are going to write a letter to a friend or relative, telling them about a time when you were trapped in a difficult situation.

Imagine

1 Imagine a situation in which you could have found yourself trapped. Write **one** sentence summarising your experience. You could write about a real experience, or make one up.

I could write about the time when I fell into a...

I remember when I got locked inside the...

When I was younger, I managed to get my hand trapped in a...

Plan

2 Look at all the information you could include in your letter.

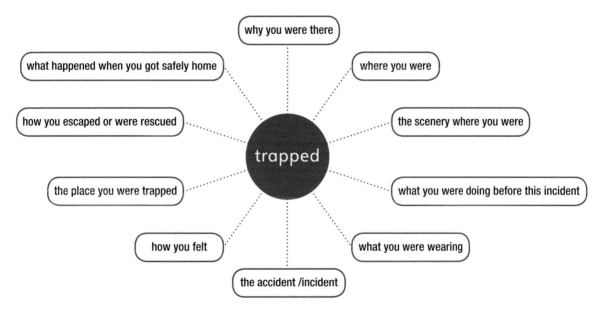

why you were there

what happened when you got safely home

where you were

how you escaped or were rescued

the scenery where you were

trapped

the place you were trapped

what you were doing before this incident

how you felt

what you were wearing

the accident /incident

   a) Write down the **four or five** details that will explain and describe your experience most fully.

   b) In what order will you sequence your chosen ideas? Number them.

Write

3 Write your letter. Aim to:
   - use the correct format and layout for a letter
   - use a first-person viewpoint
   - use a variety of sentence starts in your writing
   - tell the reader what happened
   - show the reader how you felt.

This section links to pages 40–43 of the Workbook.

Section 10
Reviewing and revising

In this section, you will develop your skills in **checking** the accuracy and effectiveness of your writing, and **revising** it to make improvements.

Activity 1: Sentence punctuation

A sentence should begin with a capital letter and end in a full stop, an exclamation mark or a question mark. One common error with sentence punctuation is using a comma to join two sentences that should be separated with a full stop.

1 Look at the following sentences:

A My alarm woke me up, it was very early.

B I put on a clean shirt, brushed my teeth and went out.

C Soon, I was ready to go.

D There was a loud noise, it sounded like something falling over.

a) Two of these sentences are punctuated correctly, and two are not. Which sentences are **not** punctuated correctly?

b) Look again at the two sentences that are not punctuated correctly. Rewrite each one as **two** sentences separated by a full stop.

Spelling Boost: Common verb suffixes

Verbs often have the suffix '–ed' added when they are in the past tense, and the suffix '–ing' when they are in the **past continuous** or **present continuous** tense:

Present tense: *I kick.* | Simple past tense: *I kicked.* | Present continuous tense: *I am kicking.*

For some verbs, you need to double the final letter when adding these suffixes.
You should double the final letter of the root verb if it:

- has one **syllable** and ends in **consonant**–**vowel**–consonant (for example, 'step' becomes 'stepped' and 'stepping')
- has two or more syllables, ends in consonant–vowel–consonant and the second syllable is stressed (for example, 'prefer' becomes 'preferred' and 'preferring').

Remember

- A syllable is a part of a word that makes a single sound.
- The letters 'a', 'e', 'i', 'o' and 'u' are vowels. All the other letters of the alphabet are consonants.

1 Which verbs are spelled correctly in the following sentences?

a) We hopped/hoped we would win the cup.

b) I love running/runing and jumpping/jumping.

c) They are shopping/shoping.

d) It was just beginning/begining to rain.

Activity 2: Proofreading

Look at the following extract from one student's writing. It contains **ten** mistakes. It is extremely important to **proofread** your writing for punctuation, spelling and grammar errors.

> I was four or five years old my sister wants to play hide-and-seek so I crept upstairs while she is counting to a hundred. I climbed inside my mum's wardrobe.
>
> I waited there for ages, I do not know how long I waitted. Eventually I give up and I tried to open the door. I could not move it. I pushed, shovved and rattled it but I could not open the door. I were traped. I began to panic, I called out but no one could hear me.

1 Copy and correct the text above. As you correct each mistake, label it to show the kind of mistake the writer made.

How do I do that?

To find **punctuation mistakes**, look closely at the full stops and capital letters.

- Some full stops and capital letters might be missing.
- There may be commas used where there should be full stops.

To find **spelling mistakes**, look closely at any words with suffixes to make sure the correct spelling has been used.

To find **grammar mistakes**, look closely at each verb.

- Does it agree with its subject?
- Does it match the tense used in the rest of the writing?

2 How many mistakes of each kind did you find? Copy and complete the sentences below.

> I found _____ of the three punctuation mistakes.
>
> I found _____ of the three spelling mistakes.
>
> I found _____ of the three grammar mistakes.

Take note of the kinds of mistakes that you had most difficulty finding. Use 'How did you score?' on page 46 to assess your ability to find each kind of mistake.

How did you score?

3/3 – Well done! You are good at spotting and correcting this kind of mistake.
2/3 – Well done, but you need to check twice for this kind of mistake.
0/3 or 1/3 – You need to look very closely at your writing for this kind of mistake.

Activity 3: Reviewing vocabulary choice

When you finish a piece of writing, you should review it to assess whether it is perfect or could be improved. Consider your vocabulary choice: have you chosen precisely the right words or could you choose more effective ones?

1 Look at the following extract from one student's writing. In his paragraph, the student has thought of some different vocabulary choices she could have made.

Mali reached a small rope bridge over the river. The river was big. The water bubbled strongly as it hurried beneath the bridge.

Vocabulary Bank

tiny	vast	boiled	angrily	rushed
little	huge	churned	violently	raced
narrow	wide	hissed	powerfully	flowed

Copy out the paragraph above, choosing the most effective vocabulary from the **Vocabulary Bank** to replace the highlighted words.

2 Look at the second paragraph from the student's writing, below.

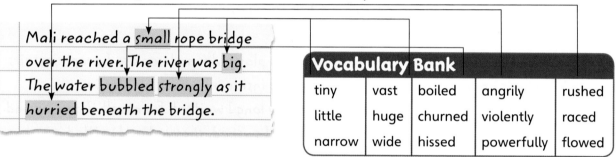

Mali began to walk over the bridge. She tried not to look down at the water below. Her hands were shaking and she could feel her heart beating. "You can do this," she said to herself. "Just take one step, then another, then another." Soon she reached the other side of the river. She felt happy.

Vocabulary Bank

a) Copy and complete the **Vocabulary Bank** with words that could be used to replace the highlighted words. Aim to add at least **two or three** options to each section of the bank.

b) Copy out the second paragraph, choosing the most effective vocabulary from your **Vocabulary Bank** to replace the highlighted choices.

Activity 4: Avoiding repetition

One way to make your meaning clearer and avoid repetition is to replace a noun with a pronoun.

1 Read the following sentences.

Reth walked to the shop. The shop was closed. Reth knew that Reth's mother was relying on Reth to buy ingredients for the big family meal that evening. Reth's family would be disappointed in Reth if Reth didn't complete the shopping. Reth decided that Reth would have to go to the shop in the next village. Reth hoped that the shop in the next village would be open.

a) Copy out the sentences, replacing any repeated nouns with the correct pronoun. You could look at the table below on pronouns for support.

b) Check that the meaning of the sentences is still clear. Would it be clearer if you put back any of the nouns you have taken out? If so, rewrite them again.

Pronouns	
Subject	I | you | he | she | it | we | they
Object	me | you | him | her | it | us | them

Activity 5: Reviewing and proofreading writing

1 Look at the following extract from one student's writing. It contains punctuation mistakes, grammar mistakes and spelling mistakes.

> I walked through the city streets. I looked at all the people walking past me.
> I look up at all the big buildings above me. I did not no where I was or where
> I was going. In the distance I could here the sound of a police siren and some
> voices, the siren and the voices made me feel worried and alone.

a) Look through the extract for the mistakes. Then copy and correct the extract. As you correct each mistake, label it to show the kind of mistake the writer made.

b) Underline **three** vocabulary choices in the extract that you think could be improved.

c) Create a vocabulary bank for each word you have underlined, and then choose the best word to replace it.

This section links to pages 44–45 of the Workbook.

Section 11
Assessment

In this section, you will answer questions on a short extract and write a short, narrative text to assess your progress in this unit.

▼ Read the extract and then answer the questions that follow it.

1 Raj was weary. He had worked all night at the office, hunched over his computer screen, peering at lines of code. Now, at last, in the early hours of the morning, he was heading home and looking forward to food and sleep. Despite his tiredness, he was calm and in good spirits. He sat easily in the saddle at the top of the steep descent into town, waiting for the lights to change. He gazed at the roofs of clustered houses glittering
5 with morning frost below. He watched the white smoke of early fires climbing from chimneys, their TV aerials gleaming against the blue sky. He turned his gaze to the familiar junction at the bottom, where the foot of the hill met the main road. The traffic was often heavy, particularly around 8.30, with a queue of impatient drivers making their way to work. But Raj figured it would be quiet so early in the morning. The light turned green, and he released his grip on the brakes, and pumped hard on the pedals. He crouched over the handlebars and began
10 to free-wheel.

Halfway down the hill he reached maximum speed, the wind billowing his jacket. A moment later he began to squeeze steadily on the brakes, so that he would slow and stop at the junction. He had made the descent so often he was confident he could judge it. Perhaps it was tiredness, or his brakes were worn, but he quickly realised that the junction was approaching too fast.

15 Panicking, he tugged hard on the brakes as his tyres hit a patch of ice. His heart thudding in his throat, he shot across the junction. From the corner of his eye, he saw a lorry heading towards him. The driver's shocked face filled Raj's vision. For an instant everything slowed,
20 and four words filled his mind…'I'm going to die…'.

A moment later he was flung through the air. He felt his left shoulder smash into the tarmac. He cannoned into a cluster of
25 dustbins and rubbish bags banked against a wall. The bins clattered and bounced like skittles; the bags exploded.

But for them, he would certainly have slammed into the bricks. Instead, he lay on
30 his back, dazed and sick, in a chaotic heap of garbage. His jacket was torn, his broken shoulder throbbing. He turned his head painfully and stared at his bike, folded and crushed beneath the wheels of the lorry.

Activity 1: Reading

1 Look carefully at the first paragraph of the extract. Identify **three** things you learn about the place where Raj crashes.

2 Continue to look at the second paragraph of the extract. What does this part of the story suggest about the character of Raj?

3 Look carefully at lines 14–19 of the extract.

   a) Give **two** descriptions from these lines that show this was a dramatic and violent crash.

   b) Which individual words in this part of the extract do you think create this effect most powerfully? Write one or two sentences explaining how these helped to form your response to the extract.

   c) How do you think the writer intended the reader to respond to this part of the story?

4 Look at the final paragraph of the extract.

   a) Where is the bike at the end of the extract?
   b) Where is Raj at the end of the extract?

Activity 2: Writing

Imagine a story in which a character is in a difficult or dangerous situation. At the end of the story, this character is rescued.

1 Write a short, narrative text telling the part of the story in which the character is rescued.

Before you start writing

- Think about the story. What was your character's difficult or dangerous situation? Who rescues your character?
- Plan your writing by gathering all the ideas you could include.
- Think carefully about how you will structure your writing. At what point in the story will you begin your text? How will you end it?

As you write

- Use a variety of sentence starts, sentence lengths and conjunctions.
- Choose your vocabulary carefully, including pronouns.

When you have finished writing

- Check the accuracy of your spelling, punctuation and grammar.
- Check the accuracy of your paragraphing.

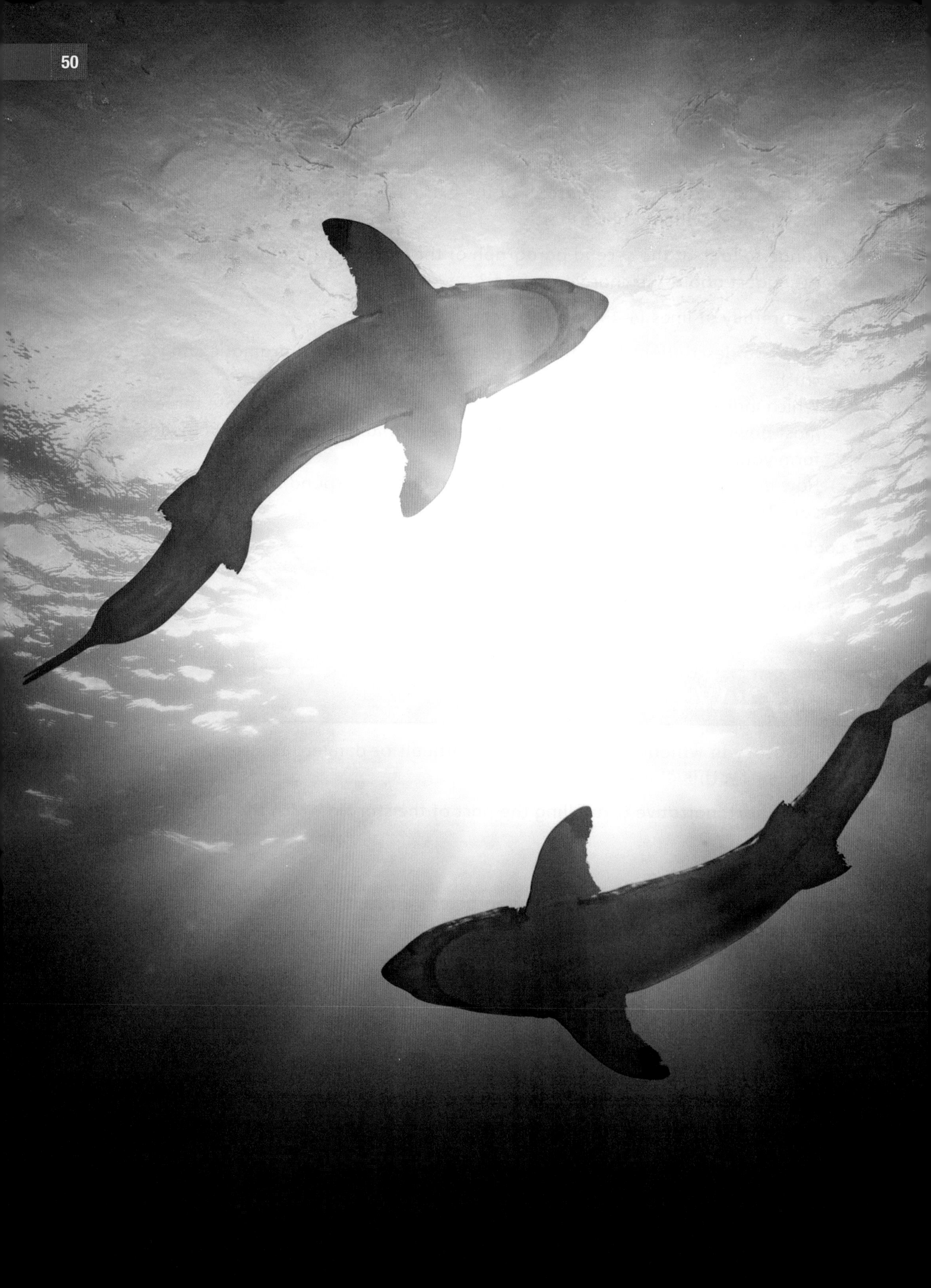

Unit 2
Danger!

In this unit you will explore a range of fiction and non-fiction texts in which people have been placed in dangerous situations. These range from natural disasters to conflict and unexpected accidents. The people featured are often tested to the limits of their strength and bravery. They include vivid descriptions of events and characters' feelings, and tense retellings of the moment the dangers occur. Would you be brave enough?

In this unit you will...

- explore different ways of reading a text and identifying key points of information.

- explore key ideas the writer has used to create a tense description.

- identify key ideas and use them to write a summary.

- identify and compare the key ideas in two extracts.

- answer questions on two short extracts to assess your progress in the unit so far.

- develop your inference skills and use them to explore a writer's intention.

- identify the writer's intention and explore your response to a text.

- explore a character's viewpoint and support your response with evidence.

- track and develop your response to a text.

- write the opening of a story. You will then write a response to it.

- answer questions on an extract from a novel to assess your progress in this unit.

By the end of this unit, you will be able to summarise, compare, and respond to narrative texts.

This section links to pages 46–49 of the Workbook.

Section 1
Reading and understanding

In this section, you will explore different ways of reading a text and identifying key points of information.

This extract is a **leaflet** designed to prepare people for a natural disaster.

> **DO NOT READ the leaflet below!**
> **Go straight to Activity 1 and follow the instructions.**

TSUNAMIS – BE PREPARED!

1 A tsunami (pronounced soo-nahm-ee) is a series of giant waves that happen after underwater movement due to natural events such as earthquakes, volcanic eruptions, landslides and meteorites. The waves travel in all directions from the area of disturbance, much like the ripples that happen after throwing a rock. The waves may travel in the open sea as fast as 450 miles per hour. As the big waves
5 approach shallow waters along the coast, they grow to a great height and smash into the shore. They can be as high as 100 feet.

BEFORE

✓ Build an emergency kit.
✓ Make a family communications plan.
✓ If the water recedes from the shoreline or
10 goes out to sea in a very noticeable way, get away from the area immediately. This is nature's warning that a tsunami is coming.

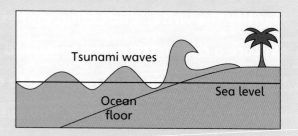

Tsunami waves

Sea level

Ocean floor

DURING

✓ Listen to evacuation orders and leave the area immediately.
15 ✓ Take any pets with you.
✓ Move inland (away from the ocean) and towards higher ground.
✓ Stay away from the beach. Never go down to the water to watch a tsunami come in. If
20 you can see the wave, you are too close to escape it.

AFTER

✓ Don't return home unless officials tell you it is safe to do so. Tsunami waves can continue for hours and the next wave may be more
25 dangerous than the first.
✓ Stay away from debris in the water. It could be dangerous.
✓ Stay out of any building with water around it. Water can make floors crack or walls
30 collapse.

Activity 1: Skim-reading

1 Spend no more than 30 seconds skim-reading the leaflet on page 52.

How do I do that?

Skim-reading means looking very quickly at a text to get an idea of what it is about. It does not mean trying to read every word in the text very quickly. One way to **skim-read** a text is to look at:

- the title and any subtitles
- only the first sentence of each paragraph or section of text.

a) Summarise in **one** sentence what kind of text the leaflet is.

b) Summarise in **one** sentence what the leaflet is about.

Skills Boost: Monitoring your understanding

As you read a text, it is important to monitor your understanding: to make sure you understand each sentence before you carry on reading.

1 Read the first paragraph of the leaflet on page 52 without pausing.

2 Copy the table below. Read the first paragraph again, pausing after each sentence to decide whether or not you have understood it. Using the table, note which sentences you understood straight away, and which ones you needed to work a little harder to understand. If you have to reread a sentence, start by rereading the sentence before it.

Sentence	1 ✓	2 ✓	3 ✓	4 ✓	5 ✓
I understood this sentence the first time.					
I needed to reread this sentence before I understood it.					
I asked a friend or adult to help me understand this sentence.					
I used a dictionary to help me understand this sentence.					
I still do not understand this sentence.					
The difficult words or features of the sentence were ...					

Activity 2: Checking your understanding

1 Now you have gained a fuller understanding of the leaflet on page 52, look again at your responses to Activity 1. How accurate were they? Write one or two sentences explaining your answer.

Activity 3: Scanning for key words

Once you have read a text, you can **scan** it to find the answers to questions about it. This means identifying a key word or phrase in the question and looking through the text for only that word or phrase. When you find it, you should find the answer to the question nearby.

1 Look at the question below. Do not answer it yet.

> How fast do tsunami waves travel in the open sea?

When you choose the key word or phrase in a question, always choose one that is unlikely to appear often in the text.

Which **one** of these words and phrases would you choose to scan for when you want to find the answer to the question above?

A	How	B	fast	C	do	D	tsunami waves
E	travel	F	in	G	the	H	open sea

2 Now scan the first paragraph of the leaflet on page 52 (below), looking for the keyword or phrase you chose in question 1. Use it to answer the question: How fast do tsunami waves travel in the open sea?

TSUNAMIS – BE PREPARED!

A tsunami (pronounced soo-nahm-ee) is a series of giant waves that happen after underwater movement due to natural events such as earthquakes, volcanic eruptions, landslides and meteorites. The waves travel in all directions from the area of disturbance, much like the ripples that happen after throwing a rock. The waves may travel in the open sea as fast as 450 miles per hour. As the big waves approach shallow waters along the coast, they grow to a great height and smash into the shore. They can be as high as 100 feet.

3 How helpful did you find scanning? Did you select a useful word or phrase? Write one or two sentences explaining your ideas.

Activity 4: Scanning for key points of information

Use scanning to help you answer the following questions about the whole leaflet on page 52. When you write your answers:

- note down the key word or phrase for which you scanned the leaflet
- use complete sentences.

For example:

1 How is the word 'tsunami' pronounced?

2 How high can a tsunami wave be?

3 What should you take with you during a tsunami?

4 When should you return home after a tsunami?

5 Why should you stay out of a building if it has water around it?

> 1 The key word I used was 'pronounced'.
> The word 'tsunami' is pronounced...

> 2 The key word I used was 'high'.
> A tsunami wave can be...

Activity 5: Combining key points of information

Scanning can help you to find and combine key points of information to answer more complicated questions.

1 **a)** Scan the leaflet on page 52 and note down any information that explains how tsunamis happen.

> **How do I do that?**
>
> 1 Look at each sentence in the leaflet.
> 2 Ask yourself: Is it relevant to the task?
> 3 If it is, note down the key information you find. If it isn't, keep reading and scanning.
>
> - caused by underwater movement, e.g. earthquake, volcanic eruption
> - waves travel in all directions

b) Referring to your notes, use your own words to write **three or four** sentences explaining how tsunamis happen.

2 **a)** Scan the leaflet and note down any information that explains how frightening and dangerous tsunamis can be.
b) Referring to your notes, use your own words to write **three or four** sentences explaining how frightening and dangerous tsunamis can be.

This section links to pages 50–53 of the Workbook.

Section 2
Combining key points

In this section, you will explore key ideas the writer has used to create a tense description.

Eight-year-old Amber Owen was in Thailand on holiday with her mother and stepfather in 2004. A deadly tsunami struck while she was riding Ning Nong* the elephant. A tsunami is an enormous wave caused by an earthquake deep beneath the sea.

▼ Read the extract and then answer the questions that follow it.

1 Amber remembers the morning of the tsunami: 'There was a small earthquake about eight in the morning, but we didn't think much about it. I was riding along the beach on Ning Nong after breakfast and I could tell he was anxious and kept turning away from the sea. As he edged inland, a huge wave rushed up to his shoulders.' Clinging to the back of the elephant as the waves threatened to engulf them, Amber watched in terror as flailing fellow holidaymakers disappeared beneath the breakers.

2 Just moments before, the tide had suddenly receded, and though Amber had no idea what was happening, a huge tsunami was about to smash across the beach. 'But Ning Nong definitely did know,' Amber recalls. 'While some people ran to pick up the fish scattered across the beach when the waves went out, he became agitated at once. He knew something was wrong and began running as fast as he could inland.

3 'The mahout [elephant trainer] kept trying to get him to come back down the beach towards the sea but he wouldn't go. He kept pulling away and trying to run from it.'

4 But it was this amazing animal instinct that saved her life when the wall of waves hit. Amber's mother was only alerted to the disaster when she heard screams from the beach. 'We ran down the sand, and because Amber was always with Ning Nong I was screaming, "Where's the elephant?" ' says Samantha, 47. 'Someone said he was dead and I panicked because I knew Amber would have been on his back. I was trying to sprint but the water was up to my knees.'

5 Meanwhile, and unbeknown to Samantha, Ning Nong was already heading inland, forcing his body forward as he waded against the strong currents now swirling around his shoulders. The sturdy elephant had managed to climb up the beach, straining to brace himself against the force of the water. As trees and houses fell, he remained standing.

6 He only stopped when he found a small wall then, wedging himself beside the stone shelf, he withstood the powerful pressure of the rising water long enough for Amber to scramble on to the wall to safety. 'I remember being so scared but so relieved,' says Amber.

7 Samantha adds: 'That's when I saw Ning Nong in the distance, at the other end of the beach, by the wall, with Amber on his back. I was almost hysterical with relief. We grabbed her, then ran to the hotel. We just made it to our first-floor room when, less than ten minutes later, the next wave came in and swept two ground-floor rooms away.'

Remember

Tracking how the writer's thoughts and feelings change can help you identify the key points in a text.

*Ning Nong is an affectionate Thai nickname in this context

Skills Boost: Understanding unfamiliar words

When you are reading a text, you may come across a word you do not know. You can often use the words around it to help you work out its meaning.

How do I do that?

Look at the clues to the missing word in this sentence:

I looked up at the tall **?**. The sunlight was shining through its leaves and branches.

(The highlighted words suggest that the missing word could be some kind of tree.)

1 Look at the following sentences. Using the clues, work out what kind of word would make sense to replace each **?**. Use the example to guide you in forming your answers.

A *wolf* was running towards me, snarling and growling and showing all its *sharp* teeth.

What kind of thing runs, snarls and growls? This must be a kind of dangerous animal.

This is probably an adjective, describing the dangerous animal's teeth.

a) When she realised she had lost the race, she was filled with a feeling of **?**. She **?** to the ground and covered her face to hide her tears.

b) They ran through the forest as **?** as they could. They were too **?** to look back.

Activity 1: Understanding new vocabulary

1 Look again at the following sentence from the extract on page 56.

Clinging to the back of the elephant as the waves threatened to engulf them, Amber watched in terror as flailing fellow holidaymakers disappeared beneath the breakers.

a) Note down any words in this sentence that you do not know or understand.
b) Using the **context** of the other words around it, try to guess the meaning of each word you have written down.
c) Which of the following sentences best describes your understanding of the quotation above?
  A There are some unfamiliar words in the sentence but they do not stop me understanding its overall meaning.
  B I do not understand the meaning of the sentence because it contains some unfamiliar words.
  C I know and understand every word in the sentence.

2 Note down any other words in the extract that you do not know or understand. Use their context to try to work out their meanings.

Activity 2: Testing yourself

When you finish reading a text, try testing yourself on it to consolidate your understanding.

1 Identify whether each of the following statements is true or false.
   a) When Amber first experienced the small earthquake, she was immediately worried.
   b) Ning Nong had no idea the tsunami was about to happen.
   c) Ning Nong charged up the beach to the hotel, with Amber on his back.

2 Look again at the extract on page 56, from paragraph 6 onwards. Write **three** true-or-false statements of your own, to test a partner's understanding of it.

Activity 3: Identifying key points

The key points in a text are the most important pieces of information the writer gives the reader about events, ideas, actions or reactions.

1 The writer of the extract on page 56 describes what happened to Amber when the tsunami hit. Look at the following list of nine things that happened.

1. Amber rode Ning Nong on the beach.
2. She clung to Ning Nong's back as the waves rose.
3. Amber's mother was worried Amber was in danger.
4. Ning Nong ran away from the sea with Amber.
5. Amber climbed from Ning Nong's back onto a small wall.
6. Amber's mother saw Amber on the wall.
7. They ran to their hotel.
8. They arrived at their hotel room.
9. Other rooms in the hotel were destroyed.

   a) Which are the **five** most important pieces of information in the extract?
   b) Look at the list of five pieces of key information you have selected. Which are the **three** most important?

Activity 4: Combining and comparing key points

You are now going to identify key points that are relevant to one important aspect of the extract on page 56.

1 Think about Amber's reactions to the things she sees. Which emotions do you think she feels? You could choose from the emotions below or use your own ideas.

enjoyment | surprise | panic | worry | relief | happiness | indifference

2 Look at the list of emotions you have identified in question 1. Copy and complete the sentences below by replacing the **?** in each sentence to combine these important key points in a summary.

a) At first, Amber feels **?**.
b) Then she starts to feel **?** because **?**.
c) Finally, Amber realises that **?** and she feels **?**.

3 Look at the extract again, focusing on Samantha, Amber's mother. Write **two or three** sentences describing how Samantha's feelings change. You could use some of the ideas and sentences above to guide your answer.

4 Look again at your answers to questions 1, 2 and 3 above. Write one or two sentences comparing Amber's reactions with Samantha's. You could use some of the following words and phrases to help you.

At first, | Eventually, | Finally,

Amber | Samantha | both Amber and Samantha

whereas | On the other hand, | However,

This section links to pages 54–57 of the Workbook.

Section 3
Summarising key information

In this section, you will identify key ideas and use them to write a summary.

This extract is from a story told by a mother about the conflict between her family and another family. The families live in neighbouring villages, in a valley in the mountains.

▼ Read the extract and then answer the questions that follow it.

1 I was chopping vegetables by our stove when I heard shouting from my son's house next door. Shouting, the noise of a struggle and then a scream. I dropped everything, not caring that I knocked the pot from the stove, and ran out of my house yelling, "Sam! Sam! What's happening? Are you okay?"

2 A tall man, his face hidden by a wrapped scarf, came out of Sam's house. Two more masked men followed him, holding an obviously hurt Sam between them. Blood trickled from a cut on Sam's face.

3 "This is your son? Where's his brother?" the man demanded. "We need to talk to him, too."

4 "I don't know. He left for work early," I replied. "Let Sam go. He's done nothing wrong, nothing!"

5 The man towered over me and I smelt chemicals. No, not chemicals – I saw the petrol can in his hand now. He held it up, threatening me, "We'll burn this village unless you tell us."

6 "I don't know which field he's working in," I lied, desperately. "Please, let Sam go."

7 "Yes you do. Tell me now, or we'll burn the village. Do you want to see your pretty painted house burnt to ashes?" He unscrewed the lid from the can and began to pour petrol on the path leading to my front door.

8 I suddenly recognised the man's voice. This attacker had a name. I knew him.

9 "Cal, how dare you threaten me," I shouted, doing my best to seem confident. Cal hesitated.

10 He had grown up in the next village along the valley. The same age as Sam, they'd quarrelled all their lives. Even as little boys, they'd argued about who owned a ball, or who was the best cricket player. Now they were fighting over who owned the land between our villages.

11 "So you think you know who I am?" he asked, reaching into his pocket and taking out a match. He lit it.

12 "Let my son go, Cal. Go home with your brothers." I sounded much braver than I felt but I couldn't take my eyes from the burning match.

13 He brought the flame up to his face and blew hard. "We'll be back," he growled. His brothers let go of Sam, who fell to the ground, and they marched down the road. Sam hauled himself to his feet and ran towards the field, where he knew his brother was working.

Remember

Check your understanding as you read. If you lose understanding, stop reading and try to find the word or part of a sentence that needs more work.

Activity 1: Checking understanding

1 Use your skim-reading and scanning skills to help you answer the following questions.

How do I do that?

1   Identify a key word or phrase in each question – a word or phrase that is unlikely to appear more than once or twice in the extract.
2   Scan the extract on page 60 for that key word or phrase.
3   When you find it, read around that word to find the answer to the question.

a) Why did the mother run out of her house?
b) What was the name of her son?
c) What did the masked man want?
d) How did the mother know who Cal was?
e) What did Cal do with the match?
f) Why might Cal not have carried out his threat?

Activity 2: Identifying key points

Before you write a summary of a text, you should identify the key points of information it contains.

How do I do that?

One way to do this is by dividing the text into paragraphs – or, if a text contains several short paragraphs, by dividing it into sections of two or more paragraphs. You can then look for the key piece of information in each paragraph or section.

1 Note down each key idea in the extract on page 60, and the number or numbers of the paragraphs that explain it. For example:

- Masked men capturing Sam: paragraphs 1–2

- Masked man speaking to the mother: paragraphs 3–7

2 Look again at the ideas you have identified. Cross out any you do not think should be included in a summary of only the key points of information.

3 To create your summary, write **one** short sentence summing up each of the remaining key ideas in your list. For example:

Sam is captured by masked men. One of the men talks to the mother.

Activity 3: Combining key points

An effective summary of an account like the mother's combines key points of information about:
- what happened
- who was involved
- where it happened
- why it happened.

1 Read the extract on page 60 carefully, noting down every piece of information you can find about each of the above elements. You could copy and complete the spidergram below, following the examples given for the 'Who' element.

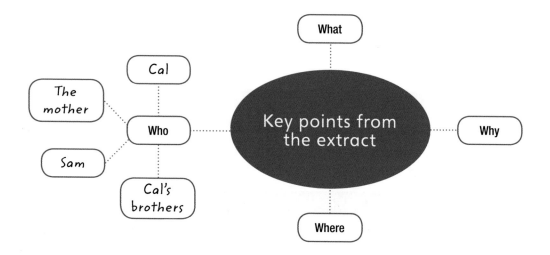

2 Look at all the pieces of information you have noted. Decide which of them are important or interesting enough to be used in a 50-word summary of the extract.

Tick (✓) any information that might be important or interesting enough.
Cross (✗) any information that is not important or interesting enough.

How do I do that?

Choose **five or six** pieces of information that help to describe the events, the thoughts or the feelings experienced by the people in the extract.

Grammar Boost: Linking clauses with conjunctions

Single-clause sentences contain one clause, which contains one verb and gives the reader one piece of information. For example:

| The mother was chopping vegetables. | | The mother heard a struggle. |

Multi-clause sentences contain two or more clauses, often linked with conjunctions. The words 'and', 'but' and 'or' are all **coordinating conjunctions**.
Subordinating conjunctions show how two clauses are linked. They could add information about cause, effect, time, condition or concession. For example:

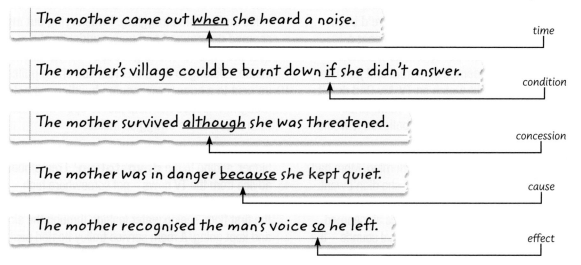

The mother came out <u>when</u> she heard a noise.   *time*

The mother's village could be burnt down <u>if</u> she didn't answer.   *condition*

The mother survived <u>although</u> she was threatened.   *concession*

The mother was in danger <u>because</u> she kept quiet.   *cause*

The mother recognised the man's voice <u>so</u> he left.   *effect*

1 Link each pair of sentences below to create a single, multi-clause sentence, choosing the conjunction that makes the clearest link between them.
  a) The mother heard a noise. She came out of her house.
  b) The man threatened to burn the village. He wanted to know where her son was.
  c) The mother knew who the man was. She recognised his voice.

Conjunction Bank

and	but
although	while
when	until
before	so
if	because

Activity 4: Summarising key information

1 Write a summary of the extract on page 60 using **50** words or fewer.
  a) Note down the key events described in the extract, in chronological order.
  b) Add any relevant or interesting details from Activity 3 to your notes.
  c) Use your notes to write your summary.
  d) Count the number of words you have used in your summary. If you have used over 50 words, cut out some of the less important information. If you have used under 50 words, could you add a little more information from your response to Activity 3?

Section 4
Comparing key points

In this section, you will identify and compare the key ideas in two extracts.

Extract A is taken from a fictional account of real events. Gulfport is a coastal city in the United States. In August 2005, it was hit by a terrible storm – Hurricane Katrina. The story is told by Anna Jackson, a fourteen-year-old girl, who lived there with her parents.

▼ Read Extract A and then answer the questions that follow it.

1 It was early in the morning that the hurricane hit. We'd been warned it was coming and there'd been pictures of it on TV hitting just down the coast a few days earlier. The local police told us we should

5 **evacuate**[1] but it all seemed so unreal and just like any other show we might watch on TV. My Dad didn't seem worried and that helped me be calm. To be honest, I don't think any of us really believed it would happen. We were wrong.

10 I'd been dragged out of bed early that morning, Mom had wanted to get to the store to stock up – she didn't want to be the last there in case panicking people bought all the food! It was quiet when we left and the air seemed still and heavy. Looking back, all the normal sounds – the

15 calling of seagulls, and barking of dogs – were missing, almost as if the animals knew danger was on the way.

As we drove, the weather got worse. To start with it was just a slight darkening of the sky but soon Mom had to turn the headlamps on. Now I began to worry.

20 I remembered the pictures of the hurricane from TV and it began to seem real. The wind began to whistle louder and louder. Litter flew across the road and hit the car like rain. I saw **white caps**[2] out at sea, growing bigger and bigger. Palm trees were whipping

25 round and bending…one snapped right in front of us. I remember screaming as Mom stood on the brakes and we skidded towards it. As we stopped dead, a trashcan slammed into the car, and the ocean raced across the tarmac, moving the car sideways.

30 I was frantic, I was just a passenger, I didn't know what to do. I was dimly aware of my Mom screaming down the phone and then the car coughing a few times and the wheels spinning as she pulled round the fallen tree and sped away.

35 I stared out of the windshield and saw cars on their sides and people struggling. I was crying but my Mom seemed determined and now, suddenly, she shouted over the wind for me to get out of the car and head inside. Looking to the side I realised she'd pulled

40 up next to a huge, grey, square building – a hotel, I thought. I needed her help just to open the door, and then together we struggled inside.

This whole time the water had been getting higher and higher, adding to the **devastation**[3]. I remembered the

45 advice from the TV news – get somewhere high – so we ran into the stairwell and headed up and up. We passed the first floor, seeing water leaking through the air vents and kept going. A room service trolley floated past and I remember wondering where the maid was. We kept

50 going, breathless now until we reached the fourth or fifth floor – it still looked dry. We found an empty room and sat down. I breathed out for what seemed like the first time in hours and clung to my Mom.

Through the window we watched the scene far below,

55 barely able to think over the noise. Roofs were being torn off houses, boats and trucks were smashing into each other. It was four hours before the water began to drop, and another eight before we crept out to join the **bewildered**[4] huddle of survivors. It was the

60 longest day of my life.

Key vocabulary

evacuate[1]: leave
white caps[2]: strong waves caused by wind
devastation[3]: destruction
bewildered[4]: scared and confused

Activity 1: Exploring Extract A

1 a) In what way does the weather change during the course of Extract A on page 64?

b) Note down **four** pieces of evidence from the extract that show how the weather changes. They could describe the weather or its effect on the setting.

2 Why did Anna's family decide to stay in Gulfport?

3 Imagine that you were living in the town of Gulfport during the hurricane. At what point during the events described in the extract would you have headed for the hotel? Why is that? Write one or two sentences to explain your ideas.

Activity 2: Identifying key points in Extract A

When you compare the information in two extracts, you first need to identify each extract's key points.

How do I do that?

One way to identify key points is to note down the most important subjects in the extract: its different characters, events and settings. Once you have identified these, you can focus on the key points that the writer makes about each.

1 Which of the following do you think are the most important subjects in Extract A on page 64?

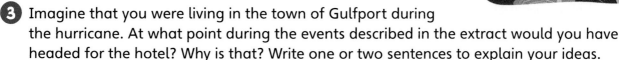

A	B	C	D
the weather	the hotel	the narrator	the sea

E	F	G	H
the narrator's family	the destruction caused	the police	the television

2 What do you learn about each of the subjects you have selected? Write down **one or two** pieces of information about each one.

3 Look at each of the points of information you have gathered. Is each point a key point? Ask yourself: Does it tell the reader something important about the setting, the events or people in the extract? If not, cross it out.

Extract B is from a fictional account of the floods which struck the UK town of Upton Upon Severn in July 2007. The narrator is a teenage girl called Mary, whose family live next to the river.

▼ **Read Extract B and then answer the questions that follow it.**

1　At certain times of year the river bursts its banks, but it's usually only the fields which are flooded. That morning, it came over the roads. My brother Phil woke me. It was raining heavily. Dad had gone out, but hadn't come back. Water was gushing into the hallway and Mum was panicking. I told
5　her to get upstairs. I phoned the police and said Dad was missing. They said boat patrols were out looking for people who were stranded, and we should wait.

　Our neighbour phoned. She said a group who own motorboats had formed a volunteer rescue squad, and were going from house to house. We raced
10　downstairs and waded out. She threw us a line, and we were dragged aboard.

　It wasn't only people who were in danger. There are some stables a couple of miles away. Fortunately, the owner got news of the rising waters in time, and transported the horses to higher ground. Some local sheep farmers
15　weren't so lucky as many sheep were lost.

Activity 3: Making connections

1 Look again at the most important subjects you identified in Extract A on page 64, in the previous lesson. Copy and complete the table below, adding the main subjects from Extract A to the first column. One example has been added for you.

2 Now complete the second column in relation to each subject. Can you make any connections between the subjects in Extract A and Extract B? Write your answers in the second column. One example has been added for you.

Subject from Extract A	Is this an important subject in Extract B? Why is that?
The weather	This is important in Extract B because the rain is so heavy it causes the river to flood over the road, threatening the lives of the local people.

3 Note down any subjects that are important in Extract B, but not in Extract A.

4 What do you learn about each of the important subjects in Extract B? Write down **one or two** pieces of information about each one.

Grammar Boost: Pronouns

Pronouns can replace or stand in for a noun. Using pronouns can help you to avoid repeating words or phrases, and to link together ideas. However, it must always be clear what subject each pronoun represents.

1 Read the sentences below. Note down each of the pronouns in the text and which noun or nouns each pronoun represents.

Clouds were gathering. They were heavy and grey. Rain began to fall. At first, it formed just a shower – but then it began to grow heavier. There was a flash of lightning, and a crack of thunder. When she heard it, my sister screamed. We ran to find our parents.

Pronoun Bank		
I	you	
he	she	it
we	they	

2 a) Copy out the extract below, underlining all the repeated nouns.

At first, the building was shaking and groaning – but then the building suddenly collapsed. People ran screaming. People were terrified. As people ran, some cracks appeared in the ground. The cracks made the people run even faster.

b) Rewrite the extract, using pronouns to replace some of the repeated nouns.
c) Check that it is still clear what subject each pronoun represents. If it isn't, change some pronouns back into nouns.

Activity 4: Making comparisons

1 Write a comparison of the key points of information in Extract A on page 64 and Extract B on page 66. Aim to write **two or three** sentences about each of the key subjects you have identified in Activity 3, comparing their key points. For example, you could write about:
- the weather
- the destruction caused
- how people react to the events described.

You could use some of the words and phrases below to help you make a clear comparison.

Extract A covers the key subjects of

Whereas in Extract B the most important subject is

However, both texts   On the other hand,

Similarly,   Also,   In the same way,

Section 5
Assessment

In this section, you will answer questions on two short extracts to assess your progress in the unit so far.

Extract A is from the opening of an old Japanese **myth**.

▼ Read Extract A and then answer the questions that follow it.

1 Lake Biwa was famous for its beauty, but in those days it had few visitors. Everyone for miles about lived in terror of a monstrous centipede that destroyed houses, and ate not only cattle but local children! However, Hidesato was a dauntless warrior, and he couldn't live for long without adventure. So he went to Lake Biwa, to see the monster for himself.

5 After many days' travel, Hidesato came to a bridge that lay across the end of the lake. The moment he set foot on the bridge, he saw a sight that made even his warrior heart tremble. A massive dragon lay coiled like a serpent across the bridge, blocking his path. Fire and smoke wreathed from its nostrils, and it appeared to be sleeping.

"Well," thought Hidesato, "I've come this far, and I can't turn back now." And he clambered over the sleeping dragon's body, trying his hardest not to wake it. It seemed
10 an eternity until he reached the far end of the bridge, with the dragon apparently slumbering on.

He had only taken a few steps away from the bridge when he heard someone calling his name. Whipping round, he saw to his shock that the dragon had vanished! In its place, a regal-looking man stood on the bridge. His hair was long, red and flowing, and
15 he wore a lavishly decorated crown in the shape of a dragon's head.

"Hidesato!" said the man. "I am the Dragon King of the Lake. I have waited many long days for a warrior brave enough to cross my bridge. I have a challenge for you, if you choose to accept it."

Activity 1: Reading Extract A

1 Look carefully at the description of Hidesato in the first paragraph. Using the context, describe what kind of meaning you think the word 'dauntless' may have.

2 Why is the dragon lying on the bridge?

3 Explain **two** ways in which Hidesato shows bravery in this extract.

4 In your opinion, will Hidesato accept the Dragon King's challenge? Write one or two sentences to explain your answer.

5 Using only **one** sentence, summarise the events described in Extract A.

Extract B tells the story of Thandi and her unexpected encounter with danger.

▼ **Read Extract B and then answer the questions that follow it.**

1   It was early in the morning when I left the cabin to walk down the narrow path to the lake. Already a haze hung over the landscape, the gentle breeze doing nothing to cool the heat.

The water looked calm and inviting, dappled with shadows and the occasional ripple from a bird darting down to snatch an insect. I took a moment to just enjoy the feeling of the sun on my skin, leaning against a tree trunk at the
5   top of the bank.

Without warning, the water erupted, and a long shape launched itself onto the bank in front of me. My heart almost stopped as I realised what that shape was – a full-grown saltwater crocodile.

I was so shocked I couldn't move at all. Then, the crocodile lashed its tail and seemed to grin at me and quicker than I could have thought possible started climbing the bank towards me.

10   Without thinking, I span and ran as fast as I could, away from the bank and towards the low-hanging branches of a nearby tree. Gasping for air, I pulled myself up and clung to the trunk.

Looking down, I saw the crocodile, so close now, nosing around the bottom of the tree. With an agility that didn't seem possible it launched itself towards me, its jaws
15   snapping closed centimetres from my feet. I desperately climbed higher into the thinning branches, as high as I dared, knowing a fall meant certain death.

For what seemed like hours I sat in that tree, waiting for the creature to move. The sun was high and I was dizzy with thirst by the time it turned and slowly walked back to the lake, slipping under the surface with hardly a splash. It was even longer before I
20   had the courage to climb down and make my way back to the cabin.

Activity 2: Reading Extract B

1 What was the narrator doing before she saw the crocodile?

2 How did the narrator feel before she saw the crocodile?

3 In your opinion, was the narrator brave or foolish to behave as she did? Write one or two sentences to explain your answer.

4 Explain **two** ways in which the narrator shows how dangerous the crocodile was.

Activity 3: Comparing

1 Write a comparison of the situations and events described in Extract A and Extract B. You may wish to:
   • compare your answers to Activities 1 and 2
   • consider the main subjects of the extracts
   • note down the key ideas in each extract.

This section links to pages 64–67 of the Workbook.

Section 6
Inferring intentions

In this section, you will develop your inference skills and use them to explore a writer's intention.

This extract is the opening to a short story set in the United States about a family living with the threat of wildfires.

▼ Read the extract below and then answer the questions that follow it.

1 The house backed onto an area of sage, buckwheat and greasewood shrubs and tall cedar trees. The setting could be beautiful, but when the plants began to wither in autumn, the area was like **tinder**. A campfire, a tossed match, or even lightning would be enough to start a blaze which could spread quickly and threaten the whole town.

2 Mum said this danger was the reason she had decided to volunteer for the local fire crew, but sometimes Brin thought it was because of what happened to her brother. The picture of Uncle Jess had hung above the fireplace in the sitting room for as long as Brin could remember. Brin couldn't recall if his mum had hung it there before or after the wildfire – in fact he could barely remember his uncle these days. The perfect, smiling man in the yellow helmet had helped him to build a picture of a hero in his mind. Jess's sacrifice was never really discussed, but its effect on the family, and on Mum in particular, was obvious. She seemed determined to carry on where he'd left off.

3 But recently, Brin had begun to worry about his Mum. She seemed to have lost weight, and her skin looked paler and paler. Sometimes he thought he could hear her coughing softly in the room across the landing and he lay awake worrying long after she stopped. Every Tuesday evening, she set out to practise with her fellow firefighters at the town hall. On those evenings, the look on Dad's face as he sat staring at the TV suggested that Brin was not the only person who worried.

4 Brin had done his best to ignore all this. After all, how hurt could she get practising? But that morning the phone had rung, calling his Mum away. A fire had started on the other side of town, and the whole crew were put on full alert. She'd gone out early, gathering her gear and quickly drinking a coffee, and left them to their breakfast. Brin paced around the house, unable to relax.

5 There was a knock at the door. Brin's stomach jumped. He ran to the door and threw it open. It was his friend, Mia – and as he tried to smile, the scent of smoke hit him and he shivered.

6 "What's wrong?" asked Mia.

7 "I need to go and see Mum," he said. "She's in trouble, I know she is. She might be hurt. Or worse. I need to go and find her."

Key vocabulary

tinder: dry flammable material used for lighting fires

Activity 1: Retrieving information

You will often be asked to retrieve information from a text. This means reading the text carefully so that you can find the information you need to answer a question. Use your skim-reading and scanning skills to help you answer the following questions.

1 What plants grew near the house?

2 At what time of year was fire most likely?

3 Whose picture is on the wall in the sitting room?

4 Where does Brin's mother go every Tuesday evening?

5 Why did Brin's mother go out that morning?

Activity 2: Using the skill of inference

Sometimes a writer will clearly and explicitly state ideas or information. However, sometimes the writer will suggest, or imply, an idea to the reader instead.

Readers must then use the skill of inference: using clues in the text, they have to infer, or work out, what the writer is suggesting.

Try using the skill of inference to answer the following questions.

1 Look again at the following sentence from the second paragraph of the extract on page 70.

> Jess's sacrifice was never really discussed, but its effect on the family, and on Mum in particular, was obvious.

What idea is the writer suggesting about what happened to Uncle Jess?

2 Look again at paragraphs 3 and 7. What can you infer about the reason Brin and his father worry? Decide whether each of the following statements is true or false.
a) Brin's mother is not a trained firefighter.
b) Brin's mother suffers with ill health.
c) Brin's mother does not have proper firefighter's equipment.

3 Look again at your answers to question 2. Note down the word or phrase from the extract that helped you to make your decision about each statement.

4 Look again at paragraphs 5–7 of the extract on page 70. What does Mia infer about Brin? What clue does she use? Write one or two sentences to explain your ideas.

Skills Boost: Using quotations

You can use a quotation from the text as evidence to support or prove your ideas.

A quotation should always be:
- entirely relevant to the ideas it supports (so shorter quotations may be better)
- accurately copied from the text, including any punctuation
- enclosed in speech marks.

1 How has the writer of the following statements **not** followed the rules for using quotations?

a) The writer uses the word 'tinder to imply that the area becomes a fire hazard in autumn.

b) The writer implies that Brin's father is not happy when his wife goes out on Tuesday evenings: 'he looked worried as he sat staring at the TV'.

c) The writer suggests that Brin is worried about his mother going to fight the fire on the other side of town because he says, 'A fire had started on the other side of town, and the whole crew were put on full alert. She'd gone out early, gathering her gear and quickly drinking a coffee, and left them to their breakfast. Brin paced around the house, unable to relax.'

Activity 3: Identifying the writer's intention

Writers select ideas and descriptive details to create a specific effect on the reader.

1 Look again at paragraph 2 of the extract on page 70. What impression is the writer trying to create of Uncle Jess?

2 Consider how you worked out your answer to question 1.
   a) Note down any clues that helped you.
   b) Choose **one** quotation from paragraph 2 that shows the writer's intended impression of Uncle Jess. Use it in a sentence, taking care to copy and punctuate it correctly.

3 Look again at paragraph 1 of the extract. Choose **one** quotation that shows what impression the writer is trying to create of the place where they live. Use it in a sentence, taking care to copy and punctuate it correctly.

4 Look again at the whole extract. Choose **one** quotation that shows what impression the writer is trying to create of Brin's thoughts and feelings. Use it in a sentence, taking care to copy and punctuate it correctly.

Activity 4: Writing to achieve your intention

You are going to write **one or two** paragraphs in which the narrator implies his or her thoughts and feelings.

Imagine

1 Imagine that you have an important test tomorrow. You are worried because you want to do well in the test, and because you want to make your family proud.

Plan

2 Plan **one or two** paragraphs implying, not explaining, your thoughts and feelings on the night before your test. You will have to explore some ways in which you can suggest ideas, meaning readers must use their skills of inference.

Note down ways in which you could:

- show the reader that you feel worried without using words such as 'worried', 'frightened' or 'nervous'
- show the reader how your family will feel if you do well or badly without using words such as 'proud' or 'disappointed'

You could describe:

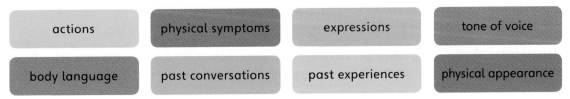

actions	physical symptoms	expressions	tone of voice
body language	past conversations	past experiences	physical appearance

Write

3 Write **one or two** paragraphs suggesting your thoughts and feelings on the night before your test. Remember not to explain these: try only to imply them.

Avoid words like these:

worried | nervous | frightened | proud | happy | disappointed

This section links to pages 68–71 of the Workbook.

Section 7
Responding to a text

In this section, you will identify the writer's intention and explore your response to a text.

This extract is from a novel about a young girl called Sunflower, who has recently moved from the city to a remote house in the countryside. In this extract, she looks across the river to the village of Damaidi, and longs to visit it.

▼ **Read the extract and then answer the questions that follow it.**

1 One day, Sunflower was down by the river. Damaidi looked like a huge boat moored in the reeds on the other side. She saw two haystacks as high as mountains, one on the left, one on the right. She saw a melia tree in blossom, clouds of pale lilac dusting the treetops. She saw milky-white cooking smoke curling up into the sky, then meeting and drifting as one over the reeds. Dogs were running through the streets. A cockerel had flown up into a mulberry tree and was crowing. There was children's laughter everywhere.

2 Sunflower longed to go there. She turned to look at the little boat that was tied to the old elm tree. She had seen it when she arrived, bobbing about on the water as though trying to attract her attention. A seed of an idea began to form in her mind. It grew like a shoot of grass pushing its way through the wet earth.

3 As the grass fluttered in the spring wind, the idea took shape: I'm going to get into that boat and go to Damaidi. But did she dare? She looked back at the Cadre School, then nervously inched towards the boat. There was no landing, just a grassy embankment, quite steep. She didn't know whether to climb down facing the river or facing the embankment. She hesitated a while, then eventually chose to face the embankment. She grabbed hold of the grass with both hands and tried to find a good place to put her feet. Slowly and steadily, she began to climb down to the water's edge.

4 Boats passed in the distance, helped along by the breeze. If anyone on board had looked her way, they might have been alarmed by what they saw but would have been unable to do anything about it. As she lowered herself down, drenched in sweat, Sunflower could hear the water gurgling below her feet. Her small hands clung to the grass, holding on for dear life.

5 A sailing boat came along. Seeing a little girl clinging to the embankment like a gecko, the man at the helm called out to her. Then, afraid that he might startle her, he stopped – although he worried about her long after he had passed by.

6 Across the river a buffalo was making a strange huffing noise like the whistles of a factory. Sunflower tried to concentrate, but suddenly the earth under her feet loosened. She clutched at the grass but the roots came away in her hands. There was nothing to hold on to, nothing to stop her slipping down. Filled with terror, she closed her eyes.

> ### Remember
> As you read, think about your thoughts and feelings. What has the writer made you think? How has the writer made you feel?

Activity 1: Exploring your first response to the extract

When you read a narrative text, think about what the characters are thinking and feeling – and how that makes you think and feel.

1 **a)** What did Sunflower think or feel when she saw the village of Damaidi?
   b) Look again at your answer to question 1a. Note down three things that made her think or feel that.
   c) Look again at your answer to question 1b. What did you think or feel when you read about those things?

2 **a)** What did Sunflower think or feel when she saw the little boat tied to the old elm tree?
   b) What do you think Sunflower was thinking or feeling when she decided to get into the boat?
   c) What did **you** think or feel when Sunflower decided to get into the boat?

3 **a)** How did Sunflower try to get into the boat?
   b) What do you think Sunflower was thinking or feeling as she tried to climb down into the boat?
   c) What did **you** think or feel when Sunflower tried to climb down into the boat?

Activity 2: Identifying the writer's intention

When a writer tells a story, they have an **intention** in mind: the effect they intend their story to have on the reader.

1 Look again at paragraphs 2 and 3 of the extract on page 74. What do you think was the writer's intention in these paragraphs? You could look at the **Intention Bank** for ideas.

2 Look again at paragraphs 4, 5 and 6 of the extract on page 74. What do you think was the writer's intention in these paragraphs? You could look at the **Intention Bank** again for ideas.

> **Intention Bank**
>
> **humour:** to make the reader smile or laugh
>
> **sadness:** to make the reader feel upset
>
> **anger:** to make the reader feel angry
>
> **sympathy:** to make the reader feel sorry for a character
>
> **empathy:** to make the reader feel how a character is feeling
>
> **tension:** to make the reader feel anxious or excited about what will happen next

Grammar Boost: Synonyms and antonyms

Synonyms are words with very similar meanings. Using synonyms can help to add variety and interest to writing.
Antonyms are words with opposite meanings.

1 Match the antonyms in column A with those in column B below.

A	B
laugh	quietly
strong	cry
create	weak
loudly	sadness
happiness	destroy

2 Organise the words below into groups of synonyms.

giggle | joy | weak | sorrow | strong | dread | happiness |
tough | sadness | chuckle | fear | delight | feeble |
misery | terror | powerful | laugh | powerless

3 Look at the sentences below. Rewrite them, replacing as many words as you can with a synonym.

> She felt strong. She was filled with happiness.
> She laughed loudly.

4 Rewrite the sentences again, replacing as many words as you can with an antonym to create the opposite meaning.

Activity 3: Exploring the writer's vocabulary choices

1 **a)** Which words and phrases in the following sentences from the extract on page 74 create an appealing image of the village?

> She saw a melia tree in blossom, clouds of pale lilac dusting the treetops. She saw milky-white cooking smoke curling up into the sky, then meeting and drifting as one over the reeds.

b) Which words in the following sentences create sympathy for Sunflower?

> As she lowered herself down, drenched in sweat, Sunflower could hear the water gurgling below her feet. Her small hands clung to the grass, holding on for dear life.

c) Which words in the following sentences create tension?

> She clutched at the grass but the roots came away in her hands. There was nothing to hold on to, nothing to stop her slipping down. Filled with terror, she closed her eyes.

Activity 4: Developing your response to the extract

Look at the following example response to paragraph 1 of the extract on page 74.

> In the first paragraph of the extract, Sunflower longs to visit the village of Damaidi. The writer describes what she sees and hears across the river.

These sentences explain what is happening in the extract, and what the writer describes.

> For example, we are told Sunflower sees that 'Dogs were running through the streets. A cockerel had flown up into a mulberry tree and was crowing. There was children's laughter everywhere.'

This quotation gives evidence of what the writer describes in this part of the extract.

> The writer makes the village sound busy, exciting and happy by choosing words like 'crowing' and 'laughter'.

This sentence explains some of the writer's vocabulary choices in detail.

> This creates empathy. It helps the reader to understand why Sunflower feels so desperate to cross the river to get to the village.

These sentences explain the writer's intention.

1 Look again at paragraphs 2 and 3 of the extract. Use the example response above and the following questions to help you write your response to them.

a) Using your answers to Activity 2 to help you, think about the writer's intention in paragraphs 2 and 3.

b) Start your response by writing one or two sentences explaining what is happening and what the writer describes in these paragraphs.

c) Choose **one** quotation that has an effect on the reader.

How do I do that?

Look at each sentence in the second and third paragraphs of the extract. Look for a sentence that proves what you have observed about the writer's intention in these paragraphs.

d) Using your answers to Activity 3 to help you, choose **one** or **two** words from the quotation that create the effect most powerfully. Describe this effect.

e) Write one or two sentences explaining the writer's intention.

This section links to pages 72–75 of the Workbook.

Section 8
Supporting your response

In this section, you will explore a character's viewpoint and support your response with evidence.

In this extract, a boy called Lucas is staying with his uncle in Paris, and has set out to explore the city. Despite his uncle's warning about staying in the areas where there are lots of people, he decides to visit the Crypte Archéologique – a system of underground excavations revealing the ancient history of the city.

▼ **Read the extract and then answer the questions that follow it.**

1　A day out in the bright, bustling avenues of Paris had become a frightening and lonely experience. Lucas thought back to the advice offered by Yves that morning, "This is your first time in the city. Stick to the main tourist areas, where there are lots of people…" At the time he was annoyed and impatient. His uncle was fussy and overprotective and didn't understand his desire to explore and see the sights of Paris. But now, his feelings had changed. He was
5　hundreds of feet underground, alone, and surrounded by cold shadows. He wished he'd taken Yves seriously.

The problem was he was just fascinated with archaeology. He had towers of books on archaeology at home that he loved reading, but he wanted to see it all in real life. He dreamt of Paris and imagined all the hidden, underground history he could see – it would be incredible! Now here he was, and his heart raced with the thrill of it all. He bought a sandwich and ate it quickly while walking to Les Invalides– a museum recommended by his uncle, knowing his
10　interest in history. But he was disappointed as it was mainly military history. He overheard someone talking about the Crypte Archéologique – a whole underground chamber with 2,000 years of history, right under the centre of Paris! – so he rushed over to find it.

At first he was excited. The dim, dank passages and crumbling walls smelt of earth and the distant past and were all an avid archaeologist could wish for. But as Lucas continued to explore, he took a wrong turn down a side-
15　passage, and realised he was lost.

He **groped** his way along. The blue light from his phone spilled against a wall to his left, illuminating a white sign with black printing. But the words meant nothing to him, and only increased his sense of being lost in a foreign world. The scrape of a footstep in the shadows ahead made his heart pound in his chest. Suddenly, a beam of yellow torchlight bathed him. Blinded, he struggled to make out the figure before
20　him. His companion guessed his confusion, and turned the torch on himself.

He saw a short, uniformed guide, with thick brows and neat hair tucked behind his ears.

"Excusez-moi. Vous êtes perdu?"

Lucas shrugged, indicating that he didn't understand. A gentle smile flickered
25　across the old man's face.

"Do you speak English?" Lucas nodded.

"Are you lost?"

He stammered, "Y...yes…"

"Come…" he murmured kindly, offering his arm,
30　"The exit is not far…"

Key vocabulary

groped: searched for something using your hands

Activity 1: Exploring setting

1 Select at least **two** adjectives that describe the way the writer presents the Crypte Archéologique. You could choose from the words below, or use your own ideas.

beautiful | frightening | dangerous | threatening | exciting

2 Select a quotation that supports each adjective you chose. You could choose from the quotations below, or select different ones from the extract on page 78.

The dim, dank passages and crumbling walls smelt of earth and the distant past

all an avid archaeologist could wish for

the words meant nothing to him, and only increased his sense of being lost in a foreign world

The blue light from his phone spilled against a wall to his left, illuminating a white sign with black printing

The scrape of a footstep in the shadows ahead made his heart pound in his chest

Blinded, he struggled to make out the figure before him

3 Write one or two sentences explaining why each quotation supports your choice of adjective.

Activity 2: Exploring character

1 Select at least **two** adjectives that describe the way the writer presents the guard Lucas meets in Crypte Archéologique. You could choose from the words below, or use your own ideas.

knowledgeable | frightened | helpful | threatening | sympathetic

2 Select a quotation that supports each adjective you chose. You could choose from the quotations below, or select different ones from the extract on page 78.

His companion guessed his confusion, and turned the torch on himself

He saw a short, uniformed guide, with thick brows and neat hair tucked behind his ears

A gentle smile flickered across the old man's face.

"Do you speak English…?"

"Are you lost?"

"Come…" he murmured kindly, offering his arm, "The exit is not far…"

3 Write one or two sentences explaining why each quotation supports your choice of adjective.

Punctuation Boost: Clauses and full stops

A **clause** is made up of one verb and all the other words that are linked to it. A sentence can be made up of one or more clauses.

Look at the single-clause sentence below. It has one verb.

We <u>went</u> to the park.

Look at the multi-clause sentence below. Each clause has one verb.
The clauses are linked using the conjunction 'and'.

We <u>went</u> to the park and we <u>played</u> football.

1 How many clauses are there in each example below?
   a) I love volleyball.
   b) I like football. I prefer cricket.
   c) I like football but I prefer cricket.
   d) I went to the park but it was raining so I came home again.

2 Rewrite each of the multi-clause sentences below as a series of single-clause sentences, adding full stops and capital letters in the correct places.
   a) I was doing my homework while my dad was cooking dinner.
   b) I finished my chores before I watched a film with my friends.
   c) She went to the park but it was raining so she came home again.
   d) We came home and I changed my clothes before I watched television.
   e) Katie went to football practice but her sister stayed in bed because she was ill.

Activity 3: Selecting relevant evidence

Short quotations are usually more effective than longer quotations. You should choose only the sentence, or part of a sentence, that directly supports your ideas.

Look at one student's comment and supporting quotation:

> Lucas was staying with his Uncle Yves, but we know he did not like him because the extract says: 'At the time he was annoyed and impatient. His uncle was fussy and overprotective and didn't understand his desire to explore and see the sights of Paris.'

▼ Not all of the quotation in the example on page 80 is relevant to the point the student has made. Using only the relevant part would make the comment more effective:

> Lucas was staying with his Uncle Yves, but we know he did not like him because he thought of him as 'fussy and overprotective'.

1 Look at the following students' comments, which use the same supporting quotation. Not all of the quotation is relevant to the points the students have made. Note down the part of the quotation that is relevant to each comment.

a)
> The writer shows that Lucas changed his opinion of the Crypte Archéologique when he got lost by saying: 'But now, his feelings had changed. He was hundreds of feet underground, alone, and surrounded by cold shadows. He wished he'd taken Yves seriously.'

b)
> Lucas seems stubborn because he did not take any notice when he was given advice. This is made clear when he says: 'But now, his feelings had changed. He was hundreds of feet underground, alone, and surrounded by cold shadows. He wished he'd taken Yves seriously.'

Activity 4: Writing a response

1 **a)** Consider your response to the extract on page 78. You could plan to comment on the effect the writer has achieved for any of the subjects below, or use your own ideas.

| the Crypte Archéologique | Lucas | the guard | the idea of becoming lost | the idea of curiosity |

b) Select words that describe your response and the effect of the extract. You could choose from the words below, or use your own ideas.

excitement | intrigue | mystery | fear | humour | anxiety | sadness

c) Select **one or two** quotations that show how the writer has achieved the response you had.

d) Write one or two sentences explaining why each quotation supports your comments.

This section links to pages 76–79 of the Workbook.

Section 9
Developing your response

In this section, you will track and develop your response to a text.

This extract is from a novel. A boy has just rushed to catch the last train home – but he soon realises that he has got on the wrong train.

▼ Read the extract and then answer the questions that follow it.

1 He stuck his face to the glass and stared, trying to figure out where he was, but there were no clues, not one – no station, no sign, nothing. He desperately wanted the train to stop so he could get off, but it just kept on going. Fifteen minutes – twenty? He sat looking helplessly at the empty car and the dark mirrors of the windows while the sound of the diesel droned on, taking him he hadn't a clue where.

2 At last, the train began to slow. For several minutes it crawled along as though on the point of stopping, but never actually did, and each time he thought it would, it began to pick up speed again. Finally the train juddered to a halt in the dark, and he didn't even know whether it was at a station or not, because when he cupped his hands to the glass, there were only a few lights and a low concrete wall to be seen out of the window. But the light on the door button came on, and being off the train seemed a better deal than being on it. So, getting out of his seat, he stepped onto the cold, dark platform before he'd even really thought through whether that was a good idea or not.

3 Hearing the doors of the train close behind him, and the engine revving up and pulling away, leaving him in the dark and the cold, he wasn't so sure it had been a good idea at all. There was no one else on the platform, but by then it was too late to do anything except watch the lights of the train disappear. When the sound of it couldn't be heard anymore, there was no sound at all.

4 Just silence.

5 It didn't even look like a real station. The slab concrete of the wall ran along the back of it and there was a little shelter with a bench, but nothing else – not a ticket office or a machine. Not even a sign to say where it was. He could see the ends of the platform sloping down to the tracks and three lamps on poles, but the light from them was thin and weak. There were no houses, no streetlights. So far as he could see, there wasn't a road, not even steps down to one. It was just a platform, dark and still, in the middle of nowhere.

6 Pulling his coat around him, he tried laughing at the dumbness of what he'd done, but in the cold silence his laughter fell from his lips like a shot bird, and that made him feel more alone. Sitting down on the bench, he turned up his collar against the cold and wondered what on earth he was going to do.

7 He'd been sitting like that for a while before he noticed the light.

8 At first it was so small that he wasn't sure what it was – just a tiny dot swinging to and fro. But as it came slowly nearer, grew larger, he realized it was a flashlight.

9 No, not a flashlight.

10 A lantern.

11 A glass lantern.

12 Someone carrying a lantern was walking along the railway tracks, out of the darkness, toward him.

Activity 1: Tracking your response

The following repeated questions will guide you as you consider your response to the extract, section by section.

1 Look again at paragraph 1 of the extract on page 82.
   a) What information have you found out from these lines?
   b) What are you thinking or feeling after reading these lines?
   c) What has made you think and feel that way?

2 Look again at paragraph 2 of the extract on page 82.
   a) What information have you found out from these lines?
   b) What are you thinking or feeling after reading these lines?
   c) What has made you think and feel that way?

3 Look again at paragraphs 3–6 of the extract on page 82.
   a) What information have you found out from these lines?
   b) What are you thinking or feeling after reading these lines?
   c) What has made you think and feel that way?

4 Look again at paragraphs 7–12 of the extract on page 82.
   a) What information have you found out from these lines?
   b) What are you thinking or feeling after reading these lines?
   c) What has made you think and feel that way?

Activity 2: Tracking the writer's intention

1 How does the boy's situation change during the extract on page 82?
   a) It gets worse and worse.
   b) It gets worse and then better.
   c) It gets better and better.
   d) It gets better and then worse.

2 Note down **three** different effects the writer intends to create. You could choose from the responses below, or use your own ideas.

   tension | mystery | humour | sympathy | fear | excitement | suspense

   In the extract, the writer's intention is to create the effects of

3 For each effect you have noted in question 2, does it get more or less intense during the extract? Write **one** sentence for each effect to explain your ideas.

   The feeling of tension gets more intense during the extract because

Activity 3: Exploring vocabulary choice

1 Look again at the following sentences from the extract on page 82.

> He stuck his face to the glass and stared, trying to figure out where he was, but there were no clues, not one – no station, no sign, nothing. He desperately wanted the train to stop so he could get off, but it just kept on going. Fifteen minutes – twenty?

a) Which **one** of the sentences above tells you most clearly about the boy's feelings?

b) Which **one** word in that sentence tells you most clearly about the boy's feelings?

c) Write **one or two** sentences to explain the effect of your chosen word, remembering to use the conventions of quotations.

2 Look again at the following sentences from the extract.

> Hearing the doors of the train close behind him, and the engine revving up and pulling away, leaving him in the dark and the cold, he wasn't so sure it had been a good idea at all.

> Just silence.

> There were no houses, no streetlights. So far as he could see, there wasn't a road, not even steps down to one. It was just a platform, dark and still, in the middle of nowhere.

a) Which **three** different words in the sentences above does the writer use to describe the station?

b) What thoughts and feelings are prompted by these vocabulary choices? Write **one or two** sentences to explain your ideas, remembering to use the conventions of quotations.

3 Look again at the following sentence from the extract.

> Someone carrying a lantern was walking along the railway tracks, out of the darkness, toward him.

The word 'someone' is used to describe the figure walking towards the boy. Why do you think the writer chose this word? Write one or two sentences to explain the effect of this word, remembering to use the conventions of quotations.

Skills Boost: Expressing your ideas precisely

When you write your response to a text, it is important to express your ideas as clearly and precisely as possible. One way to do this is to choose your vocabulary carefully.

1 Copy and complete each sentence below by replacing the **?** with **one** word. You could choose a word from the **Vocabulary Bank**, or use your own ideas to describe your response more clearly and precisely.

Vocabulary Bank

- weird
- odd
- shocking
- disturbing
- strange
- unusual
- confusing
- worrying

a) The writer of the extract on page 82 creates the impression that something **?** is happening.

b) When a mysterious figure walks out of the darkness, it is **?**.

c) It makes you want to find out what happens next because it is so **?**.

Activity 4: Writing your response

You are going to write **two** paragraphs explaining your response to the extract on page 82. Complete the following tasks to gather your ideas before you start writing.

1 a) Write **one or two** sentences summing up your response to paragraphs 1–2. To help you, you could look at your answers to Activity 1, questions 1 and 2.

b) Choose **one** quotation from the extract that shows one way in which the writer created that response.

How do I do that?

- Look for a sentence in the extract that helped to form your response.
- Choose only the part of the sentence that directly supports your ideas.

c) Write **one or two** sentences explaining how the writer created that response, aiming to comment on the writer's choice of vocabulary. Remember to use the conventions of quotations.

2 a) Write **one or two** sentences summing up your response to paragraphs 3–12. To help you, you could look at your answers to Activity 1, questions 3 and 4.

b) Choose **one** quotation from the extract that shows one way in which the writer created that response.

c) Write **one or two** sentences explaining how the writer created that response, aiming to comment on the writer's choice of vocabulary. Remember to use the conventions of quotations.

3 Use your notes to write **two** paragraphs answering the following question: How does the writer build up a sense of tension and danger in the extract?

This section links to pages 80–83 of the Workbook.

Section 10
Writing your response

In this section, you will write the opening of a story. You will then write a response to it.

Activity 1: Considering your intention and gathering ideas

You are going to write the opening of a story in which the narrator finds themselves in danger.

In your story, the narrator will:
• set off on a journey
• realise that they are lost
• meet a stranger who may be a friend or a threat.

Considering your intention

1 The purpose of any story is to engage and entertain the reader. The opening of your story could achieve this in different ways.

Select an effect that would suit the story events described above. You could choose one of the following approaches or use your own ideas.

using action to create a feeling of excitement and adventure	building up tension to create a feeling of suspense and mystery	focusing on the narrator's thoughts and feelings to create a feeling of empathy

Note down what your intended effect will be.

Selecting details

2 Note down answers to the questions below to plan your ideas. You could choose from the suggestions below each question, or use your own ideas.

a) Why is the narrator going on a journey?

going home	visiting someone	escaping	searching

b) Where will the story be set?

a forest or jungle	a busy town or city	a method of transport

c) When does the story take place?

| during the day | in the middle of the night | just as darkness is falling |

d) Why does the narrator get lost?

| travelling in an unfamiliar place | taking a wrong turn | using bad directions |

e) How should the stranger be described?

| mysterious | friendly | threatening |

Implying ideas

3 Think about your narrator's thoughts and feelings in your story opening.

a) Note down how your narrator will feel when:

- setting off on the journey
- realising they are lost
- meeting a stranger.

b) Think about how your narrator will imply, not explain, their thoughts and feelings. Note down one or two clues you could give about each of the feelings you have noted.

> ### Remember
> Implying ideas means you will have to explore some ways in which you can suggest them, meaning readers must use their skills of inference.

You could describe:

| actions | physical symptoms | expressions |

| body language | past conversations | past experiences |

Writing your story opening

4 Write the first **three** paragraphs of your story. Use all the ideas you have gathered in your plan, and the given story structure:

- The narrator sets off on a journey.
- They realise that they are lost.
- They meet a stranger who may be a friend or a threat.

Skills Boost: Proofreading

Read your story opening from Activity 1, looking for and correcting any mistakes. Use the steps below to review some of the most common errors in spelling, punctuation and grammar.

Spelling

1 **a)** Check that every verb ending is spelt correctly, including verbs ending in –s, –ed and –ing.

b) Check you have doubled the last letter of the root verb where necessary.

Punctuation

2 **a)** Check that every sentence begins with a capital latter and ends with a full stop, a question mark or an exclamation mark.

b) Check that you have not joined any full sentences with a comma.

Grammar

3 **a)** Check that every verb agrees with its subject.

b) Check that every verb matches the tense used in the rest of the writing.

Activity 2: Tracking your intention as a writer

Look again at your story opening from Activity 1.

1 How does your narrator's situation change during your story opening?
a) It gets worse and worse.
b) It gets worse and then better.
c) It gets better and better.
d) It gets better and then worse.

2 Note down at least **two** different effects that you intended to create. You could choose from the responses below, or use your own ideas.

tension | mystery | humour | sympathy | fear | excitement | suspense

> In the story opening, I intended to create the effects of

3 For each effect you have noted in question 2, does it get more or less intense during your story opening? Write one sentence for each effect to explain your ideas.

> The effect of humour gets less intense during the story opening because

Activity 3: Tracking a reader's response

The following repeated questions will guide you as you consider a reader's response to the extract, section by section.

1 Look again at the part of your story opening that describes the narrator setting off.
  a) What information have you found out from these lines?
  b) What are you thinking or feeling after reading these lines?
  c) What has made you think and feel that way?

2 Look again at the part of your story opening that describes the narrator getting lost.
  a) What information have you found out from these lines?
  b) What are you thinking or feeling after reading these lines?
  c) What has made you think and feel that way?

3 Look again at the part of your story opening that describes the narrator meeting a stranger.
  a) What information have you found out from these lines?
  b) What are you thinking or feeling after reading these lines?
  c) What has made you think and feel that way?

Activity 4: Writing a response

You are going to write **two** paragraphs explaining your response to the story opening you wrote in Activity 1.

1 Write your first paragraph, following the steps outlined below.
  a) Give your response to one aspect of your story opening. You could comment on one of the aspects of your story given below, or use your own ideas.

  | what happened in the story | the character of the narrator | the way the stranger is presented |

  b) Select words that describe your response. You could choose from the words below, or use your own ideas.

  excitement | intrigue | mystery | fear | humour | anxiety | sadness

  c) Select **one or two** quotations that show how the writer (you) achieved this response.

  > **Remember**
  >
  > Short quotations are usually more effective than longer quotations. You should choose only the sentence, or part of a sentence, that directly supports your ideas.

  d) Write **one or two** sentences explaining why each quotation supports your comments.

2 Now write your second paragraph, using the steps outlined in question 1 to help you.

Section 11
Assessment

In this section, you will answer questions on an extract from a novel to assess your progress in this unit.

This is an extract from a novel. Nisha, her father and her brother, Amil, are refugees making the long and dangerous journey from India to Pakistan.

▼ Read the extract and then answer the questions that follow it.

1   I woke up feeling terrible today. My tongue was stuck to the roof of my mouth. My head pounded. My fingers tingled. When I tried to get up, my arms and legs felt filled with sand.

‘Amil,’ I said, nudging him out of sleep. "Are you feeling strange?"

He mumbled something I couldn't understand. I looked over at Papa and he opened his eyes, and we stared in a way
5   that we never look at each other, not like father and daughter, but simply like two people who are both scared. It made me see Papa suddenly as a person, not just my papa, like a secret door had opened. Then he blinked and it was over.

I crawled over my mat, past Amil, who had fallen back asleep, and I kneeled next to Papa. He put his hand on my shoulder.

"Today we will find water," he said.

10   I nodded. I wanted to ask him how, but I didn't want him to take his hand away, so I kept silent, but he removed it anyway. I knew we couldn't walk ten miles today without water. We only had a couple of sips left in our jugs.

"Is your mouth dry?" Papa asked, sitting up cross-legged on his mat.

"Not really," I murmured in a gravelly voice, turning away from him.

He leaned over and told me to open my mouth. I did as he asked. He squinted in, examining the inside as he
15   pressed his strong fingers against the sides of my face. Then he checked my eyes by lifting up my eyelids. He checked my pulse and lightly pinched the skin on the back of my hand.

"You're okay," he said. "You have another day in you."

Another day and then what? I didn't want to know.

Then he went over to Amil. He shook his shoulder, but Amil just
20   moaned with his eyes closed.

"Amil," Papa said loudly.

Amil stirred and turned toward Papa. Dadi came over and squatted by his shoulder.

"Sit up," Papa said sternly.

25   Amil just blinked at him.

"Sit up," Papa said even louder.

Amil hoisted himself up.

"I feel sick," Amil said in a scratchy voice, his skin dry, his eyes sunken. Papa did all the things he did to me, but he didn't
30   tell Amil he had another day in him.

Activity 1: Reading

1 Why did the narrator think she and her family 'couldn't walk ten miles today without water'?

2 Identify **two** other pieces of information that suggest Nisha and her family were in a difficult situation.

3 Papa urgently tried to wake up Amil. Which words tell you how urgently he wanted to wake him?

4 In the final sentence of the extract, the narrator describes her father looking at her brother. She noticed that her father 'didn't tell Amil he had another day in him.' What does this suggest?

5 At the beginning of the extract, the narrator describes how she feels. At the end of the extract, we are told about her brother's health. Whose health was suffering the most during the long journey: the narrator's or her brother's? Explain your answer, using at least **one** quotation from the extract.

6 In **30–40** words, summarise what the extract reveals about Nisha and her family.

Activity 2: Writing a response

1 Write two paragraphs explaining your response to the extract on page 90.

Before you start writing

• Consider the focus of each of your paragraphs. What elements and effects of the extract will you select? Note your ideas in a table similar to the one below.
• Consider your response to each element you have chosen. Note your ideas in your table.
• Select **one or two** relevant quotations that show how the writer achieved this response. Note your ideas in your table.

	Focus of paragraph	Response	Quotations
Paragraph 1			
Paragraph 2			

As you write

• Describe your response in words that express it precisely.
• Use quotations as examples of the writer's effective vocabulary choices.
• Explain why each quotation supports your comments.

When you have finished writing

• Check the accuracy of your spelling, punctuation and grammar.

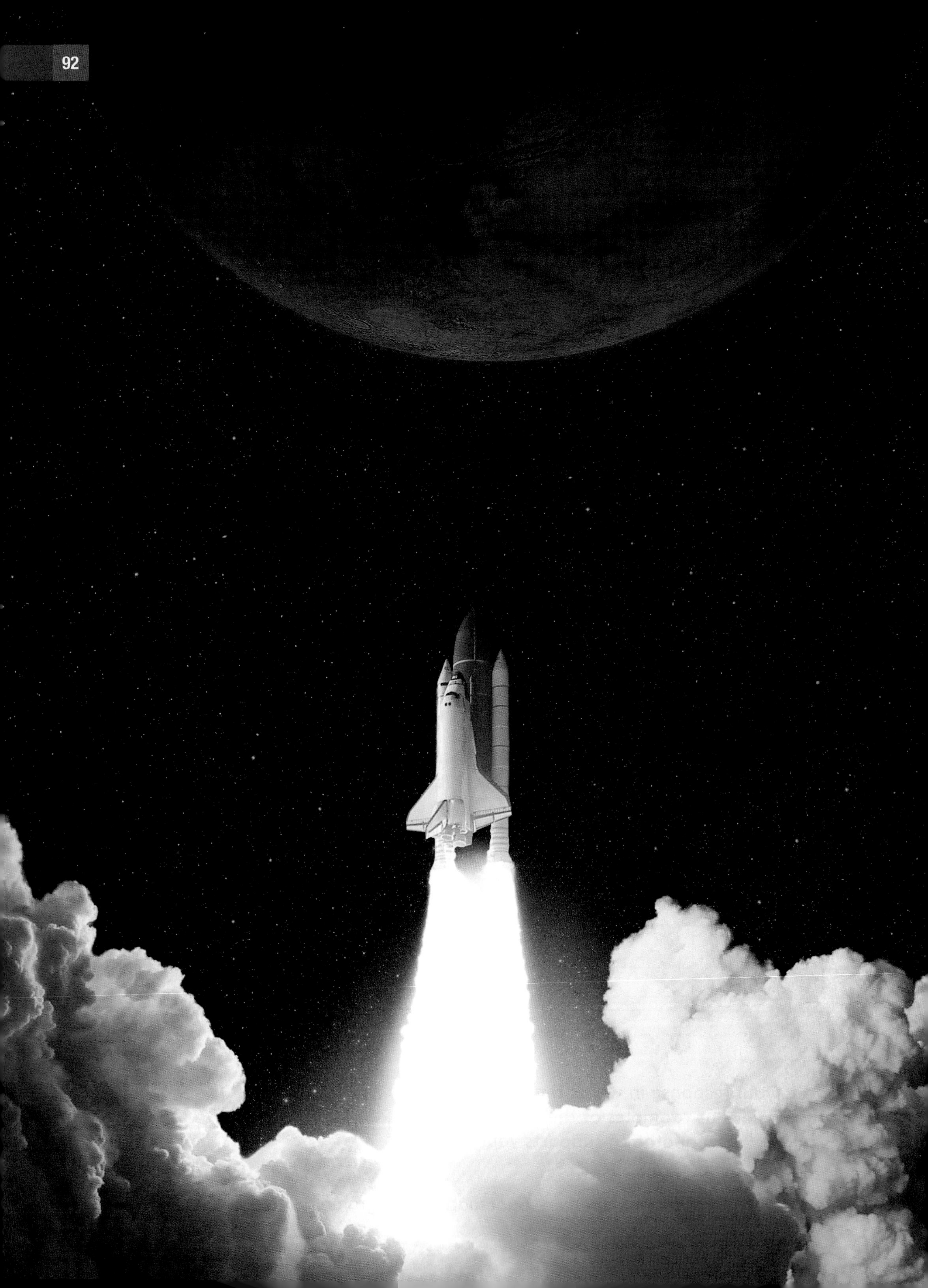

Unit 3
Travels in space

This unit focuses on the theme of travelling in space and features a variety of stories and informational texts on this fascinating topic. You will learn about a space shuttle launch, becoming an astronaut and holidaying in space. You will also discover futuristic stories about discovering new planets and life in space in the future where the possibilities are endless.

In this unit you will...

- explore the ideas and information suggested by a text and the impression the writer has tried to create.

- explore the structure of a description from a fiction text, and the effect that the writer wanted it to have on the reader.

- explore the importance of selecting precise and powerful verbs in descriptive writing.

- develop your skills in building and using noun phrases.

- answer questions on a short article and write a short descriptive text to assess your progress in the unit so far.

- explore how writers create the narrator's viewpoint in a text.

- explore how writers use description in non-fiction texts.

- explore different sentence structures in descriptive writing.

- explore different ways of planning a description.

- develop your skills of reviewing and improving the choices you have made in your writing.

- write a descriptive article.

By the end of this unit, you will be able to plan, structure and write descriptively using vocabulary choice and sentence structure to convey a viewpoint.

This section links to pages 86–89 of the Workbook.

Section 1
Creating an impression

In this section, you will explore the ideas and information suggested by a text and the impression the writer has tried to create.

This is the beginning of a short story. Two years ago, Hiroyuki and his mother left Earth on a spaceship, destined for a new life on a new planet. They were sealed into sleep pods and were told they would be woken up the day before their arrival. Now, though, something seems to have gone wrong.

▼ Read the extract and then answer the questions that follow it.

1 A loud knocking made Hiroyuki jump. Both his eyes sprang open. A girl was leaning over his sleep pod, peering through the plastic lid.

"Wake up," she was shouting, her voice muffled
5 through the plastic. "You need to get up!" she was saying. "Get up!"

"What do you want?" mumbled Hiroyuki. "Are we nearly there yet? Is something wrong?"

"Wrong?" said the girl. "Of course something's
10 wrong." She pressed the red button above his head and the lid of Hiroyuki's sleep pod opened with a hiss.

"What is it?" he asked. "What's going on?" Hiroyuki pulled himself to his feet.

"They've gone," she whispered, her dark eyes wet
15 with fear.

"Who's gone?" asked Hiroyuki.

"Everyone," she hissed. "My parents, all the other passengers, the crew, everyone. You and me are the only people left on the entire ship."

20 Hiroyuki's eyes narrowed. "But my mum," he said, turning to her sleep pod beside his. But it was gone. When he had gone to sleep, his mum was right there, beside him. There had been a long row of sleep pods, all lined up. A row of people all getting into their sleep
25 pods. Now there was nothing. An empty white space in a huge empty white room.

"This is your captain, Pilot X7," said a metallic voice from somewhere above their heads, "talking to Passenger 72350."

30 "That's you," said the girl to Hiroyuki, her dark eyes widening as she checked the passenger number beneath the barcode on his jacket.

"Passenger 72350," said the voice harshly, "you must return to your sleep pod for re-sleeping."

35 "Don't do it," said the girl. "Don't listen to it. It's just a computer. It can't hurt you. Come on."

"Ignore the human, please, passenger 72350," said the voice, "and return to your sleep pod for re-sleeping before you come to any harm."

40 The girl grabbed Hiroyuki's sleeve and tugged at it.

"Come on," she hissed urgently through clenched teeth. She pushed the door button on the sleep room. The door slid open.

"Do not attempt to leave the sleep room, Passenger
45 72350," said the metallic voice of Pilot X7. "Return to your sleep pod at once or I will be forced to take action."

Hiroyuki peered timidly through the open door into the silent shadows of a dark corridor.

"Get moving," said the girl, shoving Hiroyuki out
50 through the door, "before it's too late."

Activity 1: Thinking about action

Answer these questions to make sure you understand the strange and dramatic events in the extract on page 94.

1 When answering these questions, note down **everything** that each of the three main characters does in the extract.
a) What does the girl do?
b) What does Hiroyuki do?
c) What does the computer, Pilot X7, do?

Activity 2: Inferring ideas

In this activity, you are going to use your inference skills to work out what the characters in the extract are thinking and feeling – and what might happen next.

1 Look at everything the computer Pilot X7 says in the extract on page 94, including how it says it. For example:

"Passenger 72350," said the voice harshly, "you must return to your sleep pod for re-sleeping."

"Ignore the human, please, passenger 72350," said the voice, "and return to your sleep pod for re-sleeping before you come to any harm."

"Do not attempt to leave the sleep room, Passenger 72350," said the metallic voice of Pilot X7. "Return to your sleep pod at once or I will be forced to take action."

Use the computer's speech as clues to work out what it is thinking or feeling. Write **one or two** sentences explaining your ideas.

I think Pilot X7 is thinking

2 Look at everything the girl says in the extract. For example:

"Wake up," she was shouting, her voice muffled through the plastic. "You need to get up!" she was saying. "Get up!"

"Everyone," she hissed. "My parents, all the other passengers, the crew, everyone. You and me are the only people left on the entire ship."

"Don't do it," said the girl. "Don't listen to it. It's just a computer. It can't hurt you. Come on."

Using these clues, what can you work out about the thoughts and feelings of the girl?

I think the girl is feeling

3 Look again at what happens after the computer first speaks.
a) What do you think will happen next in the story?
b) Write down all the clues that helped you to work this out.

Skills Boost: Connotations

You can make inferences about a character based on single words, as well as on what the character says and does. The **connotations** of a word are the ideas that a word suggests or creates in a reader's mind.

1 We are told in the extract on page 94 that Hiroyuki 'peered timidly through the open door'. What does the word 'timidly' suggest about the character of Hiroyuki? Look at some connotations of the word 'timidly' below.

quietly | fearfully | shyly | unconfidently | nervously

2 We are told that the girl 'grabbed' Hiroyuki and, later, we are told about her 'shoving' him through a door. Think about the connotations of the verbs 'grab' and 'shove'. What do they suggest about the character of the girl?

Activity 3: Exploring impressions

In the extract on page 94, the writer has tried to create a strong impression of the characters and the setting. He does this in three ways:

description the words used to create a picture in the reader's mind	**dialogue** what the characters say	**action** the actions of and around the characters

1 Look at two ways in which the writer creates an impression of the setting in the extract:

> Now there was nothing. An empty white space in a huge empty white room.

> the silent shadows of a dark corridor

a) What impression has the writer created of the setting? You could choose from the suggestions below or use your own ideas.

huge | dramatic | small | dangerous | beautiful | exciting | frightening | boring

b) Has the writer used description, **dialogue** or action to create this impression?

2 You have already explored ways the writer uses dialogue to create impressions of the characters. Look at two other ways in which the writer creates impressions of them:

> "They've gone," she whispered, her dark eyes wet with fear.

> Hiroyuki's eyes narrowed. "But my mum," he said, turning to her sleep pod beside his.

a) What impressions has the writer created of the girl and Hiroyuki? You could choose from the suggestions below or use your own ideas.

clumsy | bossy | suspicious | cautious | reckless | brave | enthusiastic | scared

b) How has the writer created these impressions?

Activity 4: Planning creating first impressions

You are going to plan writing the start of a story, creating impressions of two characters taking off from planet Earth in a spaceship.

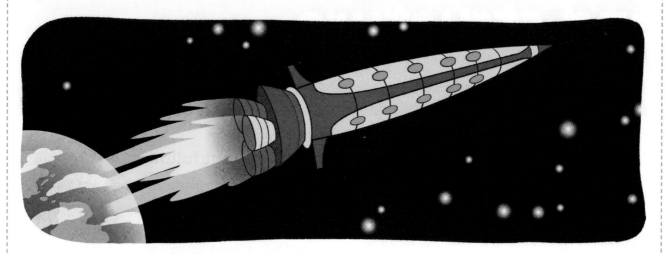

Create impressions of the setting

1 To create an impression of the setting, you will need to plan a description.
   a) What impression do you want to create of the spaceship?
   b) Imagine you are one of the characters sitting inside the cockpit of the spaceship, next to your fellow astronaut. Imagine looking around, at the spaceship's controls and out of the window. Note down **five** things that your character can see.

Create impressions of the characters

2 Who are the two characters in the spaceship? Add their names and ages to a table like the one below.

	Character 1	Character 2

3 **a)** To create an impression of each character, you will need to plan dialogue and action.

   What impressions do you want to create of these characters? You could choose from the suggestions below or use your own ideas.

   clumsy | bossy | nervous | cautious | reckless | enthusiastic | scared

   b) Think of something that each character could say that shows what they are like. Add this to the character's column in the table.
   c) Think of something that each character could do that shows what they are like. Add this to the character's column in the table.

This section links to pages 90–93 of the Workbook.

Section 2
Exploring intention and structure

In this section, you will explore the structure of a description from a fiction text, and the effect that the writer wanted it to have on the reader.

This extract is the opening to a science-fiction novel.

▼ Read the extract and then answer the questions that follow it.

1 Cas awoke with a start, disorientated and confused. It was dim in the room, despite the stars showing clearly through the window. Monitors gave out a sickly blue light and he took a moment to remember where he was. Reaching up, he unclipped the belt that held him in place and rubbed his eyes.

2 He gulped in the dry air. He felt anxious but he knew he needed to hold his nerve. He was drenched with sweat and his mouth tasted sour. A dream sat on the edge of his thoughts – a white horse surrounded by maple trees – but he couldn't keep hold of it. Something to do with home? The thoughts, the half-formed images flickered back and forth in his head unnervingly like a movie played at the wrong speed. Sensing something was wrong, he pulled himself to his feet and carefully smoothed out his clothes. He took a long drink of water, which soothed his dry throat. Straightening his shoulders, he strode out of the room and made his way towards the bridge.

3 Stopping just before the doorway, he realised that his heart was skipping but the sound of his own pulse was loud and slow in his ears. The white horse entered his thoughts again, and he remembered the sweet smell of the maple trees… but this time he pushed the image out of his mind. He walked in, doing his best to seem confident. The hum of computers and the quiet urgent voices of Premila and Niki met him. As he walked over to them he realised that the pounding in his ears was the sound of the straining engines.

4 They turned to him.

5 "Navigation's malfunctioned," said Niki.

6 Premila added, "We've drifted way off course. We're being dragged toward Monocerotis…"

7 Cas searched his memory. The name was familiar…

8 …and suddenly he felt cold. Monocerotis was a black hole, the closest to the earth. Any craft approaching within less than 1000 light years would be torn apart, its crew crushed by extreme gravity. Cas sat hurriedly at the control panel. He flicked a switch and main screen lit up in front of them. The image filling it was both terrifying and beautiful – a swirling disc of golden light, at the centre of which lay a pinprick of pure darkness. Cas realised that they might be the first people to have ever had this view. All at once he felt tiny, an insignificant speck in front of this vast awe-inspiring sight.

9 He fought to tear his view away.

10 "Can we reverse our course, Niki?" he asked, his voice determined and steady.

11 Niki stared at the monitor in front of her, moving dials and then looked up, her face creased with worry.

12 "The engines are screaming just holding us here. The slightest loss of power and we'll be pulled in…"

Activity 1: Inferring ideas

Writers do not always give you all the information you need. Sometimes you have to work it out for yourself using your inference skills.

1 Look again at the opening sentence of the extract on page 98:

> Cas awoke with a start, disorientated and confused.

    a) Where is Cas when he wakes up in the first paragraph?
    b) Which words in the extract helped you to infer this?

2 In the first half of the extract, the writer describes Cas as worried but trying to stay calm:

> He felt anxious but he knew he needed to hold his nerve. He was drenched with sweat and his mouth tasted sour.

    a) Write down all the information you can find in the extract that suggests Cas is anxious.
    b) Write down all the information you can find in the extract that suggests he is calm and in control.
    c) Look again at your answers to questions 2a and 2b. In your opinion, was Cas anxious or calm?

Activity 2: Intention and response

For every text, the writer has an intention: the response they intend to create in the reader. A successful text is one where the reader's response is the one that the writer intended.

1 How do you think the writer intended the reader to respond to the extract on page 98, as an opening to a novel? You could choose one of the responses below or use your own ideas.

That's intriguing…

I'm surprised!

This story is frightening.

It's very mysterious.

I don't understand it.

This is exciting!

2 How did **you** respond to the extract? Write **one or two** sentences to explain your ideas.

3 Do you think the writer was successful in achieving their intention? Which part of the opening was the most effective in helping the writer to achieve it? Write **one or two** sentences to explain your ideas.

Skills Boost: Paragraphing

1 Look again at paragraphs 1–3 of the extract on page 98. Each sentence below has been taken from one of these paragraphs, and each sentence is focused on a different feeling or sense.

A   It was dim in the room, despite the stars showing clearly through the window.

B   He took a long drink of water, which soothed his dry throat.

C   The hum of computers and the quiet urgent voices of Premila and Niki met him.

Remember

Descriptive texts often focus on the senses: what can be seen, heard, smelt, felt or tasted.

In which sentence (A, B or C) and paragraph of the extract (1, 2 or 3) does the writer focus most strongly on:

a) the sense of taste?   **b)** the sense of sight?   **c)** the sense of sound?

2 Look again at the following lines from the extract, which are taken from paragraphs 7 and 8. Why has the writer started a new paragraph halfway through this sentence?

The name was familiar…   …and suddenly he felt cold.

Remember

There are four reasons to start a new paragraph:
- a change of topic
- a change of scene or setting
- a change of time
- a change of speaker.

Activity 3: Structuring a text

The writer of the extract on page 98 describes three settings: Cas's cabin, the bridge of the spaceship, and the black hole.

1 **a)** Which paragraph describes the cabin? Which describes the bridge? Which describes the black hole?

b) Why do you think the writer structured the descriptions in this way? What effect does this have on the reader? Write **one or two** sentences to explain your ideas.

2 In paragraph 2, the writer describes:

A dream sat on the edge of his thoughts – a white horse surrounded by maple trees

a) Which other paragraph contains a description relating to the white horse?

b) Why do you think the writer has divided a single topic in this way? Write **one or two** sentences to explain your ideas.

Activity 4: Planning and writing a description

You are going to write **three or four** paragraphs describing a journey through the universe.

Imagine

1 Imagine you are travelling on a spaceship. Write notes in response to the following questions.
　a) What can you see on the spaceship?
　b) What can you see through the windows?

2 Write **one** sentence summing up what else you will write about in your description of the journey.

Plan

3 Picture the scenes you will describe. Think about each of your senses:

sight　　sound　　touch

smell　　taste

Note down some ideas for at least **three** of the five senses.

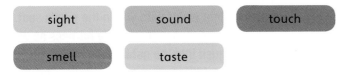

There are thousands of　　Tiny white specks of

I can hear a strange rattling sound

The air is freezing cold　　A powerful smell of　　I can taste

> ### Remember
> Describing touch could include describing the feeling of something on your fingertips, your face or your whole body – for example, the feeling of cold air or sweat.

4 What are your thoughts and feelings as you experience these sights, sounds, sensations, smells and tastes? Note down some ideas.

5 How will you structure your ideas? You could follow the suggestion below or use a structure of your own.
- Paragraph 1: Set the scene: why you are there and how you got there.
- Paragraph 2: Describe the scene using one or two of your senses. What can you see and hear?
- Paragraph 3: Describe the scene using another one or two of your senses. What can you smell, taste or feel?
- Paragraph 4: Describe your thoughts and feelings as you take in this experience.

Write

6 Use your ideas to write your description. Remember to think about your intention for what the reader's response will be.

This section links to pages 94–97 of the Workbook.

Section 3
Selecting verbs

In this section, you will explore the importance of selecting precise and powerful verbs in descriptive writing.

This is an article from a website about the history of space exploration.

▼ **Read the article and then answer the questions that follow it.**

So you want to be an astronaut...

1 Before you can even be considered for astronaut training, you will need a university degree in engineering, science or mathematics. It also helps if you are a military pilot with over 1,000 hours of flying experience. And of course, you will need to be extremely fit.

2 Once you are selected, training to be an astronaut can take two years and involves a series of gruelling challenges and tests.

3 You will be spun round and round in a machine that recreates the extreme G-forces of space travel, crushing your body and squeezing the last gasps of air from your lungs. Luckily, you will also be taught techniques that help you avoid losing your sight and passing out during the test.

4 You will be placed in a flight simulator to create the experience of flying to a height of 22,000 feet and suffering *hypoxia* where the amount of oxygen in the air and your body is reduced to the point that you feel light-headed and numbness in your face, hands and feet.

5 You will be taken up in a KC-135 aeroplane, which astronaut trainers call The Vomit Comet or The Weightless Wonder, which will help to prepare you for the weightlessness of space. The plane repeatedly soars into the air on a steep gradient, then plummets back down on an equally steep gradient. For just 20 seconds at the top of each climb, everyone on the plane floats. It is also highly likely to make you feel, or be, physically sick.

6 You will be trained for space walks – when you will leave the spacecraft to carry out repairs while floating in space at the end of a cable. This is done by spending up to seven hours underwater in a huge swimming pool containing 22.7 million litres of water and a life-size model of a space vehicle in need of repair.

7 However, perhaps the most terrifying challenge is the *dunker*. This simulates a plane or helicopter crashing into water with you in the pilot's seat. You will be strapped in with a safety harness as water starts to gush into the cabin, then climbs up your legs and rapidly covers your chest, your neck, then your mouth. Once fully submerged, and having taken a very deep breath, it's time to release yourself from the harness, escape through the cabin window, and swim to the surface. And all of this without panicking.

8 If you get through all those tests, then all that remains is training in public speaking (so you can give speeches telling huge audiences about your experiences), training for medical emergencies and survival in extreme conditions, and learning Russian so you can speak to other astronauts on the International Space Station. Then, and only then, will you be ready to go into space!

Activity 1: Gathering information

These questions will help you to check your understanding of the article on page 102 and practise your inference skills.

1 Look again at the first paragraph of the article. Using your own words, describe the kinds of people that are likely to be selected for astronaut training.

2 Look again at the third, fourth and fifth paragraphs of the article. Identify **three** things that astronauts can expect to experience in space.

3 Look again at the seventh paragraph of the article. The writer suggests that the *dunker* challenge is a frightening experience. Identify **three** pieces of evidence that the writer uses to show this.

Activity 2: Exploring verb choice

Remember

Verbs describe an action or event. For example: Sajid ate the cake.

The writer's choice of verb can make the action or event sound much more dramatic. For example: Sajid devoured the cake.

1 Look at the writer's verb choices in the following clauses taken from the article.

A This simulates a plane or helicopter crashing into water

B water starts to gush into the cabin

C The plane repeatedly soars into the air

The writer could have chosen different verbs to use. For example:

to sink | to rise | to drop | to climb | to trickle | to fly | to fall | to pour | to flow

a) Which of the verbs above could the writer have chosen instead of 'crashing'?
b) Which of the verbs above could the writer have chosen instead of 'gush'?
c) Which of the verbs above could the writer have chosen instead of 'soars'?

2 Look again at the verbs that the writer has chosen to use in the clauses above.
a) Which verb(s) use **onomatopoeia** to help the reader imagine the scene?
b) Which verb(s) make the action described sound more dramatic?

Remember

Onomatopoeia is the technique of using a word that sounds like its meaning. The words 'bang', 'crash', 'splash' and 'hum' are all examples of onomatopoeia.

Spelling Boost: Adverbs

Adverbs can add information to verbs. For example:

She shouted loudly.   *The verb tells you what she did.*   *The adverb tells you the manner in which she did it.*

Many (but not all) adverbs can be formed by adding the suffix '–ly' to an adjective. For example:

He was a quick runner.   *adjective*   He could run quickly.   *adverb*

1 Copy the sentences below and underline the adjective in each one. Then rewrite the sentences using adverbs formed from the adjectives you have underlined, following the examples given.

a) He gave a clear description of the scene.   He described the scene...

b) She was a brilliant actor.   She acted...

c) He is a persuasive speaker.   He speaks...

d) She was a wonderful singer.   She sang...

e) He had a funny voice.   He spoke...

> **Remember**
>
> For adjectives ending in 'y', change the 'y' to an 'i' before adding '–ly'.

Skills Boost: Using adverbs

Adverbs can make your writing more descriptive. However, choosing more precise verbs can be even more effective.

1 Choose a single, precise verb from the **Verb Bank** to replace the highlighted verb and adverb in the following sentences.

a) He walked quickly to school.

b) She walked slowly to school.

c) He fell suddenly to the ground

d) 'I don't want to,' she said quietly.

e) His leg was seriously broken.

Verb Bank

- hurried
- raced
- dashed
- dropped
- mumbled
- wandered
- sauntered
- muttered
- crashed
- smashed
- strolled
- collapsed
- shattered
- whispered
- fractured

Activity 3: Choosing verbs

Strong, descriptive verbs add to the impact of a descriptive text.

1 The following sentences describe an astronaut trying to steer her vessel through a cloud of asteroids. Replace the verbs to make the descriptions more powerful. You could choose new verbs from the **Verb Bank**, or use your own ideas.

Verb Bank

hurried | sped | rushed

thumping | pounding | thudding

yelling | shouting | calling

  a) She went to the control panel.
  b) Her heart was beating.
  c) The engineer was asking for help.

2 The following sentences continue the description.

> She stopped and looked out of the window, into the blackness of space.
>
> The asteroids were coming towards them.

  a) Identify the **three** verbs these sentences contain.
  b) For each of these three verbs, create your own verb bank containing **three** more verbs with the same or similar meanings.
  c) Using **one** verb from each of your verb banks, rewrite the sentences to make them more powerful.

3 What could happen next? Write **four** more sentences to conclude the description. You could use some of the ideas below, or think of your own.

  The asteroids hit the spaceship.   The spaceship shakes.

  A 'danger' light comes on.   A warning siren comes on.

  The engineer finds the damage.   The captain calls for help.

4 Look through the sentences you have written.
  a) Underline all the verbs you have used.
  b) Could any of the verbs you have chosen be more powerful or descriptive? If so, replace them.

This section links to pages 98–101 of the Workbook.

Section 4
Building noun phrases

In this section, you will develop your skills in building and using noun phrases.

This extract is the opening of a novel. The narrator and her family are going on a journey and have been told they can take very few personal items with them, including only one book each.

▼ Read the extract and then answer the questions that follow it.

1 It was easy to pack. We were allowed so little, and we didn't have to bother about leaving anything tidy behind us. Only the books caused a little delay: Father said, "I must take this." He showed us an ugly big volume
5 called *A Dictionary of Intermediate Technology*. "But you must choose for yourselves," he said. "It wouldn't be fair of me to choose for you. Think carefully."

We didn't think. We were excited, disturbed, and we hadn't really understood that everything else would be
10 left behind. Father looked wistfully at the shelves. He picked up *The Oxford Complete Shakespeare*. "Have you all chosen your books?" he asked.

"Yes," we told him. He put the Shakespeare back.

We had time to waste at the end. We ate everything
15 we could find.

"I don't want to eat iron," Pattie said, but nobody knew what she meant.

Then Father got out the **slide projector**, and showed us pictures of holidays we had once had. We didn't think
20 much of them.

"Have they all gone brownish with age, Dad?" said Joe, our brother, the eldest of us.

"No," said Father. "The pictures are all right. It's the light that has changed. It's been getting colder and
25 bluer now for years… but when I was young it was this lovely golden colour, just like this – look."

But what he showed us – a beach, with a blue sea, and the mother we couldn't remember lying on a towel, reading a book – looked a funny hue, as though
30 someone had brushed it over with a layer of treacle.

Pattie was glad that Father wasn't going to be able to take the slide projector. It made him sad.

And the next day we all went away, Father and Joe, and Sarah, and Pattie, and lots of other families, and
35 left the Earth far behind.

When this happened, we were all quite young, and Pattie was so young that later she couldn't remember being on the Earth at all, except those few last hours, and even the journey was mostly forgotten. She could
40 remember the beginning of the journey because it was so exciting. When we could undo our seat belts, and look out of the windows, the world looked like a Chinese paper lantern, with painted lands upon it, and all the people on the ship looked at it, and some of the
45 grownups cried. Father didn't cry; he didn't look, either.

Joe went and talked to Father by and by, but Sarah and Pattie stood at a porthole all day long, and saw the world shrink and shrink and diminish down 'til it looked like a round cloudy glass marble that you
50 could have rolled on the palm of your hand. Pattie was looking forward to going past the Moon, but that was no fun at all, for the ship passed by the dark side, and we saw nothing of it. And then we were in a wide black starry sky, where none of the stars had names.

55 At first there were voices from the world below, but not for long. The Disaster from which we were escaping happened much sooner
60 than they had thought it would, and after two days the
65 ship was in radio silence, alone.

Key vocabulary

slide projector: device for projecting images onto a screen

Activity 1: Inferring ideas

1 What can you infer about the planet Earth from the extract on page 106? Write **two or three** sentences explaining your ideas. Think about:
- the pictures the family are looking at, and how they suggest the Earth has changed since they were taken
- how the Earth is described as the family leave it.

How do I do that?

- Find and reread the relevant parts of the extract: the part where the family are looking at pictures, and the part where they are leaving the planet Earth.
- Look for clues that give you information you about the Earth.

2 Think about the character of the father in the extract.
a) Which of the following words best describe him? Choose **two**.

kind | upset | thoughtful | tough | loving | sad | worried | unemotional

b) Find **one** piece of evidence for each of the descriptions you have chosen.

Activity 2: Exploring noun phrases

A **noun phrase** is a group of words containing a noun and all other words that add information to it. Noun phrases often include one or more adjectives.

1 **a)** Copy out the noun phrases below. Circle the nouns and underline the adjectives.

a round cloudy glass marble   a wide black starry sky

b) The adjectives in a noun phrase can describe any of the noun's qualities. Copy the table below and add all the adjectives in the noun phrases to it.

What it is made of	Its shape	Its colour	Its size	Other qualities

2 Look again at the adjectives in the noun phrases. In your opinion, what impression do they create of:
a) planet Earth?
b) the Universe?
When writing your answer you could use words from the **Adjective Bank** or use your own ideas.

Adjective Bank
- small
- fragile
- frightening
- weak
- mysterious
- empty

Grammar Boost: Prepositional phrases

A **prepositional phrase** is a group of words that begins with a **preposition**. For example:

under the table | in the house |
with blue spots | near the park

1 Copy and complete the sentences below to describe the picture, replacing each **?** with a prepositional phrase. Use the **Preposition Bank** to help you.
a) The astronaut is standing **?**.
b) The astronaut's helmet is **?**.
c) The engineer is **?**.
d) The bird is **?**.
e) The cat is hiding **?**.

Preposition Bank

- in
- from
- underneath
- next to
- with
- of
- near
- on top of
- to
- on
- inside
- above

Activity 3: Building noun phrases

You are going to create **five** detailed noun phrases describing a unique place.

1 Imagine you are in an imaginary city on an imaginary planet. What can you see or hear in the city? Write down **five** nouns.

2 Now look at each of the nouns you have noted. Add **one, two or three** adjectives describing each one. You could use the suggestions below, or your own ideas.

What it is made of	Its shape	Its colour	Its size
metal	stone	glass	ice	round	square	thin	thick	green	blue	brown	black	tall	wide	long	huge

3 Finally, add a prepositional phrase to each noun, to describe its position or appearance further. For example: 'in the sky', 'with green spots', or 'on the ground.'

Activity 4: Using noun phrases

Imagine you have journeyed through space and have just arrived on a strange new planet that will become your home. You are going to write a short description of the planet, focusing on your use of noun phrases.

Imagine

1 Imagine the door of your spaceship slowly opening. What do you see? Note down **five or six** ideas. You could use some of your ideas from Activity 3.

Plan

2 Look over the ideas you have noted. Which will you include in your description? Tick them.

3 In what order will you use them? Number all the ideas you have ticked.

4 Underline all the nouns in your plan: the things, people or places you have named.

5 Build noun phrases from each noun by adding adjectives and prepositional phrases.

Write

6 Use your plan to write your description. Aim to write **one or two** paragraphs.

Review

7 Underline all the noun phrases you have used in your description.

8 Note down any improvements or additions you could make to any of the adjectives or prepositional phrases in your noun phrases.

Section 5
Assessment

In this section, you will answer questions on a short article and write a short descriptive text to assess your progress in the unit so far.

In this newspaper article, the writer describes a visit to Cape Canaveral in the USA to see the launch of the space shuttle, *Atlantis*.

▼ Read the article and then answer the questions that follow it.

Like nothing else on Earth

1 I sat on a grassy bank and looked out over the Florida swamp. Beside me, a big digital countdown clock stood frozen at nine minutes. There was an anxious pause, then the announcement the crowd of 10,000 had been waiting to hear came over the **tannoy**[1]: 'All final checks complete. Recommence the countdown. Go for launch!'

2 Five miles away, across the Indian River, the space shuttle *Atlantis* stood silently on Launch Pad 39A. In her cockpit were five astronauts and in her cargo bay was the *Destiny* module, the latest component of the International Space Station. I had dreamt of watching a shuttle blast off ever since the first, *Columbia*, was launched in 1981. Several times I had booked a flight to Florida from the UK, only for NASA to postpone the launch – a common occurrence. Now, the digital clock was moving again and the hairs on the back of my neck were standing on end.

3 **T (take-off) minus five minutes**[2]. Just across the water, five people sat in a capsule the size of a **family saloon**[3], directly beneath them 4.5 million lbs of liquid hydrogen and oxygen delivering the same explosive force as the Hiroshima bomb. And the clock ticked on.

4 At T-minus one minute the tension was unbearable. Dusk had fallen and a full moon hovered over Cape Canaveral. *Atlantis* stood lifeless.

5 Ten seconds. Sparks appeared at the base of *Atlantis*. It was the first outward sign of activity. It looked like a cheap firework, fizzing feebly. Five seconds. The boosters were fired, generating a huge **nimbus**[4] of steam as the flames hit the vast tank of water positioned beneath the shuttle. Obscured within the cloud, *Atlantis* was straining to break free.

And then she was off. A dazzling light pierced the cloud, then she exploded into view like a meteor, belching fire.

6 The power the shuttle needed to rip itself from the Earth's gravity meant that 20 seconds into the flight it had halved its take-off weight. At 25 seconds two remarkable things happened. First, the noise finally arrived, a crescendo that began with a low, throaty growl. You could tell it was coming because the flocks of birds that live on the river scattered in terror. Second, the shuttle burst into the full glare of the sun. *Atlantis* was now a silver bullet and her smoke trail glowed crimson, then orange. It was quite a show.

7 Within three minutes Atlantis was gone, the smoke trails, now billowing in the wind, the only sign that she had ever been there. Fifteen minutes later she would be over Paris, and by the time I had queued to get off the Cape and driven the three miles to my hotel, she would have travelled one and a half times around the Earth.

Key vocabulary

tannoy[1]: loudspeaker for making announcements to an audience or crowd
T (take-off) minus five minutes[2]: five minutes until the rocket takes off
family saloon[3]: car large enough for five people
nimbus[4]: cloud

Activity 1: Reading

1 Look again at the first two paragraphs of the article on page 110. Identify **three** things that the writer could see during the wait for the space shuttle to take off.

2 How did the writer feel when the digital clock started moving and the countdown began again? Which word or phrase tells you this?

3 Look again at the third paragraph of the article. How does the writer imply that the astronauts were in a dangerous position?

4 Look again at paragraphs 5–7. Identify **two** ways in which the writer suggests the power of the space shuttle.

Activity 2: Writing

Imagine you are one of the five astronauts in the *Atlantis* space shuttle and you have been asked to write a description of your experiences. You could describe:
- the cockpit of the space shuttle
- the other astronauts in the cockpit with you
- waiting for take-off
- take-off
- travelling away from Earth and out into space
- your thoughts and feelings.

1 Write your description of your experience on the *Atlantis*.

Before you start writing
- Plan your writing by gathering all the ideas you could include.
- Think carefully about the order in which you will describe your ideas.

As you write
- Choose your vocabulary carefully.

When you have finished writing
- Check the accuracy of your paragraphing.

This section links to pages 104–107 of the Workbook.

Section 6
Creating a viewpoint

In this section, you will explore how writers create the narrator's viewpoint in a text.

This is an extract from a short story. Pan is the only survivor on the space ship *The Unicorn*, travelling through the universe to a new planet.

▼ Read the extract and then answer the questions that follow it.

1 The alarm sounded about twenty seconds ago. I turned off my music, pulled out my headphones and called up the ship's manual on my screen.

"In the event of an emergency," says the manual, "the alarm will sound. After thirty seconds, all power will be diverted to the automated repair system."

5 "Shutting down in 5 seconds," says my screen. "4… 3… 2… 1." The screen goes blank. The lights in my cabin darken to a dull red glow. And I remember I am completely alone on a spaceship, about a billion miles from everywhere. Fear hits the bottom of my stomach like it's been kicked.

I run to the ship's cockpit, my thoughts racing. The first thing I notice is the darkness. Normally the drive-display fills the room with dancing light as it monitors the engine health, mapping, steering, air supply, all the stuff the ship
10 needs to get it from one end of the universe to the other. Now all it says is *Error. Estimated time of repair: 4 minutes.*

I stare through the windscreen into the blackness of space, and watch specks of stars approach and pass. Streaks of blinding white light flash above the ship as meteors burn up, lumps of rocks burnt and shattered to dust and scattered into infinity. And all the while I hear the distant whirr of the ship's engines.

Then the sound of the engine changes. And it feels as though the nose of the ship is dipping and I'm leaning
15 forward. It feels like we're speeding up.

"Computer?" I say. I can hear my voice is shaking. "Computer, show me our speed."

Silence.

Error. Estimated time of repair: 2 minutes, says the screen.

Then the screen goes completely blank for a couple of
20 seconds, flashes bright white and says *Rebooting…*

A wave of relief washes over me. After thirty seconds, the screen adds, *Rebooting… Failed.*

I feel the ship lurch and drop. The nose of the ship is dipping. I'm being tipped forward, tipped out of my seat. With fumbling
25 fingers, I clip the safety harness around myself, strapping myself to the chair, and look out of the windscreen to the vast blackness through which I am plummeting, trapped in a tiny tin can plunging to the bottom of the universe.

I feel tears stabbing at the back of my eyes. And I tighten
30 my sweaty fingers around the arms of my chair, close my eyes and try to keep breathing.

Activity 1: Tracking thoughts and feelings

The extract is written in the first person. This means that one of the characters narrates the story, giving the reader their viewpoint: the reader sees what the character sees, and has access to the character's thoughts and feelings.

1 The following questions will help you to track the thoughts and feelings of the narrator in the extract on page 112.

a) Using **bullet points**, write a summary of the events described in the extract. Use the notes to the right to help you get started, and the quotations below to help you finish off your summary.

- The ship's alarm has sounded.

- Pan's screen goes blank and the lights in her cabin dim.

> I run to the ship's cockpit

> *Estimated time of repair: 4 minutes.*

> it feels as though the nose of the ship is dipping

> It feels like we're speeding up.

> *Estimated time of repair: 2 minutes*

> *Rebooting… Failed.*

> I'm being tipped forward, tipped out of my seat.

> I feel tears stabbing at the back of my eyes.

b) Look at your summary. Next to each of the bullet points, add a note about how Pan is feeling. For example:

> Pan feels anxious and tense.

> Pan feels frightened.

> Pan is panicking.

Activity 2: Choosing vocabulary

One way in which the writer sets the scene and builds tension is through the choice of vocabulary.

1 Look again at the first two paragraphs on page 112. Which words and phrases tell you that there is a problem on board *The Unicorn*?

2 Look again at the final two paragraphs of the extract. Identify **three** words or phrases from this section that the writer has chosen to show that Pan is in a very dramatic and dangerous situation.

Skills Boost: Past and present tense

Verb forms change depending on the person doing the action. For example:

Present tense	**First person**	I	I watch. | I have. | I do.
	Second person	you	You watch. | You have. | You do.
	Third person	he | she | it	He watches. | It has. | She does.

Verb forms also change to indicate when the action happened. The past tense shows that action happened in the past. To show the past tense, the most common suffix added to verbs is '–ed', but there are some irregular past-tense forms. For example:

Past tense	**First person**	I	I watched. | I had. | I did.
	Second person	you	You watched. | You had. | You did.
	Third person	he | she | it	He watched. | It had. | She did.

1 Rewrite the sentences below, changing the sentences that use the past tense to the present tense, and the sentences that use the present tense to the past tense.
a) I decided to check the ship's manual.
b) The ship flies through the darkness of space.
c) I do not know what to do.
d) He did not have time to check the data.
e) She spoke quickly to the computer.

Activity 3: Viewpoint and tense

The extract on page 112 is written in the first person and the present tense. Look again at the last two paragraphs.

1 Identify **three** words from the last two paragraphs that show the extract is written in the first person and the present tense.

2 Rewrite the last two paragraphs of the extract using the third person and the past tense. Circle all the words you have changed.

> She felt the ship lurch and drop. The nose of the ship was dipping

3 Compare the last two paragraphs of the extract with the version you have written in answer to question 2. Which version do you prefer, and why? Write **one or two** sentences explaining your ideas.

Activity 4: Plan and write

You are going to write a paragraph of description, using the first person and the present tense.

Imagine

1 Imagine you are on a spaceship. The emergency alarm sounds, and a warning message appears on the ship's computer screen. What has happened? You could choose one of the following ideas or use your own.

- A huge asteroid is heading straight for your spaceship.
- The ship's air supply is failing and breathing will soon become difficult.
- An enemy spaceship is rapidly approaching.

Plan

2 What would you think and feel in the situation that you have imagined?

Note down some ideas, using the spidergram below to help you.

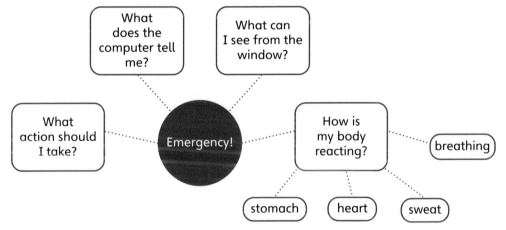

3 Now add some possible vocabulary choices to your plan. Aim to note at least **ten** nouns, verbs and adjectives. You could choose from the following suggestions or use your own ideas.

hurtling | crashing | gasping | dangerous | destroyed | panic | fear | trembling

Write

4 Using your plan, write your description using only **50–75** words. Remember, you need to write in the first person and the present tense.

Review

5 Look again at your writing.
   a) Circle all words that show it is written in the first person and present tense.
   b) Rewrite your description in the third person and the past tense.
   c) Compare the two versions of your description. Which do you prefer, and why?

Section 7
Explaining and describing

In this section, you will explore how writers use description in non-fiction texts.

In this article the writer imagines what it might be like to take a holiday in space.

▼ **Read the article below and then answer the questions that follow it.**

Holidays in space

1 Imagine orbiting our planet in a spaceship, travelling 100 miles above the surface of the Earth. From the window on your right, you stare into the blackness of space and the lights of a billion stars. From the window on your left, far below, you can see the whole of the blue and green planet, its seas, mountains and valleys. Then, as your orbit continues, night falls and the city lights dot the blackness of the land.

2 How many people have escaped the Earth and experienced this extraordinary sight? Around five hundred professional astronauts and a handful of space tourists. American businessman Dennis Tito was the first to buy a ticket to space, in 2001. His ticket, with eight days on board the International Space Station, 250 miles above the Earth, cost 20 million US dollars.

3 Soon, though, the number of space travellers could grow. Several companies are planning to offer holidays in space, travelling around the Earth, around the Moon and beyond – and are spending billions trying to make it possible. Most companies are working on a re-usable rocket. One company is planning to float tourists into space in a capsule suspended from a huge balloon. However, developing any vehicle that can take off, travel through space and return to Earth is difficult. Developing one that can do it safely, and do it over and over again, is even harder. It may be several years before holidays in space become a reality.

4 When they do eventually take off, space tourists may not find themselves sitting comfortably and gazing out of the window at the wonders of the universe. With little or no gravity in space, your body floats and your blood gathers in your head, so for the first twenty-four hours, before your body adjusts, you feel sick and dizzy and your brain struggles to know which way is up. And there is, of course, the small possibility that you may not return safely: experts have estimated the risk at a one percent chance that your spaceship will fail.

5 But if none of that puts you off, why not sign up? You will need to be (according to one company) between the ages of 10 and 90, physically fit, and have an estimated 10 million US dollars to spend.

Activity 1: Identifying purpose

Look at these definitions of two writing purposes for **non-fiction** texts.

- **description:** writing that aims to create a vivid image in the reader's mind
- **explanation:** writing that makes information and ideas clear and easy to understand

Explanation and description are different. However, explanation writing often uses description to achieve its purpose: to make ideas clear and easy to understand.

1 Look closely at the article on page 116.

   a) Which of the ideas below does it make clear and easy to understand?

   A The experience of being a traveller in space.

   B The different people who have already travelled in space.

   C How much it will cost to travel in space.

   D The kinds of vehicles that will take travellers into space.

   E What it would be like to land on the Moon.

   F What it would be like to travel in space.

   b) Which of the ideas above are made clear using description, to create a vivid image in the reader's mind?

   c) For each of your answers to question 1b, write down a phrase or sentence from the article that uses description to explain the idea.

Activity 2: Structuring an explanation

1 Writers often structure **explanation texts** to answer the kinds of questions readers might have. Each paragraph in the article on page 116 focuses on the answer to one of the following questions.

A
> What would it be like to travel in space?

B
> Who has already been to space?

C
> How will people travel to space?

D
> Who will be able to go into space?

Which paragraphs in the article answer which questions?

The writer answers question A in paragraphs 1 and

2 Writers often structure explanation texts with the intentions of:

- engaging the reader's attention from the very beginning
- leaving the reader interested by using a surprising or engaging idea at the end.

In your opinion, how effectively has the writer of the article achieved both of these intentions? Write **two or three** sentences explaining your ideas, using examples from the article.

Activity 3: Exploring explanations and descriptions

Look at the following extracts from the article on page 116.

A From the window on your right, you stare into the blackness of space and the lights of a billion stars. From the window on your left, far below, you can see the whole of the blue and green planet, its seas, mountains and valleys.

B American businessman Dennis Tito was the first to buy a ticket to space in 2001. His ticket, with eight days on board the International Space Station, 250 miles above the Earth, cost 20 million US dollars.

1 a) Which extract uses **facts** and **statistics** to explain information to the reader?
   b) Identify **three** facts or statistics that the writer uses in that extract.
   c) What impression of space travel is created by these facts and statistics?

2 a) Which extract uses description to convey ideas and information to the reader?
   b) Identify **two** words or phrases for each extract that the writer uses to describe space travel.

Skills Boost: Writing in a formal register

Explanation texts are often written in a formal **register**. A formal register should feature:

- no **contractions** or **abbreviations**   ~~don't~~ | ~~can't~~

                                                            do not ✔ | cannot ✔

- no **slang**.   ~~cool~~ | ~~OK~~

                                                            good ✔ | agreed ✔

1 Rewrite the following sentences, replacing the contractions with full words.

> You wouldn't believe how much it's going to cost. If you're going into space, you'll need a huge amount of money. I don't think many people could afford it.

2 a) Choose and note down **two** examples of slang or informal language that show you like something, and **two** examples that show you dislike something.
   b) Use your informal words in **two** sentences: **one** positive and **one** negative.
   c) Alter your sentences to use formal language to express the same ideas.

Activity 4: Writing an article

You are going to write an article explaining an imaginary holiday on which customers visit another planet.

Imagine

1 What kind of planet will your article be about? Note down **four or five** adjectives. You could choose some of the suggestions below, or think of your own.

warm | beautiful | relaxing | icy | exciting

2 What differences from Earth will visitors find there? Note down **four or five** nouns. You could choose some of the suggestions below, or think of your own.

oxygen | gravity | plant life | animals | water | food

Plan

3 Plan your article in **three** paragraphs by adding **one or two** questions to each row of a table like the one below. You could use some of the suggestions of questions below to help you, or your own ideas.

Paragraph 1	What will the planet be like?
Paragraph 2	
Paragraph 3	

What will the planet be like?

What will the journey be like?

What will we do when we get there?

4 How will you engage your reader from the beginning of your article? Add some ideas to paragraph 1 of your plan.

5 How will you explain the holiday to your readers? You could use facts and statistics that answer any of the following questions. Add some ideas to paragraphs 2 and 3 of your plan.

How old? | How much? | How long? | How far? | How big?

Remember

Facts, statistics, description and opinion are all effective ways to explain ideas to the reader.

Write

6 Write your first line, choosing vocabulary carefully to ensure it engages the reader's attention immediately.

7 Write your article, using formal Standard English. Remember, you are aiming both to explain and to describe the holiday, making ideas clear and creating vivid images in the reader's mind.

This section links to pages 112–115 of the Workbook.

Section 8
Exploring sentence structure

In this section, you will explore different sentence structures in descriptive writing.

In this extract a team of space explorers has lost contact with their fleet. Their spacecraft is damaged, supplies are running out, and they are beginning to give up hope. By chance, they land on a strange planet.

▼ Read the extract and then answer the questions that follow it.

1 Mina was woken by a soft, jolting thud. For a moment, she failed to realise the meaning of the sound. Then she sat up with a start. They had landed! Breathlessly, she clambered up the ladder from her cabin. Dazzling light blinded her as she emerged onto the main bridge of the spacecraft. Weak with hunger, she grabbed at a handrail. Steadying herself, she shaded her eyes with the other hand, and looked out.

2 She saw a landscape of sand and rock, similar to the harsh deserts of earth. The only obvious difference was in the sky, where twin suns blazed fiercely. Briefly, her spirits sank. No food or water. But as her eyes adjusted to the light, she noticed a dome of rocky ground, roughly half a mile from one end to the other, crowned with a black conical peak, and surrounded by a forest of dense green trees. An oasis! Hope filled her heart.

3 She sounded the siren to rouse her three companions – Margot, their leader, who emerged first, looking tense and exhausted, followed by Karson the science officer, who went straight to the instrument panel, and Sully the engineer, frowning and rubbing his eyes. The weary crew had drifted for twenty days since the radio and navigation system failed, and they lost contact with the rest of the fleet. Now hope gave them new energy. Karson reported that the atmosphere was breathable, and Margot decided they should make for the oasis.

4 As they marched, Mina was able to study the features of the strange new world more closely. The sand was not red or gold, as on Earth, but pale blue, fashioned into patterns of ridges and dunes by the wind, and littered with tiny pink gemstones of a type she had never seen before. Pulling binoculars from her backpack, she focused on the forest surrounding the oasis. Wind rippled through the tops of the trees, twisting their leaves this way and that, so that they fluttered and flashed in the light of the twin suns. Rising from the trees was a grey cliff dotted with small black holes, which she guessed were the nesting sites of birds. At the base of the cliff was a cave, in front of which was a patch of thin yellow grass, strewn with grey boulders of various sizes and shapes. Her eye lingered on the sight. Something about the arrangement of the boulders puzzled her… they seemed neatly ordered, almost as if they had been deliberately rolled into place, to provide a barrier against the wind. She dismissed the idea, and turned back to her companions. Perhaps, she thought, the cave was somewhere they could shelter and build a fire.

5 She shared this thought with Sully. He frowned; "Maybe…" he said. "The place looks safe enough, but there's no guarantee of food or fresh water. What's left of our stores is on board the ship, and I don't fancy carrying boxes and packets all the way across this desert".

6 Margot joined them; "Sully's right. We'll explore now, and find out what we can, but I think we should return to the ship before it's dark. Our best chance of rescue is fixing the radio".

7 Suddenly, a cry halted their discussion. Karson was calling to them, pointing eagerly. They followed his gaze. What they saw startled them. Smoke was rising above the trees in a thin white trail. With racing hearts, the four companions looked at each other, their eyes bright with excitement and uncertainty. They were not alone.

Activity 1: Following the camera

One way to think about writing a description is to imagine a camera moving through a scene, filming everything it sees.

1 Look again at the first four paragraphs of the extract on page 120. Imagine this part of the story being made into a film. Copy the storyboard outline below and complete it with the first four frames, showing what the audience would see. Following the example below, you can use stick figures and labels to show your ideas.

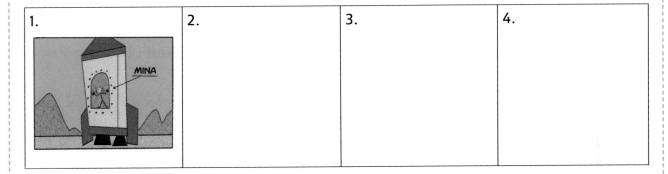

1.	2.	3.	4.

Activity 2: Looking at sentence length

Different sentence lengths suit different purposes.
- Short sentences are good for:
  - highlighting dramatic moments in a description
  - highlighting key ideas.
- Longer sentences are good for:
  - building up descriptive detail
  - showing a sequence of events.

1 Look at the following sentences from the extract on page 120. Which of the purposes above does each sentence have?

  a) They had landed!

  b) She sounded the siren to rouse her three companions – Margot, their leader, who emerged first, looking tense and exhausted, followed by Karson the science officer, who went straight to the instrument panel, and Sully the engineer, frowning and rubbing his eyes.

  c) Now hope gave them new energy.

  d) The sand was not red or gold, as on Earth, but pale blue, fashioned into patterns of ridges and dunes by the wind, and littered with tiny pink gemstones of a type she had never seen before.

Skills Boost: Adverbials

Adverbials add information to a verb, adjective or other adverbial. They can be one-word adverbs, adverbial phrases (more than one word without a verb) or adverbial clauses (more than one word with a verb). For example:

She started a new school recently.   *adverb*

She started a new school a month ago.   *adverbial phrase*

She started a new school after moving house last month.   *adverbial clause*

An adverbial can be put in different positions in a sentence without changing its meaning. For example:

A month ago, I started a new school.   I started a new school a month ago.

1 Rewrite the following sentences, moving the adverbial to a different position without changing the sentence's meaning.
a) Suddenly, we realised we were lost.
b) In the darkness, strange lights flickered and flashed.
c) At the edge of our solar system, a planet called Neptune can be found.

Remember

Adverbials often add information about position (where something is) or time (when something happened).

2 Add an adverbial to the following sentences, using the **Adverbial Bank** to help you.
a) A meteor shower exploded.
b) I heard the roar of the ship's engines.
c) I thought I saw something.

Adverbial Bank

in the distance | for a moment | outside the window | after an hour had passed | above our heads | the next day

Activity 3: Sentence openings

There are lots of ways in which a sentence can begin.
- Some sentences begin with a noun: Mina was woken by a soft, jolting thud.
- Some begin with a noun phrase: Dazzling light blinded her
- Some begin with a pronoun: She saw a landscape of sand and rock
- Some begin with an adverbial: For a moment, she failed to realise the meaning.

1 Identify **five** sentences in the extract on page 120 that begin in different ways. Write down the first **five or six** words of each sentence and whether it starts with a noun, a noun phrase, a pronoun or an adverbial.

Activity 4: Writing a description

You are going to write a description of your arrival on a hostile new planet.

Imagine

1 Imagine you have landed, and that your spaceship door has hissed open. You see the planet for the first time. What makes it hostile? You could choose from the ideas below, or use your own.

| wild alien creatures | terrible weather conditions | a hazardous landscape |

Write **one** sentence summing up the planet on which you have landed.

2 Imagine a camera moving through the scene in front of you, filming everything it sees. What would appear in that film? Note down around **ten** ideas. You could choose from the ideas below, or use your own.

| the ground | the sky | the weather | rocks |
| water | plants | animals | mountains |

Practise your sentence-writing skills

3 Write a long, descriptive sentence using **two or three** of the ideas you have gathered. You could:
- create long, detailed noun phrases
- use adverbials
- link the clauses using coordinating and subordinating conjunctions.

4 Look again at the details you have included in your long, descriptive sentence. Think about how you feel as you open the hatch and see what you have described.
a) Write a short sentence describing your feelings.
b) Add an adverbial to your short sentence.
c) Rewrite your short sentence, beginning it in a different way.
d) Decide which version of your short sentence you will use in your description.

Write

5 Continue and complete your description. Aim to:
- write **75–100** words in total
- open your sentences in a variety of different ways
- use adverbials to add information about when or where things happened
- use some longer sentences and some shorter sentences.

Remember
Different sentence lengths suit different purposes.
- Short sentences are good for highlighting a dramatic moment or a key idea.
- Longer sentences are good for descriptive detail or showing a sequence of events.

Section 9
Gathering ideas for a description

In this section, you will explore different ways of planning a description.

One way of planning a vivid description of a place you have imagined is to draw it, and map it out. The image below is one student's drawing of a strange new planet, which will form the basis of a writing plan. Your task is to continue planning a description of this experience.

Activity 1: Picturing the scene

1 Imagine yourself in the landscape pictured above, taking in everything you can see. Use all the details to add nouns to a table like the one below, answering the questions to help you. Make your table quite large – in the next few activities, you will be gathering lots of ideas to fill it.

What is immediately in front of you?	What is a little closer to you?	What is in the distance?
footprints	rocks	sky, mountains

Activity 2: Using descriptive vocabulary

Look again at all the ideas you noted in Activity 1. You are now going to add some descriptive vocabulary to each of the nouns you have noted, to create descriptive noun phrases.

1 Add **one or two** adjectives to each of the nouns you have noted, giving information about their shape, colour or size. You could choose some of the ideas below, but you should also use your own ideas. Do not use any adjective more than once.

lumpy | red | round | deep | tiny | jagged | wide | orange | huge | vast | brown | towering

2 Now add adverbials to around half of your nouns, describing their positions. You could choose one or two of the ideas below, but you should also use your own ideas. Do not use any adverbial more than once.

on the ground | in the distance | near the horizon | under my feet | to the left | ahead of me

Activity 3: Thinking about all of your senses

Remind yourself of the things you have noted about the strange new planet on which you landed. So far, they are all things you can see. You now need to think about the rest of your five senses.

1 Look again at the picture on page 124. Think about things that you can:

hear   touch or feel   taste or smell

Add at least one idea for each sense to your table, linking it to the feature that has caused it. You could choose some of the ideas below, but you should also use your own ideas.

heat | smoke | howling | wind | soft | hard | gritty | ringing | dusty | crunching | whistling | rattling | fumes

Activity 4: Describing your thoughts and emotions

Describing your thoughts and emotions can be an effective way of engaging the reader's interest.

1 Think about how your thoughts and emotions are affected as you look around. How do you respond to the different things you experience? Add at least **two** responses to your table, linking them to the features that have caused them. For example:

I feel frightened.   I'm excited!   I'm worried...   This is confusing.

2 Look at the responses you have noted. How does each one feel, physically? Add your ideas to your table, linking them to the thoughts or emotions that have caused them. You could choose one or two of the ideas below, but you should also use your own ideas.

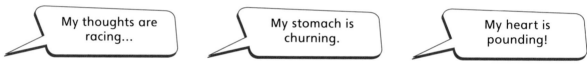

My thoughts are racing...   My stomach is churning.   My heart is pounding!

Skills Boost: Understanding story structure

Stories create tension by putting characters in difficult situations. They create satisfying endings by resolving those difficult situations. Sometimes they are resolved happily – but sometimes they are not.

One way to think of a simple story structure is in these three steps:

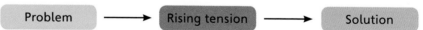

Problem   ⟶   Rising tension   ⟶   Solution

1 Look at the following story summaries.

   A   Panit is searching in his school bag for his homework. He cannot find it. The teacher is collecting the homework. It's nearly Panit's turn to hand in his homework. At the last moment, he finds his homework and hands it in.

   B   The planet that Jen has been exploring is about to be hit by a speeding asteroid. Jen races to her spaceship. She can see and hear the asteroid approaching. Jen starts the rocket's engines. Her spaceship takes off just as the asteroid hits the planet.

Copy out sentences from the summaries above to answer the following questions.
a) Which sentences describe the two problems?
b) Which sentences describe the rising tension in each story?
c) Which sentences describe the two solutions?

Activity 5: Developing your ideas

Everything you have planned so far is setting the scene by describing what you can see, hear, smell, feel and taste. Now you will develop your ideas by adding some tension to your description. One way to do this is to think about the image in your mind as part of a sequence of events.

1 Look again at the picture on page 124, seeing it as one moment in time. Think about what might have happened just before this moment. You could consider:
- How did you get here?
- Why are you here?
- What were you doing in the moments before this one?
- Was there something you saw, heard, smelled, felt or tasted just before this moment?

Write your ideas above your table.

2 **a)** Now think about what might be about to happen. One way to do this is to think about what you cannot see in the picture. You could consider:
- Could there be something just out of sight?
- Are you waiting for something specific to happen?
- Are you afraid of something happening?

   b) Finally, think about how could you use descriptions of changing sights, sounds, smells, sensations, thoughts and emotions to build up to the change.

   Write your ideas below your table.

Activity 6: Structuring your ideas

1 Look at all the ideas you have gathered in your table, and decide which ones you want to include in your description. Circle each of the key nouns that are connected to these ideas.

Imagine walking through the landscape from your starting position, seeing the features you have highlighted – you will see the features at the top of the table first, and move towards the features furthest towards the bottom. This order shows one way in which you could structure what you are going to describe.

This section links to pages 120–123 of the Workbook.

Section 10
Reviewing and revising

In this section, you will develop your skills of reviewing and improving the choices you have made in your writing.

This is an extract from one student's descriptive text, written in response to the image it accompanies.

▼ **Read the extract and then answer the questions that follow it.**

1   I had landed my spaceship on a planet. I had never visited this planet before. I pressed a button and the door on my spaceship slowly opened. I could see the sun shining in an orange sky. I
5   breathed in the warm air. I felt hot and my mouth was dry. I could not see any plants or animals or any living things, except for one tiny purple flower. I felt alone. There were lots of rocks on this planet and some were very tall and thin and
10   the ground was dusty and when I walked the dust went up into the air and I could taste the dust and I coughed. I could see mountains a long way away in the distance. I began to walk towards them. I noticed some marks on the ground as I walked along. I thought they looked like footprints.

Activity 1: Checking paragraphing

The extract above has not been paragraphed.

Remember

There are four reasons to start a new paragraph:
- a change of topic
- a change of scene or setting
- a change of time
- a change of speaker.

1 Look closely at the extract and work out where the topic or focus of the description changes. Note down the first few words of each sentence that should begin a new paragraph.

Paragraph 1: I had landed

Paragraph 2:

Activity 2: Reviewing and revising sentence structure

When you have finished a piece of writing, you should check that you have used a variety of sentence lengths and sentence openings.

1 Look at the following long, multi-clause sentence from the extract on page 128.

> There were lots of rocks on this planet and some were very tall and thin and the ground was dusty and when I walked the dust went up into the air and I could taste the dust and I coughed.

a) Rewrite the sentence by breaking it down into shorter, single-clause sentences. For example:

> There were lots of rocks on this planet.

b) Check that all the shorter sentences you have written make sense. Now try joining some of the sentences back together using conjunctions, to create variety in sentence lengths.

c) Which of the three versions do you prefer? Why is that? Write **one or two** sentences to explain your ideas.

2 Look again at the first half of the extract.
a) What do you notice about the first word of each sentence?
b) Look again at the following two sentences.

> I could see the sun shining in an orange sky.   I felt hot and my mouth was dry.

Rewrite each sentence so that neither begins with 'I', but their meaning does not change. You could try restructuring them. For example:

> I had landed my spaceship on a planet.

> My spaceship had landed on a planet.

c) Look at all of the other sentences in the extract that begin with 'I'. Rewrite **one** so that it begins with a different word.

Remember

There are lots of ways in which a sentence can begin.

- Some sentences begin with a noun: Smoke filled the air.

- Some begin with a noun phrase: Thick black smoke filled the air.

- Some begin with a pronoun: It was so thick I could see nothing.

- Some begin with an adverbial: Suddenly, the smoke cleared.

Skills Boost: Checking spelling

If you are unsure of a spelling, one way to check it is to try two or three different spellings to see which seems more familiar.

1 Look at the pairs of spellings in A–H below. Write down the correct spelling for each pair. If you are not sure, check the **How do I do that?** box.

   A flyying | flying   **B** lately | latley   **C** startted | started   **D** fixed | fixxed

E suddenly | suddenley   **F** stepped | steped   **G** lovely | lovley   **H** grabbed | grabed

How do I do that?

- When adding the suffixes '–ed' or '–ing', you double the final letter of a root verb if:
  - the verb has one syllable and ends consonant-vowel-consonant (so 'run' becomes 'running', and 'stop' becomes 'stopping')
  - the verb has two or more syllables, ends in consonant-verb-consonant and the second syllable is stressed (so 'begin' becomes 'beginning').
- The letters 'w', 'x' and 'y' are never doubled.
- Many adverbs are formed by adding the suffix '–ly' to an adjective (so 'quick' becomes 'quickly').

Remember

- A syllable is a part of a word that makes a single sound.
- The letters 'a', 'e', 'i', 'o' and 'u' are vowels. All other letters are consonants.

Activity 3: Reviewing and revising vocabulary choice

You can create vivid and interesting pictures in a reader's mind by using detailed noun phrases and precise verbs. When you review your work, you can **revise** your vocabulary to achieve this.

1 Look again at the extract on page 128.
  a) Identify **three** nouns with no related adjectives.
  b) Add **two** adjectives to each noun to create a clearer picture in the reader's mind.

2 The writer of the extract describes a hot, dusty, uncomfortable place. Look at the highlighted verbs in the following descriptions.

A   I could **see** the sun **shining** in an orange sky   **B**   when I **walked** the dust **went** up into the air

Replace the highlighted verbs with verbs that show more clearly how hot, dusty and uncomfortable this planet is. You could choose from the suggestions below or use your own ideas.

blazing | glowing   flew | rose

Activity 4: Proofreading

This is an extract from a different student's descriptive text, written in response to the same image. Read the extract and then answer the questions that follow it.

> I am walking slowley towards the mountains in the distance. It is so hot. Sweat is runing down my face, I feel so tired. I am covered in dust.
>
> Eventually I decide I have to rest. The ground is scattered with huge red rocks, I decide to sit down on one for a rest. Then I notice the footprints.
>
> I am filed with panic. My heart is beating realey fast and my hands are shaking. I cannot believe anyone else is here. The whole planet looks empty. There were no sign of another living thing but someone or something have made those footprints, I had to find out who or what it was.

It is extremely important to proofread your writing for spelling, punctuation and grammar errors.

1 Check and correct any spelling mistakes. If you find a spelling that looks incorrect, try writing it in two or three different ways before choosing the correct version.

When you find a mistake, copy it exactly and then write your correction next to it. Mark the incorrect version with a cross and the correct version with a tick. For example:

lovley ✗   lovely ✔

2 Check the student's punctuation. Should any of the commas be full stops? Note down any mistakes in the way described above.

Remember
- Sentences cannot be linked with a comma: they should be separated by a full stop or linked with a conjunction such as 'and', 'but' or 'when'.
- If you create a new sentence by adding a full stop, the new sentence should start with a capital letter.

3 Look carefully at the first two or three sentences of the extract.
   a) In which tense are these sentences written: the past or present tense?
   b) In which person are these sentences written: the first or third person?
   c) Check that the student has used the same tense and person throughout the whole extract.

Note down any mistakes in the way described above.

This section links to pages 124–125 of the Workbook.

Section 11
Assessment

In this section, you will write a descriptive article.

Activity 1: Planning

Imagine you are an astronaut, and that your job is to travel through space exploring new planets. You are going to write an article describing one of your experiences. You could write about one or two of the following experiences, or use your own ideas:
- taking off in your rocket or spaceship
- flying through outer space
- landing on a new planet.

1 Write **one** sentence summing up what you will describe in your article.

2 Think about the actions that happened during the experience, and how you will structure them.

Remember

One way to think of a simple story structure is in these three steps:

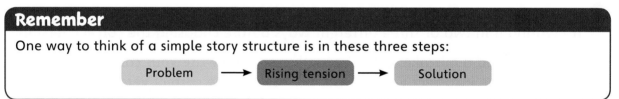

Problem ⟶ Rising tension ⟶ Solution

Think about how you could add some tension to these events. You may wish to include some hints you could give about things that are about to happen.

3 Picture in your mind each part of the experience you will describe. You may wish to draw a picture or a storyboard. Note down all the different details you could include in your article, thinking about how you will divide them into paragraphs. Add them to a paragraph planning table like the one below. Aim to write between **three** and **six** paragraphs in total.

Problem	Paragraph 1
Rising tension	Paragraph 2
	Paragraph 3

4 Look at all the ideas you have noted. Add some details about all the things you saw, heard, smelled, touched or tasted during the experience.

5 Think about your thoughts and emotions as you experienced these sights, sounds, sensations, smells and tastes. Add your ideas to your plan.

6 Look carefully through all the ideas you have noted. Add some powerful, descriptive adjectives and precise verbs you could use to describe them.

Activity 2: Writing

1 Write your article. As you write, you will need to think about making your writing as clear and engaging as possible. You can do this by using:
- accurate paragraphing
- an appropriate register (formal, informal or a mixture of both), remembering Standard English
- precise, varied and interesting vocabulary
- a variety of sentence lengths, with a variety of conjunctions
- a variety of sentence openings
- accurate sentence punctuation.

Activity 3: Reviewing and revising

1 Read through the article you have written. As you read, ask yourself:
- Is my article clear and easy to understand?
- Is it interesting and engaging?

Check that:
- the register you have chosen suits your content
- you have made vivid vocabulary choices, selecting powerful verbs, descriptive adjectives and adverbials
- you have used a variety of single-clause and multi-clause sentences
- you have consistently used the same tense and person throughout your writing
- all your pronouns agree with the nouns they represent
- your spelling is accurate
- each sentence begins with a capital letter and ends with a full stop, exclamation mark or question mark.

Unit 4
Love and hate

In this unit you will study a series of poems based on relationships. These poems express themes of love and hate in different ways, allowing you to understand the viewpoints of several poets and consider how you might feel in their place. You will explore a range of poetic techniques and examine their effects and why they have been used. You will also compare poems and write your own examples.

In this unit you will...

- **explore the ways in which poetry can be understood and the effects it can have.**
- **develop your response to some of the ideas in a poem.**
- **develop your response to a poem as a whole text.**
- **respond to the viewpoint expressed in a poem and select evidence from the poem to support your response.**
- **answer questions about a poem to assess your progress in the unit so far.**
- **explore the poet's vocabulary choices and experiment with your own.**
- **explore the poet's use of figurative language, and the effects this can create.**
- **look at how poets shape poetry.**
- **explore the form and structure of a poem and then write your own.**
- **compare the features and effects of two different poems.**
- **answer questions on a poem to assess your progress in this unit.**

By the end of this unit, you will be able to express a written response to poetry, supported with evidence.

This section links to pages 126–129 of the Workbook.

Section 1
Exploring and responding

In this section, you will explore the ways in which poetry can be understood and the effects it can have.

Poetry can form ideas and images in the reader's mind using just a few words.

Reading a poem three or four times will help you to understand a poem's ideas and images, to explore them, and to develop your response to them.

▼ **Read the poem and then answer the questions that follow it.**

Some people
by Rachel Field

1 Isn't it strange some people make
   You feel so tired inside,
   Your thoughts begin to shrivel up
   Like leaves all brown and dried!

5 But when you're with some other ones,
   It's stranger still to find
   Your thoughts as thick as fireflies
   All shiny in your mind!

Activity 1: Reading the poem

1 The poem 'Some people', above, is about different kinds of people. How many different kinds of people are described?

2 Write down **one or two** differences between the different kinds of people that the poet describes. You could choose from the adjectives below or use your own ideas.

exciting | inspiring | joyful | lively | interesting | fascinating | invigorating

boring | uninteresting | uninspiring | annoying | dull | ordinary | exhausting

One group of people is

whereas the other group is

Skills Boost: Poetry terms

Poetry	Poetry is written in **lines**: a sentence or part of a sentence that finishes at the end of the line. Sentences in poetry often continue over more than one line.
Stanza	A **stanza** is a group of lines. A poem can be written in one, two or several stanzas. People sometimes refer to stanzas as 'verses'.
Rhyme	**Rhyme** is where the last syllable or two of some lines has a similar sound to the last syllable or two at the end of another line. For example, 'line' rhymes with 'mine'.
Syllable	A syllable is a part of a word that makes a single sound. A word can consist of one, two or more syllables. For example, the word 'remind' has two syllables, and the word 'reminding' has three syllables.
Rhythm	**Rhythm** is the beat or pulse created by the words in a poem. Some poems have a regular rhythm.

1 How many lines are there in the poem, 'Some people', on page 136?

2 How many stanzas are there?

3 What are the rhyming words?

4 How many syllables are there in lines 1, 3, 5 and 7?

5 How many syllables are there in lines 2, 4, 6 and 8?

6 Read the poem aloud: does it have a regular rhythm?

Activity 2: Exploring the poem's key ideas

1 Look at the first stanza of the poem on page 136.

   a) What happens to the poet when she meets these people?

   b) Look at the simile the poet uses in this stanza. What does this image suggest about the poet's thoughts?

   c) Choose **two or three** of the words in this stanza that most clearly describe the poet's thoughts.

> **Remember**
>
> A **simile** is a comparison made by using the words 'like' or 'as'.

2 Look at the second stanza of the poem.

   a) What happens to the poet when she meets these people?

   b) Look at the simile the poet uses in this stanza. What does this image suggest about the poet's thoughts?

   c) Choose **two or three** words in this stanza that most clearly describe the poet's thoughts.

Activity 3: Responding to the poem

Responding to a poem means thinking about how the poem makes you think and feel – and how the poet has made you think and feel that way.

1 Read the poem on page 136 again, considering what your thoughts and feelings are.
   a) Note down **two** different responses you have to the poem. You could choose one or two of the suggestions below, or use your own words.

> It's a funny poem. It made me laugh.

> It's a happy poem. It made me smile.

> I know exactly what the poet means. I have met lots of people like that.

> The poem made me think about all the different people I know and how they make me feel.

> The poem made me look at people and think about them in a different way.

> It was interesting to consider the poet's thoughts and feelings.

   b) For each response you identify, write one or two sentences explaining how and why the poem made you think or feel this way.

Activity 4: Writing a simile

Look again at the similes the writer uses in the poem on page 136.

- Some people make the writer's thoughts feel: Like leaves all brown and dried!

- Other people make the writer's thoughts feel: as thick as fireflies
All shiny in your mind!

1 Write a new simile to describe your thoughts when you see something exciting.

How do I do that?

A Write down an adjective or a verb to describe your thoughts. You could choose some of the following words or use your own.

My thoughts are: quick | loud | lively | busy | energetic

My thoughts: buzz | run | fly | float | race | flutter

B Think of something else that your chosen adjective or verb could describe. You could choose one of the following ideas or use your own.

clouds in a storm | children in a playground | a bird's wings | bees in summer

C Use your choices and the words 'like' or 'as' to write a comparison.

When I see **?** my thoughts are as **?** as **?** .

When I see **?** my thoughts are like **?** .

2 Write a new simile to describe your thoughts when you are bored and tired.

Activity 5: Writing a poem

You are going to write a short poem expressing your thoughts and feelings.

1 Write a short poem about friends:
- write **one or two** stanzas with four lines each, about how friends can make you feel
- use **one** of the similes you wrote in answer to Activity 4 or write a new one
- use rhyming words at the end of the second and fourth lines of your stanza.

You could choose some of these rhyming words, or use your own:

friend | end | mend | send | spend

play | day | say | way

Remember

Poems do not have to rhyme, and they do not have to have a regular rhythm.

This section links to pages 130–133 of the Workbook.

Section 2
Responding to ideas

In this section, you will develop your response to some of the ideas in a poem.

This poem was written over a hundred years ago, and was first published in 1897. At that time, wealthy people's young children were often looked after by a nanny or a nurse.

▼ **Read the poem and then answer the questions that follow it.**

If no one ever marries me
by Laurence Alma-Tadema (1865–1940)

1 If no one ever marries me, —
   And I don't see why they should,
   For nurse says I'm not pretty,
   And I'm seldom very good —

5 If no one ever marries me
   I shan't mind very much;
   I shall buy a squirrel in a cage,
   And a little rabbit-hutch:

   I shall have a cottage near a wood,
10 And a pony all my own,
   And a little lamb quite clean and tame,
   That I can take to town:

   And when I'm getting really old, —
   At twenty-eight or nine —
15 I shall find a little orphan-girl
   And bring her up as mine.

Remember

Fiction texts and poetry can be about strange and impossible things. You may disagree with things in any text – and this may be more likely if the text was written a long time ago!

Activity 1: Understanding and thinking about the poem

Read the poem on page 140 again carefully, and then check your understanding with these questions.

1 The **speaker** in the poem is imagining her future.
   a) What does the speaker think will happen in the future? Note down at least **five** things.
   b) What does she think will **not** happen in the future, and why?
   c) What do you think about this? Write **one or two** sentences explaining your ideas.

2 The speaker in the poem thinks about what she will do when she is 'really old'.
   a) How old is 'really old', according to the speaker?
   b) What will the speaker do when she is 'really old'?
   c) What do you think about this? Write **one or two** sentences explaining your ideas.

3 Look again at your answers to question 1a. How old do you think the speaker expects to be when she does all the things you have noted?

> **Remember**
> You will often need to use your inference skills when answering questions about texts.

Activity 2: Understanding the voice of the poem

Poems are often written in the first person, using the pronouns 'I' and 'me'. However, the person speaking in the poem is not always the poet: sometimes the poet takes on the voice of a character.

1 Think about the speaker in the poem on page 140. You could consider:
   • how old the speaker in the poem may be
   • the kind of person the speaker in the poem may be
   • what the speaker's nurse says about her.

   a) Note down **three** things you can work out about the speaker.
   b) Write **one or two** sentences explaining how you worked out each thing you noted.

2 Now think about the poet's intention.
   a) What response in the reader do you think the poet wanted to create? You could choose one or two of the example responses below, or use your own ideas.

I feel sorry for the speaker in the poem.	The poem is humorous.	The poem shows that children do not understand love and marriage.
	The poem shows the things that children think are important.	The poet wants the reader to think about the meaning of marriage.

   b) For each response you identify, write one or two sentences explaining how the poem could make a reader think or feel this way.

Punctuation Boost: Poetry punctuation

Poems are not punctuated in the same way as other kinds of writing.
- In most poems, each line of poetry begins with a capital letter, even if it is in the middle of a sentence.
- There is often a comma or full stop at the end of each line of a poem.
- Poems, especially ones written a long time ago, often use colons and semicolons in an unusual way, for example just to show pauses.

1 Write out the second stanza of 'If no one ever marries me', on page 140, as if it were not a poem. You should:
- use capital letters and full stops correctly
- miss out any unnecessary punctuation
- circle any changes you make to the punctuation used in the poem.

2 The words below are from a stanza of a poem you will explore later in this unit.

> If you're cross then I will glare. If you're sad then I don't care.
> If you say that I am bad, I will say, 'Oh good, I'm glad!'

Write out the words using the layout and punctuation you would expect to see in a poem.

Activity 3: Developing your response to the poem

To develop your initial responses, you are going to compare your own ideas about adult life with the attitude shown in the poem.

1 According to the speaker in the poem on page 140, what are the **three** most important things about being an adult?

2 What do you think are the **three** most important things about being an adult?

3 How are your views different to the views expressed by the speaker in the poem?
    a) Write **two or three** sentences explaining how your views are similar or different.
    b) Which do you think is the most surprising or shocking view expressed by the speaker in the poem? Write **one or two** sentences explaining your opinion.

4 How would you describe the views expressed by the speaker in the poem? Write **one or two** sentences explaining your ideas.

Activity 4: Writing a response

You are going to write three paragraphs in response to the poem on page 140 using some of the ideas you have noted in this section.

Look back at all your answers to Activities 1, 2 and 3 before you complete this activity.

1 Write a paragraph explaining your reaction to the voice in the poem. In your paragraph, you could comment on:
- your impression of the person speaking in the poem
- the ideas or information in the poem that gave you this impression.

2 Write a paragraph explaining your reaction to the speaker's attitude. In your paragraph, you could comment on:
- what the speaker believes about adult life
- what the speaker thinks will happen in the future
- what this tells you about the speaker.

3 Write a paragraph about why you think the poet wrote the poem, and what response he wanted to create in the reader. You could comment on:
- whether you find the poem surprising, humorous, shocking or something else, or if you had a mixture of different responses
- the ideas in the poem that created those responses in you
- whether you think these things were what the poet intended
- whether you think the poet intended anything else.

This section links to pages 134–137 of the Workbook.

Section 3
Responding to a poem

In this section, you will develop your response to a poem as a whole text.

This poem was written more than 200 years ago, and first published in 1794.

▼ **Read the poem and then answer the questions that follow it.**

A poison tree
by William Blake

1 I was angry with my friend;
   I told my **wrath**[1], my wrath did end.
   I was angry with my **foe**[2]:
   I told it not, my wrath did grow.

5 And I watered it in fears,
   Night & morning with my tears:
   And I sunned it with smiles,
   And with soft **deceitful wiles**[3].

   And it grew both day and night.
10 Till it bore an apple bright.
   And my foe **beheld**[4] it shine,
   And he knew that it was mine.

   And into my garden **stole**[5],
   When the night had **veiled**[6] the **pole**[7];
15 In the morning glad I see;
   My foe outstretched beneath the tree.

Key vocabulary

wrath[1]: anger
foe[2]: enemy
deceitful wiles[3]: dishonest tricks
beheld[4]: saw
stole[5]: crept
veiled[6]: hidden
pole[7]: pole star, also called the north star

Activity 1: Exploring the first stanza

Look carefully at the first stanza of the poem above.

1 The speaker in the poem says he was angry with his friend.
   a) What did the speaker do to solve this problem?
   b) What was the result?

2 The speaker in the poem says he was angry with his foe.
   a) What did the speaker do to solve this problem?
   b) What was the result?

3 What lesson might the poet be trying to teach the reader in this first stanza?

Activity 2: Exploring the metaphor

In the poem on page 144, the poet uses the image of a tree to describe his anger. He does not use a simile to make a comparison:

> My anger was like a tree.

Instead, he uses a **metaphor**: he speaks about anger as though it really is a tree. The poison tree is an imaginary symbol of the speaker's growing feelings.

1 Look at the second stanza of the poem.

a) Note down all the different ways that the speaker says he made the poison tree grow.

b) Choose **one** of the ways in which the speaker says he made the poison tree grow. Imagine a situation that the poet might be describing with this metaphor, and write **one or two** sentences to describe it.

2 Look at the third stanza of the poem.

a) How did the poison tree change?

b) How do you think the speaker's foe felt as he looked at the apple?

Activity 3: Connecting key points

The end of the poem on page 144 tells us what happened metaphorically, but it does not explain the event this metaphor describes. To work out what may have happened, you need to connect the key ideas in the poem.

1 Look at the events from the poem summarised below. Copy and complete the sentences by replacing the **?** in each sentence. Then number the sentences to show the order the events occur.

> The speaker is **?** with his foe.

> **?** is outstretched beneath the tree.

> An **?** grows on the tree.

> The speaker's foe creeps towards **?**.

> The speaker's foe sees the **?**.

> A **?** tree grows.

2 Look at your answers to question 1.

a) What happens to the speaker's enemy at the end of the poem?

b) Why you think this happens to the speaker's enemy?

c) How does the speaker feel at the end of the poem?

d) Why you think the speaker feels this way?

e) What do you think the metaphor may be suggesting?

Grammar Boost: Linking ideas with conjunctions

Conjunctions are used to link two clauses in a sentence.

Coordinating conjunctions	e.g. and | but | or	These are used to link two clauses of equal importance.
Subordinating conjunctions	e.g. because | when | although | as | until | now | that | before | in | order | that | if | where | as long as | after | since | so | while	These show much more clearly how the two clauses are linked. They add information about things such as cause, effect, time, condition or concession.

Here are some examples of subordinating conjunctions:

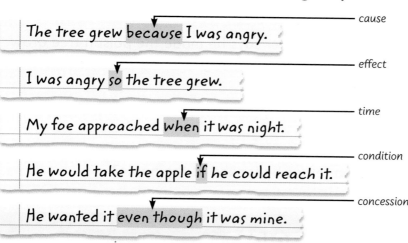

The tree grew because I was angry. —— cause

I was angry so the tree grew. —— effect

My foe approached when it was night. —— time

He would take the apple if he could reach it. —— condition

He wanted it even though it was mine. —— concession

1 The following pairs of sentences explain what happens in the poem on page 144. Link each pair of sentences to create a single, multi-clause sentence, choosing the conjunction that makes the clearest link between them.
   a) The speaker's anger ends. He tells his friend that he is angry.
   b) The speaker's anger grows. He does not tell his foe that he is angry.
   c) The speaker grows a shiny apple on the poison tree. The speaker's foe takes it.
   d) The speaker's foe eats the apple. He dies.
   e) The reader might expect the speaker to feel upset. He feels glad.

Activity 4: Responding to the poem

1 Think again about the speaker and his foe in the poem on page 144.
   a) Write one or two sentences explaining the way you feel about the speaker, and how the poem has made you feel this way.
   b) Write one or two sentences explaining the way you feel about the speaker's foe, and how the poem has made you feel this way.
   c) Which person do you think is more responsible for what happened? Write **one or two** sentences explaining your ideas.

Activity 5: Writing a poem

The poem 'A poison tree', on page 144, shows the consequences of keeping angry feelings hidden. The poet uses the metaphor of a tree to show the poisonous feelings that grow inside us when we decide not to speak out.

You are going to write a poem that shows the consequences of a different decision. It does not need to be true.

1 You could use the suggestions in the table or your own ideas to help you plan your poem.

Your decision	A What could your poem describe?	telling a lie, but not admitting it was a lie | being unkind to someone, and not apologising afterwards | learning a secret, and not being able to tell anyone
The consequences of your decision	B What could grow because of your decision?	a weed | a strange creature | a raging fire
	C Where could it grow?	in your home | in your garden | inside you

2 Answer the questions below to form the lines of your poem. You could choose from the suggestions to help you start each line, or use your own ideas.

a) What did you do?   I said to my

b) What should you have done next?   I should have

c) What did you actually do?   But I

d) What was the consequence?   Very soon, there grew

e) How did it feel?   It was

f) How did the feeling develop?   It grew

g) What happened in the end?   One day, I

Remember

Poems do not have to rhyme, and they do not have to have a regular rhythm.

Section 4
Selecting evidence

In this section, you will respond to the viewpoint expressed in a poem and select evidence from the poem to support your response.

▼ **Read the poem below and then answer the questions that follow it.**

Bookworm
By Jill Carter

1 My sister's bigger and tougher than me,
　She's in charge of our precious den.
　She can climb the side of a crumbling cliff –
　But it's me who's good with a pen.

5 She's the one with the fishing rod,
　Skewers lugworms onto her hooks,
　The one who runs faster and leaves me behind –
　But I'm the one who reads books.

　She's the hero of every game,
10 The one with the makeshift sword –
　But I'm the one who can always think
　Of exactly the perfect word.

　They say that we are "chalk and cheese"
　They can't work out why we bicker:
15 They say that we're just opposites,
　That we have to agree to differ.

　She's the one who laughs at my fears,
　The one who's brave in the dark –
　But I'm the one with the torchlight
20 And those stories leave their spark.

Activity 1: Gathering key information

1 The speaker in the poem on page 148 describes her sister and herself. Copy the table below and complete it with as much information as you can find in the poem.

How the speaker's sister is described	How the speaker is described

2 In the fourth stanza, the speaker tells us: They say that we are "chalk and cheese"

   a) Who do you think 'they' are?
   b) What does this description mean?

3 How would you summarise the speaker's opinion of her sister in **two or three** words? You could choose from the suggestions below or use your own ideas.

   The speaker thinks her sister is

   admirable | bossy | brave | annoying | energetic | competitive | sporty | mean

4 Using **15** words or fewer, write a sentence explaining what this poem is about.

Activity 2: Inferring key ideas

1 Look at the following ideas from the poem on page 148. What do they suggest about the speaker's sister?

   we're just opposites   But it's me who's good with a pen.

2 Think about all the information you have gathered about the speaker's sister.
   a) How old you do think the speaker's sister is?
   b) What clues did you use to answer question 2a?

3 Think about all the information you have gathered about the speaker.
   a) How do you think the speaker feels about herself?
   b) What clues did you use to answer question 3a?

4 The poem you have been exploring is called 'Bookworm'. Does the poem reveal more about the speaker's sister or the speaker herself?

Punctuation Boost: Punctuating quotations

When you use a quotation in your writing, you should enclose the quotation in speech marks (also known as quotation marks). This shows the reader which words are taken directly from the text.

Remember

You must copy quotations exactly, including any punctuation. Unlike in speech punctuation, you do not need to add a punctuation mark before the closing speech marks if it isn't in the text.

1 Add speech marks to the sentences below by working out exactly which words and punctuation marks are taken from the poem on page 148.
   a) The speaker in the poem says that her sister is bigger and tougher than her.
   b) The speaker knows that she can always come up with exactly the perfect word.
   c) The speaker knows that her stories leave a spark, which means that they are powerful and have an effect on the reader.

Activity 3: Supporting your response with evidence

When you write a response to a poem, you should explain your impressions of the people, places or ideas in it, and explore the impact it had on you.

You should always be able to support your response with evidence from the text. The best pieces of evidence to choose will be short and clearly relevant to the point you are making.

1 What are your impressions of the speaker in the poem on page 148? You could choose one or two of the suggestions below or use your own ideas.

   thoughtful | clever | witty | imaginative | quiet | jealous | competitive | powerful

2 Which line or two from the poem gives you that impression most strongly? You could choose one of the following quotations from the poem, or select one of your own.

   A The one who runs faster and leaves me behind   **B** I'm the one who reads books

   C She's the hero of every game   **D** I'm the one who can always think of exactly the perfect word.

   E we bicker   **F** But I'm the one with the torchlight and those stories leave their spark.

How do I do that?

Look at each line or group of lines in turn. Ask yourself: Is this the part of the poem that created my impression most strongly?

3 Write **one or two** sentences explaining how your choice of quotation created a strong impression of the speaker.

4 Answer questions 1–3 again, choosing a different word to describe your impressions of the speaker in the poem and a different quotation to support it.

Activity 4: Writing a response

You are going to write a response to the poem 'Bookworm' on page 148. You will need to write:

- **one** paragraph giving your impressions of the sister described in the poem
- **one** paragraph giving your impressions of the speaker in the poem.

Planning your response

1 Plan each of your two paragraphs, ensuring that you include the following:

- Your response. What impression is created in the poem?

  The poet creates the impression that

  The speaker is presented as

- A quotation to support your response.

  For example, we know that

  This impression is very strongly created when the speaker says that

- A comment on **how** the ideas or words in the quotation created that impression.

  This suggests that

  These words make the speaker sound

Writing your response

2 Write your response. Remember to use quotation marks to show exactly which words in your response are quotations from the poem.

This section links to pages 142–143 of the Workbook.

Section 5
Assessment

In this section, you will answer questions about a poem to assess your progress in the unit so far.

▼ **Read the poem below and then answer the questions that follow it.**

Friends
by Elizabeth Jennings

1 I fear it's very wrong of me,
  And yet I must admit,
  When someone offers friendship
  I want the whole of it.
5 I don't want everybody else
  To share my friends with me.
  At least, I want one special one,
  Who, indisputably

  Likes me much more than all the rest,
10 Who's always on my side,
  Who never cares what others say,
  Who lets me come and hide
  Within his shadow, in his house –
  It doesn't matter where –
15 Who lets me simply be myself,
  Who's always, always there

Activity 1: Reading

1 Look again at these lines from the poem on page 152.

> When someone offers friendship
> I want the whole of it.

What is the speaker suggesting they want from a friend? Write **one or two** sentences explaining your ideas.

2 The speaker says they want one special friend who is always, always there .
a) What do you think the speaker is suggesting here?
b) Identify **three** other things the speaker would like from this one special friend.

3 The speaker suggests that they are not sure it is right for them to express these thoughts and feelings about friends. Which words tell you this?

Activity 2: Responding

Write a detailed description of your response to the poem on page 152 by answering the following questions.

1 What are your impressions of the speaker in the poem?

Write a paragraph in which you:
• give your response
• support it with evidence from the poem
• explain your ideas.

2 a) What do you think was the poet's main intention in writing this poem? Choose **one** answer.

    A to make the reader laugh
    B to make the reader think about friendship
    C to show how important friends are

  b) Write a detailed explanation of your choice, using evidence from the poem.

This section links to pages 144–147 of the Workbook.

Section 6
Exploring vocabulary

In this section, you will explore the poet's vocabulary choices and experiment with your own.

▼ **Read the poem below and then answer the questions that follow it.**

Grrr
by Francesca Beard

1 I don't want to, I don't like you,
  If you touch me, I will fight you!

  If you're cross, then I will glare,
  If you're sad then I don't care,
5 If you say that I am bad,
  I will say 'Oh good I'm glad!'

  I don't want to, I don't like you,
  If you touch me, I will fight you!

  If you try and calm me down,
10 I will roll round on the ground,
  If you try and make me stop,
  I'll hold my breath until I pop!
  If you Shhhhh me,
  I will yell and Yell and YELL AND YELL!

15 I don't want to, I don't like you,
  If you touch me, I will fight you!

  If you try and make me eat,
  I'll spit my food out on the floor,
  If you try and make me sleep,
20 I'll throw myself against the door,
  If you sing a lullaby,
  I'll join in the key of 'Y!'

  I don't want to, I don't like you,
  If you touch me, I will bite you!

25 I'm the worst you've ever seen,
  I'm the worst there's ever been!
  I'm a single-handed riot –
  Now, I'm ready to be quiet…

  … Now, I like you, yes, I love you,
30 If you kiss me, I will hug you.

Activity 1: Exploring the poem

1 Identify **three** things that the speaker is refusing to do in the poem on page 154.

2 Look at the second stanza. What does this stanza suggest is being said to the speaker of the poem?

3 Think about what you can infer about the speaker, and about the person he or she is addressing.
- **a)** Who is the speaker of the poem?
- **b)** Which line or phrase gives you the biggest clue about the speaker's identity?
- **c)** Who is being addressed?
- **d)** How can you tell?

4 Imagine and describe the scene in which the speaker expresses the content of the poem. Think about:
- where the speaker is
- what the speaker is doing
- when the scene is taking place
- who else is there, and what they are doing.

Activity 2: Responding to the poem

1 **a)** How do you imagine the speaker in the poem on page 154 feels? Write **one or two** sentences explaining your ideas.
- **b)** What parts of the poem helped you to imagine that?
- **c)** How does the poem make you feel? Write **one or two** sentences explaining your ideas.

2 **a)** What are your impressions of the speaker in the poem?
- **b)** How has the poet created that impression?
- **c)** Choose two or three quotations and explain how each one helps to create this impression.

The speaker in the poem is

For example, the speaker says '_____'

This creates the impression that the speaker is

... because

Punctuation Boost: Apostrophes of possession

Adding an apostrophe and the letter 's' to a noun can show belonging, ownership or 'possession'.

> If a game belongs to the girl it is the girl's game.

> If this is the front door of the house, it is the house's front door.

If the noun is a **plural** that ends in an 's', there is no need to add an extra 's'. You just need to add an apostrophe to show possession.

> If this is the homework of the boys, it is the boys' homework.

However, if a **singular** noun or a name ends in an 's', you should add another 's'.

> If the book belongs to James, it is James's book.

1 Rewrite the following sentences using an apostrophe to show possession.
   a) The name of the poet is Francesca Beard.
   b) The voice belonging to the speaker is angry.
   c) The title of the poem is 'Grrr'.
   d) The titles belonging to most poems help you understand what the poem is about.

Activity 3: Responding to vocabulary choices

Vocabulary choice is one of the most important ways in which writers create characters and voices.

1 Look at the following lines from the poem on page 154.

> I don't want to, I don't like you,   If you touch me, I will fight you!   If you're cross, then I will glare,

   a) Underline all the verbs in these lines. Remember, contractions can be verbs.
   b) Which verbs help to create the speaker's voice most powerfully? Write one or two sentences explaining your ideas.

2 Lines 1 and 2 are repeated throughout the poem.
   a) How many times are they repeated?
   b) Why do you think the poet chose to repeat them?

3 Look at the final two lines of the poem.

> … Now, I like you, yes, I love you,   If you kiss me, I will hug you.

   a) How are these lines similar to the lines that are repeated?
   b) How are they different from the lines that are repeated?

Activity 4: Experimenting with vocabulary choice

Different vocabulary choices can have different effects. It is important to think about why the writer has made them.

1 Look at the following lines from the poem on page 154, and the alternative vocabulary choices the poet could have made.

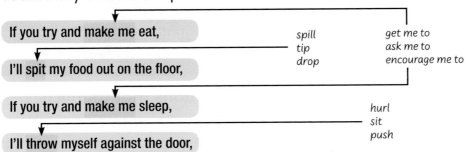

If you try and make me eat,   spill / tip / drop   get me to / ask me to / encourage me to

I'll spit my food out on the floor,

If you try and make me sleep,   hurl / sit / push

I'll throw myself against the door,

Think about what different choices you would have made. You could choose some of the options given above, or use your own ideas.

a) Write out the above lines from the poem using your choices.

b) Write a sentence explaining each choice you have made.

2 Write **one or two** more stanzas for the poem, remembering the tone of the speaker's voice. You could use the ideas below or your own ideas.

If you tell me to

Tidy your room!   Go to bed!   Turn off the television!

I will

What noise could show how you feel?   What spoken words could show how you feel?   What actions could show how you feel?

3 Rewrite the poem's second stanza as if the speaker in the poem is a stern teacher, choosing words and phrases that show the teacher's character and behaviour.

If you're cross, then I will

If you're sad then I

If you say that I am bad,

I will say '_____!'

This section links to pages 148–151 of the Workbook.

Section 7
Exploring figurative language

In this section, you will explore the poet's use of figurative language, and the effects this can create.

▼ **Read the poem below and then answer the questions that follow it.**

Eye-phone
by Jill Carter

1 Once upon a time,
  I had a phone: a my-phone, a 'Hi!'-phone,
  A smooth operator, sleek and chic,
  Cool in the palm of my hand,
5 Bleeping and buzzing,
  Chattering smiles of light –
  A gold and **titanium**[1] friend.

  I could text, share, tweet, post,
  Stream, message, follow:
10 A hand-sized vault of precious metals,
  A global power in a protective case.

An aluminium **pupa**[2],
It morphed into the eye-phone, watching and winking,
15 The tie-phone, constantly calling for me:
  A hungry chick,
  A baby croc snapping at my heels.

  Lost in myselfie,
  It became the lie-phone,
20 Casting a net of untruths –
  And I was caught – a **phish**[3] out of water.

  It was the all-alone-phone,
  The stay-at-home-phone:
24 The my-phone, the **foe**[4]-phone.

Key vocabulary

titanium[1]: a strong, light metal
pupa[2]: an insect in a hard covering as it develops from a larva into an adult
phish[3]: use lies to get at private information online (included in the poem as a pun)
foe[4]: enemy

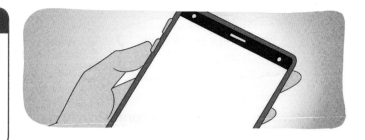

Remember

A **simile** is a comparison. For example:

| His face was grey, like a storm cloud. | His face was as grey as a storm cloud. |

A **metaphor** describes something as though it really is something else. For example:

| His face was a storm cloud. |

Activity 1: Understanding figurative language

1 In the poem 'Eye-phone', on page 158, the speaker uses different **figurative language** to describe the phone. For example, in the first stanza, a metaphor is used to describe the phone as:

> A gold and titanium friend.

   a) Look again at the second stanza of the poem. Identify **one** metaphor in that stanza.
   b) Rewrite the two metaphors as similes, using the word 'like'.

2 Look again at the two metaphors you explored in question 1. What positive qualities do these metaphors suggest? You could choose from the ideas below or use your own.

value | strength | support | company | beauty | security | status | influence | glamour

3 In the third stanza, the phone is described as: An aluminium pupa
   a) What does this comparison suggest about the phone?
   b) What other metaphors does the speaker use to describe the phone in the third stanza?
   c) How do these metaphors suggest that the relationship between the speaker and the phone has changed? Write **one or two** sentences explaining your answer.

   ## How do I do that?

   Think about the qualities implied by the metaphors in the first two stanzas. Then think about the qualities implied by the metaphors the third stanza. Ask yourself: What has changed?

4 **a)** In the fourth stanza, the speaker uses a metaphor about the lies that have been created:

   > a net of untruths

   How does the speaker feel as a result of these lies?
   b) The speaker also uses a metaphor about these feelings:

   > a phish out of water

   This metaphor includes a pun on the common saying 'a fish out of water'. What image does that saying create in your mind?
   c) What connections does the pun prompt the reader to make?

Activity 2: Exploring figurative language

1 In the poem on page 158, the speaker suggests that the phone 'morphed' from being a 'friend' into a 'foe'. The writer uses the metaphor of the 'pupa' to suggest this change. Look at some of the qualities of the pupa:

protected | natural | changing | hidden | complex |
living | growing | developing

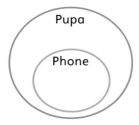

Which of these qualities could also describe the speaker's feelings towards the phone? Copy the diagram on the left, and add the words to show what they describe. The ones that describe both the pupa and the phone should be added to the inner circle.

2 Look at the qualities that are in the inner circle of your diagram. Choose **two** qualities that describe the phone accurately or interestingly. Use them to write **two** similes by replacing the **?** in each sentence. One of your similes should be positive and the other should be negative.

My phone is as **?** as a pupa.

My phone is as **?** as a pupa.

Skills Boost: Similes and clichés

A **cliché** is a phrase or idea that is overused and so has lost its impact. In English, there are several similes that have become so well known that they have become clichés. For example:

as free as a bird

1 Good writers do not use old, clichéd similes: they create new, powerful ones. For example:

as free as the wind

Rewrite the following similes, replacing the final word with a new, imaginative comparison.
a) as green as grass
b) as white as snow
c) as cold as ice
d) as old as the hills

Activity 3: Experimenting with figurative language

The poem on page 158 uses metaphors to describe a relationship between a phone and its owner. You are going to develop a simile and a metaphor that will help you write a poem about **your** relationship with an item of technology.

1 Choose **one** item of technology. You could choose one of the suggestions below or use your own ideas.

a phone | a laptop | a computer | a TV | a smart speaker | a tablet

2 Explain **one** positive quality of the technology. For example:

> My computer hosts lots of games and I enjoy choosing which to play.

3 Choose **one** object that shares an element of the quality you chose, and explain the connection. For example:

> My computer gives me lots of great options, and so does a box of chocolates.

4 Form the comparison into a simile. For example:

> My computer is like a box of chocolates.

5 Turn your simile into a metaphor. For example:

> ~~My computer is like a box of chocolates.~~

> My computer is a box of chocolates.

6 Write a stanza about your chosen item of technology. You could structure it in a similar way to the descriptions in 'Eye-phone'. For example:

> Once upon a time,

> I had a computer, packed full of games:

> A box of delicious chocolates

> Overwhelming me with choice,

> Beckoning and enticing.

Section 8
Exploring form

In this section, you will look at how poets shape poetry.

▼ **Read the poem below and then answer the questions that follow it.**

Nettles
by Vernon Scannell

1 My son aged three fell in the nettle bed.
  'Bed' seemed a curious name for those green spears,
  That regiment of spite behind the shed:
  It was no place for rest. With sobs and tears
5 The boy came seeking comfort and I saw
  White blisters beaded on his tender skin.
  We soothed him till his pain was not so raw.
  At last he offered us a watery grin,
  And then I took my **billhook**[1], **honed**[2] the blade
10 And went outside and slashed in fury with it
  Till not a nettle in that fierce parade
  Stood upright any more. And then I lit
  A **funeral pyre**[3] to burn the fallen dead,
  But in two weeks the busy sun and rain
15 Had called up tall recruits behind the shed:
  My son would often feel sharp wounds again.

Key vocabulary

billhook[1]: a large knife for cutting through plants and tree branches
honed[2]: sharpened
funeral pyre[3]: a fire on which dead bodies are cremated or burned

Activity 1: Reading the poem

1 Who is speaking, and telling the story of the poem on page 162?

2 How old is the child in the poem?

3 What happened to the child?

4 Write down **two** things that the speaker did when this happened.

5 Why do you think the speaker says the word 'bed' is a 'curious' name for a group of stinging nettles?

6 Look again at the following lines.

> At last he offered us a watery grin,

> And then I took my billhook, honed the blade

> And went outside and slashed in fury with it

How did the child feel after he sought comfort? How did the speaker of the poem feel?

7 What happened two weeks after the child's accident?

8 Look again at the final line: My son would often feel sharp wounds again.

What do you think the speaker means? Write **one or two** sentences explaining your ideas.

Activity 2: Exploring the poet's ideas

1 Look at all the words and phrases that the poet uses to describe the nettles in the poem on page 162.

green **spears**	**spear:** long weapon with a sharpened tip
regiment of spite	**regiment:** unit or group of soldiers
that fierce **parade**	**parade:** procession of marching soldiers
the **fallen dead**	**fallen dead:** people killed in war
tall **recruits**	**recruits:** new soldiers joining the army

a) What do these descriptions have in common?

b) Why do you think the poet chose to describe the nettles in this way? Write **two or three** sentences explaining your ideas.

Grammar Boost: Using paragraphs

Prose is written or spoken language in its ordinary form. Most things you read are prose, such as stories, instructions and explanations. Poems are written in stanzas. Prose is written in paragraphs. These are similar because they are both blocks of text. However:

- The poet chooses how to structure the stanzas in a poem. There are no rules.
- There are rules about starting a new paragraph when you are writing prose.

Remember

You should start a new paragraph in your writing when there is:

- a change of topic   • a change of time   • a change of setting   • a change of speaker.

Look at this summary of the poem 'Nettles' on page 162:

A A 3-year-old child fell into a nettle bed.

B The child cried.

C The child was comforted.

D The child's parent cut down the nettles and burned them.

E Two weeks later, the nettles had regrown.

F The son felt 'sharp wounds' again.

1 Imagine you are writing this story using prose instead of poetry. Write down what would happen in each paragraph.

Activity 3: Exploring rhyme

1 Look at this revised version of the beginning of the poem on page 162:

My son aged three fell in ~~the nettle bed.~~ *a patch of nettles.*

'Bed' seemed a curious name for those green ~~spears,~~ *spikes,*

That regiment of spite ~~behind the shed:~~ *at the bottom of the garden:*

Write out the next **three** lines of the poem. Cross out and replace the final word or phrase of each line, like in the example above. Try to replace each one with a word or phrase with a similar meaning, but make sure your new line endings don't rhyme.

2 Compare the new version of the first six lines with the original. What effect do you think the rhyme has? Write **one or two** sentences explaining your ideas.

Activity 4: Exploring punctuation

Some of the sentences in the poem on page 162 continue from one line to the next, but some end with full stops.

1 Which is the longest sentence in the poem? How many lines does it cover?

2 Think about the effect caused by the longest sentence. Which of the statements below do you think is most accurate?

   A The long sentence shows how quickly the parent's reactions happen.

   B The long sentence makes the speaker sound hurried and breathless.

   C The events in the long sentence seem to be less important than others.

3 How many lines in the poem end with full stops?

4 Reread the lines that end with full stops. Which of the statements below do you think is most accurate?

   A The lines that end in full stops are the most effective lines in the poem.

   B The lines that end in full stops describe the most important events in the poem.

   C The lines that end in full stops are more interesting than the ones that don't.

Activity 5: Exploring form

The **form** of a poem means its shape and structure: the way in which the writer has set out its lines, stanzas, rhymes and punctuation.

1 How many stanzas are there in the poem 'Nettles' on page 162?

2 Do the lines have similar, regular lengths, or irregular, different lengths?

3 Look back through this Student Book, and find **one** poem that has a very different form from 'Nettles'.

   a) Write down the name of the other poem you have found.

   b) Compare the voices of the speakers in the two poems: Which is louder? Which is faster? Which is calmer?

   c) Consider the form of the poem you have found: the number of stanzas and lines, and the lengths of the lines.

   d) Do you think the two poems' different forms help to create the different voices of the speakers? Why do you think this?

This section links to pages 156–159 of the Workbook.

Section 9
Exploring structure

In this section, you will explore the form and structure of a poem, and then write your own.

▼ **Read the poem below and then answer the questions that follow it.**

Mum
by Andrew Peters

1 She's a:

   Sadness stealer
   Cut-knee healer
   Hug-me-tighter
5 Wrongness righter
   Gold star carer
   Chocolate sharer (well, sometimes!)

   Hamster feeder
   Bedtime reader
10 Great game player
   Night fear slayer
   Treat dispenser
   Naughty sensor (how come she
      always knows?)

15 She's my
   Never glum,
   Constant chum
   Second to none
   We're under her thumb!
20 Mum!

Spelling Boost: Verbs and nouns

Some nouns are created by adding the suffix *–er* to a verb. These nouns usually refer to a person or thing that is doing the action described by the verb. For example:
- If you **read**, you are a **read<u>er</u>**.
- If you **heal** people, you are a **heal<u>er</u>**.

If the verb has one syllable and a short vowel sound, double the final consonant:
- If you run, you are a **ru<u>nn</u>er**.

if the verb ends in an *e*, just add *–r*.
- If you **care** for someone, you are a **care<u>r</u>**.

1 Turn these verbs into nouns. Each noun will refer to a person doing the action described by the verb.
   a) teach   **b)** call   **c)** knit   **d)** compute   **e)** drive   **f)** swim

Activity 1: Exploring ideas

1 Look again at some of the ways the speaker in the poem on page 166 describes his mother:

   A Sadness stealer

   B Night fear slayer

   C Treat dispenser

   D Naughty sensor

   E We're under her thumb!

   Write a sentence explaining what you think each description means.

2 Does the speaker describe their mother in only positive ways? Which description, if any, do you think is the most negative one?

3 How would you describe the mother in this poem?
   a) Choose **two** words from the suggestions below and add **two** more of your own.

   comforting | happy | helpful | affectionate | strict

   b) Write **one or two** sentences explaining each of your choices.

4 In your opinion, what qualities should a perfect parent have that are **not** described in the poem?

Grammar Boost: Pronouns and repetition

In some writing, **repetition** can be effective by creating **emphasis**. However, in most writing, it is better to replace repeated nouns or noun phrases with a pronoun such as 'he', 'she', 'it' or 'they'. You can also replace other repeated phrases with the pronouns 'this', 'that' or 'these'.

1 Read the following student response to the poem on page 166.

> The poem is all about the speaker's mother. The speaker's mother is very kind and thoughtful as the speaker's mother looks after the speaker, comforts the speaker, and is a good friend to the speaker. The poem is written in very short lines that all rhyme. The very short lines that all rhyme make the speaker's voice sound fast and enthusiastic.

a) Copy the response above, underlining all the repeated nouns and phrases.

b) Replace the repetitions with pronouns. Remember, the first instance of each noun or phrase should be left in.

c) Check your writing very carefully. Is its meaning still clear? Could it be made clearer by putting some of the nouns or phrases back in?

Activity 2: Exploring form

Read the poem aloud. Then answer these questions to help you explore its form.

1 Look at the first two stanzas of the poem on page 166.

a) How many lines does each of these stanzas have?

b) What is similar about all the lines' final words, in these stanzas?

c) Which lines in the first two stanzas rhyme?

d) Why do you think some words are in brackets at the end of each stanza?

2 Look at the final stanza of the poem.

a) How many lines does the final stanza have?

b) Which lines in this stanza rhyme?

c) What do you notice about these lines' length, compared to the other lines in the poem?

d) How does the final stanza's form suggest the speaker's voice changes? Think about any suggested changes in volume, speed and mood. Write **one or two** sentences to explain your ideas.

Activity 3: Writing your own poem

You are going to write a poem describing the qualities of a family member or a good friend. All the qualities could be positive, or you could include one or two that are more negative.

Gather your ideas

1 Which family member or good friend will be the subject of your poem?

2 Write at least **15** short sentences about this person, with each sentence describing just **one** quality.

Organise your ideas

3 **a)** Highlight the verb in each of your sentences. For example:

> She gives me hugs.

b) Use the suffix –er to turn each verb into a noun. For example:

> giver

c) Add any words that are important to the meaning of this quality. For example:

> Hug giver

4 Look at the ideas you have gathered.
a) Do any of them rhyme? Organise them into pairs. Could you add any new rhymes?
b) Select which ideas you will include in your poem.

> **Remember**
> Poems do not have to rhyme, and they do not have to have a regular rhythm.

5 Decide how to organise your lines into stanzas, and how many lines each stanza will have. You could use the poem 'Mum' as a guide.

Write

6 For your title, use the name of the person described in your poem.

7 Write your poem using the lines you selected in answer to question 4.

8 Finally, write the last line of your poem. Like in the poem 'Mum', it should be the same as your title.

Section 10
Comparing poems

In this section, you will compare the features and effects of two different poems.

▼ **Read the two poems below and then answer the questions that follow them.**

Dad
by Andrew Peters

Mum
by Andrew Peters

1 He's a:

   Tall-story weaver
   Full-of-fib fever
   Bad-joke teller
5 Ten-decibel yeller
   Baggy-clothes wearer
   Pocket-money bearer
   Nightmare banisher
   Hurt-heart vanisher

10 Bear hugger
   Biscuit **mugger**[1]
   Worry squasher
   Noisy **nosher**[2]
   Lawn mower
15 Smile sower

   Football mad
   Fashion sad
   Not half bad
   So glad I had
20 My
   Dad!

1 She's a:

   Sadness stealer
   Cut-knee healer
   Hug-me-tighter
5 Wrongness righter
   Gold star carer
   Chocolate sharer (well, sometimes!)

   Hamster feeder
   Bedtime reader
10 Great game player
   Night fear slayer
   Treat dispenser
   Naughty sensor (how come she always knows?)

   She's my
15 Never glum,
   Constant chum
   Second to none
   We're under her thumb!
   Mum!

Key vocabulary

mugger[1]: a slang term for 'stealer'
nosher[2]: a slang term for 'eater'

Activity 1: Exploring ideas

Before you can compare two texts, you need to be sure you have understood and explored **both** of them. Read 'Dad' on page 170 again, and then answer the questions below.

1 Look again at some of the ways the speaker in the poem describes his father:

A Ten-decibel yeller

B Pocket-money bearer

C Hurt-heart vanisher

D Noisy nosher

E Smile sower

F Fashion sad

Write a sentence explaining what you think each description means.

2 Does the speaker describe his father in only positive ways? Which description, if any, do you think is the most negative one?

Activity 2: Beginning a comparison

One way to begin comparing texts is to think about how the writer presents the subject.

1 Look again at both poems on page 170, focusing on how the speaker presents each parent.
   a) Copy and complete the table below, ticking just **one** box in each row.
   b) If you tick 'Dad', 'Mum' or 'Both' on any row, add a quotation from one or both poems to show how they are presented in that way.

	Dad	Mum	Both	Neither
embarrassing	✔ 'Fashion sad'			
fun				
greedy				
generous				
gloomy				
caring				
affectionate				
kind				

Skills Boost: Making comparisons

When you compose a comparison of two texts, you need to plan and write it carefully. Look at the two pictures below.

A

B

Plan

1 First, identify some ideas and features that could be relevant to both poems on page 170. Which of the following ideas and features could you compare in the two pictures?

time of day | weather | buildings | animals | people

When you have identified which ideas and features to compare, you need to note the similarities and differences. You could structure them in a table like the one below.

Time of day:	DIFFERENT. It is daytime in picture A but night time in picture B.
Weather:	

Write

2 When you have finished your planning, write a comparison that clearly signals similarities and differences. You can do this using adverbials and conjunctions that show comparison. Use the **Adverbials and Conjunctions Bank** to help you.

Adverbials and Conjunctions Bank

whereas | however | on the other hand similarly | also | as well | too

For example:

Similarities

| In both pictures, there is... |
| Picture A shows... |
| In Picture B, there is also... |

Differences

| In Picture A, there is... whereas Picture B features... |
| In Picture A... However, in Picture B... |

Activity 3: Writing a comparison

You are now going to plan a comparison of the two poems on page 170, 'Mum' and 'Dad'.

Plan

1 What do you notice that is similar in the two poems? What is different?

Using the ideas below to help you, select **three or four** comparable features of the poems.

> Their subjects   The way the subjects are presented   Their rhymes

> The kinds of words used   Their organisation into lines and stanzas

Write

2 Write about each comparison using **two** paragraphs. One should identify similarities. The other should identify differences.

In each paragraph, you should:

- identify a significant similarity or difference

  > Both poems are

- explain that similarity or difference

  > In the poem 'Mum', the writer
  > However, in 'Dad', he

- signal the similarity or difference clearly by using adverbials and conjunctions of comparison

  whereas | however | on the other hand
  similarly | also | as well | too

- use evidence from the poems to support your explanation.

  > For example, in 'Dad' the speaker describes the father as a 'Nightmare banisher'.

This section links to pages 164–165 of the Workbook.

Section 11
Assessment

In this section, you will answer questions on a poem to assess your progress in this unit.

▼ **Read the poem and then answer the questions that follow it.**

That time so long ago
by Steve New

1 That time my uncle sang
Silence fell
Jokes stopped mid-punchline
The party turned its head
5 Conversations
Frozen –
That time my uncle sang.

Those words my uncle sang
Some old song
10 Meant nothing; just an echo
Of all the times
Before
All *that* –
That time my uncle sang.

15 That tune my uncle sang
Out of key
Rasping, old but somehow
Beautiful enough to
Bring us
20 To tears –
That time my uncle sang.

That time my uncle sang
Like rainfall
That clears the suffocating air
25 That says: we'll live on
Beyond
This pain –
That time – so long ago.

Activity 1: Reading

1   **a)** Look again at the first stanza of the poem on page 174. Identify **three** reactions to the speaker's uncle's song.

     b) What do these reactions suggest about the uncle?

     c) What do these reactions suggest about the people around him?

2   Look again at the second and third stanzas of the poem.

     a) What do we learn about the words of the song?

     b) Identify **two** negative descriptions of the tune of the song.

     c) Identify the **one** positive description of the tune of the song.

     d) Which has the most powerful effect on the listeners: the words or the tune?

3   Look again at the second and fourth stanzas. What do you think the speaker means by the words 'All *that*' in the second stanza?

Activity 2: Writing a response

1   Look again at this simile from the final stanza of the poem on page 174:

> That time my uncle sang

> Like rainfall

> That clears the suffocating air

Do you find this an effective simile? Why is this? Write one or two sentences explaining your ideas.

2   What overall impression of the uncle and the song do you think the writer intends to create?

Remember to:
- give your response
- explain your ideas
- support your ideas with evidence from the poem.

3   Look again at the title of the poem. Write **three or four** sentences explaining what you understand about the 'time', or different times, it refers to.

Unit 5
Eat it

This unit focuses on presentations of food in fiction and non-fiction texts. You will explore persuasive texts and their features, analyse descriptive language and study examples of food writing that express people's love of making, sharing and eating food. A range of texts for different purposes and audiences are explored as the unit takes you on a sensory and persuasive journey of food writing.

In this unit you will...

- explore how writers craft descriptions to achieve their intention.
- explore a persuasive text and its structure, and then write your own.
- explore the writer's choice of vocabulary in a descriptive text and then try writing your own.
- explore the writer's choice of vocabulary in a persuasive text and then try writing your own.
- answer questions on an extract and write a short descriptive text, focusing on effect, to assess your progress in the unit so far.
- explore the structure of a persuasive text, and craft some persuasive writing of your own.
- explore how sentences can be structured in different ways to make meaning clear or to make a point more persuasive.
- explore how writers use language devices to make their ideas more persuasive.
- explore the key features of a persuasive leaflet.
- check and improve the accuracy and effectiveness of a student's persuasive leaflet.
- create a persuasive leaflet advertising a restaurant, café or takeaway.

By the end of this unit, you will be able to write persuasively using a range of organisational features and language techniques.

This section links to pages 166–169 of the Workbook.

Section 1
Describing

In this section, you will explore how writers craft descriptions to achieve their intention.

In this extract from a novel, the narrator has come to visit his father and his father's new wife, Mary.

▼ Read the extract and then answer the questions that follow it.

1   My father folded his paper and stood up.

'Right, let's eat.'

Under my father's watchful eye, I ate all the food that Mary set out. Like before, it was a mushy school dinner with piles of meat, slippery stewed vegetables, lumpy mashed potato and glutinous gravy. Having drunk so much water in the
5   bathroom a few minutes ago, eating it was like putting sand into a bucket of water. Solid food went easily into my stomach at first, then suddenly it was bulging and full and could take no more. Straining to finish the last few mouthfuls, I sat back. Father wasn't going to let me get away so easily:

'Mary, give him some seconds.'

I couldn't refuse. Another heaped plate came and I had to start
10 again. With absolute determination I ate each forkful. Even so, I was going more and more slowly, and my father was enjoying the discomfort he was causing me. The food was cold and congealed before I was able to heave in the last scrapings and, by that time, my father had returned to the lounge. Mary was doing the dishes.
15 I stood up, speaking clearly so my father could hear.

'Thank you very much.'

Mary didn't respond, and I went straight up to my room. Lying down, my bulging stomach was so heavy it slopped menacingly, like a greasy balloon stretched to bursting and filled with rancid,
20 lumpy fat.

Remember

After reading, consider how you feel about the people in the story and the things the writer is describing. Think about how the writer has made you feel that way.

Activity 1: Checking understanding

Before you develop your response, check your understanding of the extract above.

1 In the narrator's father's house, who decides when it is time to eat?

2 Who serves the food?

3 Who decides that the narrator should be given a second helping?

4 The narrator is given a lot of food. How much of it does he eat?

5 For what other reason does the narrator feel so full after the meal?

Activity 2: Responding to the writer's intention

1 The writer creates impressions of all the following things in the extract on page 178:

the food	the father	the narrator	Mary

a) For each thing, choose **one or two** words from the **Word Bank** below that best describe the impression the writer creates.

b) Choose a short quotation of just a few words to show how the writer created each impression.

c) Use the words to write a sentence explaining each impression created, supporting your responses with the quotations.

Word Bank

bossy	cruel	domineering	bullying	malicious
silent	quiet	worried	afraid	anxious
bullied	friendly	kind	generous	thoughtful
polite	revolting	disgusting	awful	dreadful
horrible	rude	tasty	delicious	tempting

2 How do you think the writer wants readers to respond to the extract as a whole? Choose **one or two** of the answers below, and then write one or two sentences explaining your ideas.

sympathy	anger	humour	disgust

Think about explaining what specifically creates the response, and to which character(s) and situations it relates most strongly.

Grammar Boost: Checking for comma splices

A **comma splice** is the incorrect use of a comma to link two separate clauses. Instead, the two separate clauses should be separated by a full stop or linked with a conjunction.

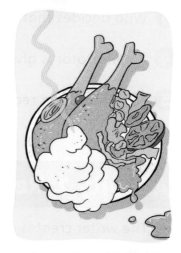

1 Each of the sentences below contains a comma splice.

A   I could smell the food, it was disgusting.

B   I chewed and chewed, I could not swallow it.

C   I did not want to eat the food, it was cold.

a) Rewrite each sentence, using a full stop to separate the clauses.

b) Rewrite each sentence again, using a conjunction to link them. You could use the **Conjunction Bank** on the right to help you.

Conjunction Bank

and	but
although	as
when	until
before	after
if	because

2 In the sentences below, some uses of commas are correct and others are not. Rewrite the sentences that contain commas splices, correcting them using either a full stop or a conjunction.

How do I do that?

Look at the two clauses in each sentence.
- If they are linked by a conjunction, the comma is correct. A conjunction could be **fronted**, rather than appearing between the two clauses.
- If they are linked by a comma but **not** by a conjunction, the comma splice should be corrected.

A   When my plate arrived, my heart sank.

B   The vegetables were raw, the potatoes were burnt.

C   Finally I finished, but they asked if I would like more.

D   I said it tasted delicious, I did not mean it.

E   As I took my first taste, I tried to smile.

Activity 3: Positive and negative vocabulary choices

One way to create effective descriptions is to think about your five senses. This means considering what you can:

| see | hear | smell | taste | feel |

1 Imagine **three** of your favourite foods. Write a sentence describing each of them as positively as possible. You could use the **Word Bank** below to help you.

Word Bank

| fresh \| crunchy \| crumbly aromatic \| rich \| sweet spicy \| creamy \| tangy | brown \| bright \| dark \| green \| yellow sizzling \| warm \| cold \| icy sharp \| bitter \| sour | chewy \| raw \| burned tasteless \| stale \| soggy stringy \| gritty \| oily |

Activity 4: Writing a description

You are going to write a short description of a horrible meal. You can base your description on a real or imagined experience.

Plan

1 One way to plan a piece of writing is to ask yourself lots of questions. Copy out this three-part table to organise your descriptive writing.

Part 1: You wait for the food.	Part 2: Your food arrives.	Part 3: You eat the food.

2 Fill the table with the answers to the following questions, deciding which of the columns you should use for each.
- What meal did you eat?
- Where did you eat it? What was that place like?
- Who were you with? How did the people with you act?
- How did you feel after the meal?

Write

3 Write **three** short paragraphs describing the meal, using one column of your table for each paragraph. As you write each part of your description, think about how you can describe what you see, hear, smell, taste and feel.

This section links to pages 170–173 of the Workbook.

Section 2
Persuading

In this section, you will explore a persuasive text and its structure, and then write your own.

This extract is taken from the introduction to a recipe book aimed at children.

▼ Read the extract and then answer the questions that follow it.

1   Cooking is one of the most useful, rewarding and fun things that you'll ever learn to do. Whether you hope to become a rocket scientist, play international football or breed ferrets, one thing's for sure: you'll always have to eat. When you can make your own food, the whole business of eating becomes much more exciting and enjoyable.

Food is so important: it's not just about grabbing a snack every time you feel peckish or even feeling full at the
5   end of a meal; it's about fuelling your body with the right food so that it runs like a well-oiled engine. When you're young, the body has so much to do; you're constantly learning, growing and running circles around all the adults in your life. You've probably heard people say 'you are what you eat', and it's pretty true. If you eat lots of junk food and sugar, you won't have as much strength and drive to do all the challenging things in life. Don't worry: this certainly
10 isn't a diet book, and it's not full of strict rules to follow, but there will be plenty of healthy food facts along the way.

Being adventurous in the kitchen gets you trying lots of different ingredients, and the more variety we have in our diets the better. Every fruit, vegetable, fish or whatever else you choose to put on your plate has a different mix of the vital calories and nutrients that
15 we all need. So, get out there, tasting and discovering new foods – and EAT TO THRIVE, NOT JUST TO SURVIVE.

This book is filled with real dishes, not children's food: stuff that you'll still love making when you're a teenager, a student and for many years to come. So, what are you waiting for? Let's get going with some REAL COOKING.

Remember

This extract is trying to persuade the reader that it is important to be able to cook. As you read, look out for words, phrases and ideas that the writer is using to persuade you.

Activity 1: Identifying intention and key ideas

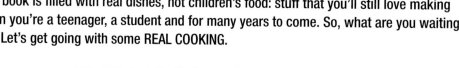

1   The extract above originally appeared on the first page of a recipe book.
   a) What is the writer's **main** intention in this extract? Choose **one** answer.
      A   to persuade the reader that food is important
      B   to persuade the reader that being able to cook is important
      C   to persuade the reader that the recipe book will be useful
   b) Write **one or two** sentences explaining your choice.

2 The extract gives the writer's opinion; there are very few facts in it. Which of the ideas below are facts and which are opinions?

A Cooking is one of the most useful, rewarding and fun things that you'll ever learn to do.

B When you can make your own food, the whole business of eating becomes much more exciting and enjoyable.

C One thing's for sure: you'll always have to eat.

D This book is filled with stuff that you'll still love making for many years to come.

3 Look again at the ideas in A–D above.
  A Which do you think are key ideas in this extract?
  B Which do you think is the **most** important key idea in this extract?

Remember

You often find key ideas near the beginning or end of a paragraph. They are the most important pieces of information in a text. In this extract, they are the ideas that the writer uses to persuade the reader.

Activity 2: Inferring key ideas

The writer of the extract on page 182 does not clearly state all of her key ideas: some are only suggested. The reader has to use inference skills to work out the key point she is making.

Remember

Inferring means you have to work out the ideas or information the writer is trying to give you using clues in the text.

1 What meaning can you infer from each of the following sentences?

a) When you're young, the body has so much to do; you're constantly learning, growing and running circles around all the adults in your life.

b) It's about fuelling your body with the right food so that it runs like a well-oiled engine.

c) This book is filled with real dishes, not children's food.

Activity 3: Exploring structure

1 In a **persuasive text**, the first and last sentences are usually very important.
- The first sentence often introduces the topic and the writer's opinion on that topic.
- The last sentence often tells the reader to act or think in a certain way, if they agree with the writer's opinion. This is sometimes called a 'call to action'.

Is this true of the first and last sentences of the extract on page 182?

2 In each paragraph of a persuasive text, the writer will often draw the reader's attention to the benefits of their ideas. For example, an advert for toothpaste might tell the reader how clean it will make their teeth. What benefits of learning to cook does the writer give? Look for **one** in each of the four paragraphs.

Punctuation Boost: Apostrophes in contractions

Persuasive texts are often written informally, to connect with the reader in a friendly way. When you are writing informally, you can use contractions. Contractions are shortened forms of two or more words. An apostrophe is used to show where one or more letters have been missed out. For example: The word 'cannot' can be shortened to 'can't'.

1 Look at the pairs of words below. For each one, write the letters that have been replaced with an apostrophe.

a) would not | wouldn't   **b)** I have | I've   **c)** he will | he'll

d) she is | she's   **e)** we are | we're   **f)** they had | they'd

2 Rewrite the phrases below as contractions. Make sure you put the apostrophe in the correct place.

a) I am   **b)** you have   **c)** they are   **d)** are not   **e)** we will   **f)** it is

3 Some contractions sound the same as other words, but have both different spellings and different meanings:

they're means 'they are' | **their** means 'belonging to them' | **there** means 'in that place'
you're means 'you are' | **your** means 'belonging to you'

Copy out the following sentences, choosing the correct spellings from the underlined options.

a) When I see they're/their/there car parked over they're/their/there, I know they're/their/there at home.

b) Remember, you're/your meant to bring you're/your exercise book to class.

Activity 4: Planning to be persuasive

You are going to plan and write a text persuading young people that they should learn a specific new skill.

Plan

1 What skill do you think it is important that young people learn? You could choose:
- an academic skill, such as learning a foreign language or doing mental maths
- a practical skill, such as making a fire or building a shelter
- a sporting skill, such as keeping fit or playing team games.

2 In the first sentence of the text, the writer clearly states her opinion:

> Cooking is one of the most useful, rewarding and fun things that you'll ever learn to do.

Think about how you could state your opinion and describe your chosen skill in an attention-grabbing first sentence.

3 In the last sentence of the text, the writer encourages the reader to take action:

> Let's get going with some REAL COOKING.

Think about what you want your reader to do or think when they have finished reading your text.

4 In each paragraph of the text, the writer states and then explains at least one benefit of learning to cook. For example, in the third paragraph:

The writer states that learning to cook means trying new ingredients.

> Being adventurous in the kitchen gets you trying lots of different ingredients, and the more variety we have in our diets the better. Every fruit, vegetable, fish, or whatever else you choose to put on your plate has a different mix of the vital calories and nutrients that we all need.

The writer explains the benefit that different ingredients contain different nutrients.

Note down at least **two** benefits of learning the skill you have chosen.

Write

5 Write your persuasive text. Remember to include:
- a clear opinion in your opening sentence, introducing the skill appealingly
- a benefit of learning the skill in each paragraph, writing one or two sentences explaining it
- an encouragement for the reader to take action in your final sentence.

This section links to pages 174–177 of the Workbook.

Section 3
Vocabulary choice

In this section, you will explore the writer's choice of vocabulary in a descriptive text and then try writing your own.

This is an extract from a story about a successful chef in New York, whose love of cooking began when he was 15 on a trip to Thailand.

▼ Read the extract and then answer the questions that follow it.

1 When I was a boy, cooking was really just a chore for my busy parents. Food was a necessity, while books were their passion. Since then, I have shown them the joy of cooking and how it takes you into a new universe bursting with countless flavours.

My parents met as language students in Bangkok in the 1980s, married, and then moved to London where they
5 found jobs as translators. I was born three years later and discovered the thrill of cooking when I was fifteen.

We were on a family holiday at my aunt's beach house in Thailand. I was amazed when I walked into Aunt Chinda's kitchen. I'll never forget that moment: the pans that steamed and bubbled, and the mouth-watering aromas of garlic, cinnamon and peppercorns. She gave me a spoonful of aromatic coconut sauce to try, which made me desperate to eat the whole lot!

10 Our first feast was a fiery sweet curry with Thai steamed rice, prepared with care and eaten in minutes. Both were delicious but the rice – lightly salted, and perfectly fragrant with lemon grass, ginger and basil – was an inspiration. I spent the rest of the holiday in my aunt's kitchen. I needed to learn. She kindly shared her knowledge and secrets. Together, we made
15 simple and complicated dishes – all of which gave my taste buds a new experience.

Back home, I set my goal: to become a chef and run the best Thai restaurant in New York. I practised my aunt's recipes at home, went to college and got a job in the kitchen of a top restaurant. After two years of chopping ingredients and preparing only
20 parts of dishes I became frustrated. I decided to take my skills out to the streets.

I booked a stall at a market and cooked my aunt's two favourites: hot and sour crinkly noodles – a buzz for anyone's taste-buds – and crispy pillows of deep-fried tofu with a shockingly tangy eggplant sauce. The stall was a huge success.

Within a year, I had enough money to set up a restaurant. My aunt came to the opening and she'll be coming to cut
25 the ribbon at my new restaurant too. This time, my leading dish will be her stir-fry, vibrant with spices, and topped with an explosion of bright green, peppery basil.

Aunt Chinda always gives me a few tips that improve my cooking, and on this trip, she is going to help me plan my first recipe book. I'm hoping my mum or dad will translate it into Thai.

Remember

Look closely at the positive language the writer has chosen to describe the food that his aunt cooks.

Activity 1: Identifying and inferring key ideas

1 Check your understanding of the key points in the extract on page 186.

a) Which of the pieces of information below do you learn from the extract?

A	B	C
The writer was inspired by his aunt to become a chef.	The writer's aunt opened a restaurant.	The writer's parents got jobs as translators.

D	E	F
The writer was born in New York.	The writer's parents did not enjoy cooking.	The writer is planning to write a recipe book.

b) Look again at your answer to question 1a. In which order did these key events take place?

2 The writer suggests that his aunt was very good at cooking. Note down as much information as you can find in the extract that supports this idea.

3 The writer suggests his love of food and cooking. Note down **two** words or phrases from the text that support this idea.

> **Remember**
>
> Use your inference skills to work out important information from clues in a text.

Activity 2: Choosing adjectives and adding details

Adjectives and other language techniques can help to create vivid descriptions.

1 Look at the following description of the writer's aunt's food.

> Our first feast was a fiery sweet curry with Thai steamed rice, prepared with care and eaten in minutes.

a) What **two** adjectives does the writer use to describe the curry?

b) Why do you think the writer chose these two adjectives?

Look again at the second part of the description: prepared with care and eaten in minutes.

c) What do the phrases 'prepared with care' and 'eaten in minutes' suggest about the curry? Write one or two sentences explaining your ideas.

2 Look at the following description of the writer's aunt's kitchen.

> I'll never forget that moment: the pans that steamed and bubbled, and the mouth-watering aromas of garlic, cinnamon and peppercorns.

a) There is only **one** adjective in this description. What is it?

b) Why do you think the writer chose this adjective?

c) What other details does the writer add to the description?

d) What do these details suggest about the writer's aunt's cooking?

Grammar Boost: Exploring nouns

Nouns are used to name people, places, objects and ideas. Look at the list of words below from the extract on page 186, most of which are **concrete nouns**, and some of which are **abstract nouns**.

Concrete nouns	These name physical things you can see, hear, smell, taste or touch.	e.g. 'tree' and 'cat'
Abstract nouns	These name ideas that you **cannot** see, hear, smell, taste or touch.	e.g. 'happiness' and 'idea'

1 Look at the list of words below.

boy | chore | parents | money | curry | students | thrill | flavours
pans | cooking | aunt | kitchen | aromas | feast | cinnamon | tofu
spices | secrets | knowledge | sauce | delicious | success | time | explosion

a) Only **one** of the words is not a noun. Which one?
b) Some of the words are plural nouns. Write down **three** of them.
c) Some of the words can act as nouns **or** verbs. Write down **one** of them.
d) Some of the words are abstract nouns. Write down **two** of them.

Activity 3: Choosing nouns

Nouns are usually chosen for their meaning: to convey information as clearly and precisely as possible. However, sometimes nouns are also chosen for impact: to have a particular effect on the reader.

1 Look at the writer's choice of nouns in the following sentences, and then answer the questions.

> Our first feast was a fiery sweet curry with Thai steamed rice, prepared with care and eaten in minutes. Both were delicious but the rice – lightly salted, and perfectly fragrant with lemon grass, ginger and basil – was an inspiration.

a) The writer could have chosen the noun 'food', 'meal' or 'supper' here. Why do you think he chose the word 'feast'?

b) The writer could have used the noun 'herbs' here. Why do you think he chose to name three different herbs?

c) The writer could have used the noun 'joy', 'achievement' or 'surprise' here. Why do you think he chose 'inspiration'?

Activity 4: Writing a description

You are going to write **two** paragraphs of description.

Imagine

1 Imagine that you have walked into a café or restaurant. What can you see? What can you hear? Note down some nouns.

table	chairs	people

2 Imagine that a plate of delicious food is put in front of you. What can you see? What can you smell? Note down some nouns.

Plan

3 Think about the nouns you might use in your description. You could choose some from the extract as well as some of your own.

4 Choose **five** of the nouns you have noted. Add **one or two** adjectives to each one, describing different elements of your nouns. For example:

Size	Shape	Colour	Temperature
small	round	bright red	hot
tiny	long	golden brown	steaming
huge	thin	deep yellow	cold
vast	plump	fresh green	frozen

5 Think about the effect the food would have on you. How would you feel when you saw it? What effect would it have on your body? Note down some ideas using the words below to help you.

eyes | nose | mouth | lips | fingers | belly

Write

6 Write **two** paragraphs giving a detailed description of the food in the café or restaurant.
   • In your first paragraph, describe arriving and sitting down.
   • In your second paragraph, describe the food that is put in front of you.

Use some or all of the ideas you have noted.

This section links to pages 178–181 of the Workbook.

Section 4
Persuasive vocabulary

In this section, you will explore the writer's choice of vocabulary in a persuasive text and then try writing your own.

This is the home page of a restaurant's website. It is the first thing customers see when they visit the website.

▼ Read the webpage and then answer the questions that follow it.

● ● ● Search...

Book a table   **Our menu**   **Reviews**   **Contact us**

A warm welcome, a relaxing atmosphere and truly beautiful food are waiting for you at A Taste of China.

1 More than thirty years ago, our family opened a
   small restaurant, which became more and more
   popular with every year that passed. Many of our
   customers have been eating with us for years –
5 and now they bring their children, and even their
   grandchildren!

   Every day, our award-winning chefs select the
   freshest ingredients, the most authentic spices
   and the finest recipes to create a menu to appeal
10 to everyone.

   Choose from our delicious dumplings, succulent
   seafood, tender chicken, crisp vegetables, sizzling
   stir-fries and mouth-watering sauces, served on a
   generous bed of fluffy rice or delicious noodles.

15 Whether it's a quiet meal for two or a family celebration for twenty,
   our friendly, helpful staff are waiting to create a memorable meal
   for you.

   Just five minutes from Central Station, a meal at our restaurant is
   the perfect way to end a busy day in the city – or the best possible
20 start to a great night out.

   Please book your table in advance to avoid disappointment.

Opening times

Monday: Closed
Tuesday: 5:30–11:30 pm
Wednesday: 5:30–11:30 pm
Thursday: 5:30–11:30 pm
Friday: 5:30–11:30 pm
Saturday: 5:30 pm–midnight
Sunday: 5:30 pm–midnight

Activity 1: Inferring the writer's intention

1 The webpage for 'A Taste of China' on page 190 is a persuasive text. What is the writer trying to persuade the reader to do? Write **one or two** sentences explaining your ideas.

2 The writer gives lots of information about different aspects of the restaurant.
   a) What do you learn about the restaurant's customers?
   b) What do you learn about the chefs at the restaurant?
   c) What do you learn about the staff working at the restaurant?

Remember
Use your scanning skills to identify a key word in the question and then scan the extract for the answer.

3 Look again at each of your answers to question 2. How might each of these persuade you to visit this restaurant? Write **one or two** sentences relating to each answer explaining your ideas.

4 Look again at the final line of the webpage:

   Please book your table in advance to avoid disappointment.

   What does this sentence suggest about the restaurant? Write **one or two** sentences explaining your ideas.

5 What other aspects of the restaurant does the writer describe in order to persuade you to visit it?

Activity 2: Identifying persuasive points

1 Look again at the webpage on page 190. Can you identify any sentences or phrases that are **not** trying to persuade you to visit the restaurant?

2 Choose the **three** ideas or pieces of information in the webpage that you find the most persuasive.

3 Look again at your answer to question 2. Which **one** piece of information most strongly persuades you to visit this restaurant? Write a sentence explaining your choice.

Grammar Boost: Noun phrases

A noun phrase is a group of words containing a noun and other words that are linked to that noun. For example, 'the best restaurant in the world.' In this noun phrase, 'restaurant' is the noun. All the other words in the phrase add more information about the restaurant.

Words linked to a noun could be of different **word classes**. For example:

a determiner	an adverb	one or more adjectives	a noun	a prepositional phrase
the | a | an | some	very | extremely | really | most	large | healthy | expensive | delicious	plate | snack | dessert | helping	of salad | with ice cream | in the evening | for breakfast

A prepositional phrase is a phrase that is linked to a noun or verb by a preposition. Prepositions include words such as 'in', 'of', 'with', 'near', 'under' and 'behind'.

1 Using the examples above to help you, write a noun phrase:
   a) using **two** different word classes
   b) using **three** different word classes
   c) using **four** different word classes
   d) using **five** different word classes.

Remember

A noun phrase must contain a noun!

Activity 3: Building persuasive noun phrases

1 Look again at the extract on page 190. Identify **one** noun phrase in which the writer has used **two** adjectives.

2 **Alliteration** is the use of one sound to begin two or more words. For example:

> salty sardine sandwiches

Identify **one** noun phrase in which the writer has used alliteration.

3 **Superlatives** are formed by adding the suffix –*est*, or by positioning the word *most* in front of an adjective. They show the highest level of the quality described by the adjective. For example:

> We climbed the <u>biggest</u> hill in the park. It was the <u>most tiring</u> thing I have ever done.

Identify **one** noun phrase in which the writer has used a superlative.

4 Imagine a delicious plate of food. Write a noun phrase describing the food on your plate. Aim to use:
   • **two** adjectives, including at least **one** superlative
   • alliteration.

Activity 4: Writing persuasively

Imagine you are about to open a new restaurant or café. You are going to write a menu for its first week.

Plan

1 First, you need to plan the dishes that you will serve in your restaurant. Write down **five** nouns naming items you will have on your menu.

> fish

> curry

> chicken

2 Choose **one** of the items on your menu.
   a) Add **three** adjectives to the noun:

> crisp, golden, fried fish

   b) Now add an adverb to the noun phrase:

> beautifully crisp, golden, fried fish

   c) Finally, add a prepositional phrase:

> beautifully crisp, golden, fried fish with lemon sauce

3 Look at the noun phrase you have created.
   • Could you make it more persuasive by taking out any of the words?
   • Could you make it more persuasive by using a superlative or alliteration?

Try adding, taking away or changing words in your noun phrase until you are happy that you have made it as persuasive as possible.

Write

4 Now write the rest of your menu, making all five items sound as persuasively delicious as possible.

This section links to pages 182–183 of the Workbook.

Section 5
Assessment

In this section, you will answer questions on an extract and write a short descriptive text, focusing on effect, to assess your progress in the unit so far.

In this extract, a student describes the experience of eating fresh fruit for the first time in several months.

▼ Read the extract and then answer the questions that follow it.

A healthy luxury: The pleasure of fresh fruit

1 In my first term at college I lived away from home. The fact that I was constantly busy, and had little money to spare, meant that my diet became dull and unhealthy. Mostly I ate stodgy white bread and peanut butter. My only treat was an occasional greasy takeaway. So when I came back home, and entered my parents' kitchen, the sight which met my eyes made me gasp with excitement. In the centre of the table was a bowl overflowing with fruit…

5 bright yellow bananas, fragrant oranges, gleaming grapes and shiny apples. After months of boring meals, these **humble**[1] items suddenly seemed exotic and luxurious.

The first thing I grabbed was a banana. I peeled it, exposing the pale flesh, and sank my teeth in. It was perfectly ripe, creamy and mellow. I was **ravenous**[2],

10 and made short work of it. As I swallowed the last morsel, I felt a sense of healthy energy filling my body.

Then I started on the grapes. Purple, plump, and cool to the touch, each one exploded on my tongue, filling my mouth with pleasure. Next was an orange. I chose

15 the largest one in the bowl and dropped it onto a plate with a satisfying thud. I sliced it into glistening discs, inhaling the heady scent, which reminded me so strongly of my childhood it almost brought a tear to my eye. I peeled each slice, careful to remove every shred

20 of bitter **pith**[3], and cut it into segments. I took my time, **relishing**[4] the patient **ritual**[5] of preparation. At last I popped a segment into my mouth, savouring the combination of acidity and sweetness as the juice trickled down my throat.

By now I'd probably eaten enough for a large breakfast, but the apples looked so tempting I had to have one. I selected a perfect specimen – the skin smooth and golden, with a slight blush of rosy red on one side. The loud

25 crunch as I bit into it was wonderfully satisfying. I smiled contentedly. Forget the three-course meal that was planned for that evening…this was my idea of a **banquet**[6]!

Key vocabulary

humble[1]: simple
ravenous[2]: mad with hunger
pith[3]: the white layer under the skin of an orange
relishing[4]: really enjoying
ritual[5]: ceremony
banquet[6]: feast

Activity 1: Reading

1 In the extract on page 194, the writer describes eating four different types of fruit. What effect does the writer want her description to have on the reader?

2 **a)** Look again at the first paragraph. Find two examples of negative vocabulary the writer uses to describe her college diet, and two examples of positive vocabulary the writer uses to describe the fruit.
   b) For each example you've chosen, explain what effect you think the writer wants to have on the reader

3 **a)** In the first sentence of paragraph 2 the writer says she 'grabbed' a banana from the bowl. Why do you think she has chosen this word?
   b) What word does she use to suggest that she was hungry?
   c) Explain the effect of this choice of vocabulary.

4 Identify one adjective the writer uses to describe each of the fruits. For each phrase you have chosen, write one or two sentences explaining its effect.

5 Does the writer enjoy the experience of eating the fruit? Explain your answer, using evidence from the extract to support your ideas.

Activity 2: Writing

Imagine that you have been asked to try a new fruit or vegetable that you have never seen before.

1 Write a description of the fruit or vegetable, and the experience of eating it, focusing on the effect you hope to have on a reader.

Before you start writing:

• Plan your writing by gathering all the ideas and descriptions you could include.
• Think carefully about the effect you want your description to have. What vocabulary and comparisons could you use to build a vivid picture in the reader's mind?
• Consider how you will structure your writing. How will you begin your description? How will you end it?

As you write:

• Choose your vocabulary carefully.
• Continue to think about the most effective structure for your description.

When you have finished writing:

• Check the accuracy of your punctuation, especially full stops.

This section links to pages 184–187 of the Workbook.

Section 6
Structuring persuasive writing

In this section, you will explore the structure of a persuasive text, and craft some persuasive writing of your own.

This is an extract from a leaflet giving information about eating a healthy diet.

▼ **Read the extract and then answer the questions that follow it.**

EAT WELL; BE WELL!

Eat well

1 Food is our fuel. It gives us the energy, nutrients and vitamins we need to stay alive and keep well. To be sure of getting everything you need to stay healthy, eat a wide range of different foods, with different tastes and different colours. As the poet William Cowper said, 'Variety is the spice of life that gives it all its flavour'!

Eat breakfast

Some people miss out breakfast because they're in a hurry or they
5 think it will help them lose weight. However, research shows that eating breakfast every day means you're less likely to be overweight, and more likely to be able to concentrate and think clearly.

Eat carbohydrates

Experts recommend that around a third of our diet should be starchy carbohydrates, such as potatoes, bread, pasta or rice. Have at least
10 one starchy food with every main meal.

Eat fruit and vegetables

Fruit and vegetables give us plenty of the vitamins, minerals and fibre we need to keep healthy. They're big on flavour and small on fat, so you can fill up with plenty of vegetables on your plate. Aim to eat at least five portions of different
15 fruits and vegetables every day.

Cut down on salt, fat and sugar

We do need fat, sugar and salt, but too much of them can be bad for our health. Too much salt can give us high blood pressure, making us more likely to develop heart disease or have a stroke. You should have no more than one teaspoon of salt a day. Too much fat and sugar can make us overweight, making us more likely to develop diabetes or heart disease. Many foods contain a lot of fat and sugar that we cannot see.
20 A medium-sized portion of fast food fries contains nearly a quarter of the fat an adult should eat in one day, and a can of soda can contain the equivalent of 13 cubes of sugar: more than 150% of the amount an adult should eat in a day!

Activity 1: Exploring the extract

1 The writer of the extract on page 196 has included lots of information about eating a healthy diet. What is the writer's intention?

2 The writer uses different features to influence the reader's opinion and actions. Which of the following features can you identify? Write down **one** example of each.

a) **imperative verbs:** verbs that give the reader a command or instruction, such as 'stand up', 'talk to me' or 'don't move'

b) **facts:** information that is true and can be proved

c) **evidence:** examples that prove the point the writer is making, such as statistics, expert opinions or scientific research

d) **reasoning:** clear explanations of why something is important

3 Based on the information given in the leaflet, plan a plate of healthy food you could eat for your midday or evening meal. Write **two or three** sentences explaining your choices.

Activity 2: Organising a persuasive text

1 Look at the subheadings in the extract on page 196.
a) How many subheadings has the writer used?
b) Why do you think the writer has used these subheadings?

2 How many pieces of advice does the writer give?

3 How many key points does the writer make?

4 How many paragraphs does the writer use?

5 Why has the writer started each new paragraph?

Remember

A writer could start a new paragraph when there is:
- a change of setting
- a change of time
- a change of topic
- a change of speaker.

6 Plan **three** subheadings using imperative verbs that you would include in a leaflet with **one** of these titles:

Exercise is good for you! | Making the most of school

Punctuation Boost: Speech and quotation punctuation

When you write the exact words spoken by a real person or a fictional character, you need to enclose the words they speak in speech marks, which are also known as quotation marks.

The rules of speech punctuation:

- Speech marks are always used in pairs.
- There should be a punctuation mark before the closing speech mark.
- If an **identifier**, such as 'he said' or 'they shouted', follows the speech, the punctuation mark before the closing speech mark should be a comma, question mark or exclamation mark.
- If the speech is not followed by an identifier, the punctuation mark before the closing speech mark should be a full stop, question mark or exclamation mark.

For example:

William Cowper said, "Variety is the spice of life."
"Variety is the spice of life," said William.

Variety is the spice of life.

1 Copy and correct the sentences below, adding the correct punctuation.

You're going to be late for school said Dad.

I've got plenty of time I replied.

You're still in bed! Dad pulled the covers off me and stormed out of the room.

2 When you have finished, check you have followed **all** the rules above.

Activity 3: Structuring persuasive paragraphs

Look again at the extract on page 196. In each paragraph, the writer:
- tells you what to do   • explains why you should do it.

1 Look at these three sentences from the fourth paragraph:

A   Fruit and vegetables give us plenty of the vitamins, minerals and fibre we need to keep healthy.

B   They're big on flavour and small on fat, so you can fill up with plenty of vegetables on your plate.

C   Aim to eat at least five portions of different fruits and vegetables every day.

a) Which sentence or sentences tell you what to do?
b) Which sentence or sentences tell you why you should do it?

2 Choose another paragraph from the leaflet.
a) Write down **one** sentence that tells you what to do.
b) Write down **one** sentence that tells you why you should do it.

Activity 4: Writing a persuasive paragraph

1 Write a paragraph for a leaflet called 'Cutting back on snacks', persuading readers to follow your advice.

How do I do that?

1 Write **one** sentence telling your readers what to do. You could use an imperative verb to do this.

2 Write a sentence explaining **one** reason why they should do what you have told them to do. You could use some of the information in the extract on page 196 to help you.

3 Write a second sentence explaining another reason why they should do what you have told them to do.

2 Try **two or three** different ways to sequence the three sentences you have written, and then decide which order makes your paragraph most persuasive.

Activity 5: Writing a persuasive leaflet

You are going to write **two or three** paragraphs from a persuasive leaflet.

1 Choose **one** of these titles:
- Exercise is good for you!
- Making the most of school

2 Plan your subheadings. You could use the ones you planned in Activity 2, question 6, or choose new ones.

3 Plan to use an expert opinion to support **one or two** of your paragraphs. You could use a quotation researched on the internet, or you could make up a quotation.

4 Under each subheading, write a paragraph that:
- tells your reader what to do, using an imperative verb
- explains why your reader should do this
- gives an expert opinion to support the idea, using speech marks.

Section 7
Structuring persuasive sentences

In this section, you will explore how sentences can be structured in different ways to make meaning clear or to make a point more persuasive.

This extract is from a newspaper article. It tells parents how to cope with a child who refuses to eat foods that they do not like or do not know.

▼ **Read the article and then answer the questions that follow it.**

STEPS TO REFORM A PICKY EATER

1 Cook a meal together. Let your child be part of the process of actually cooking the meal, allowing them to feel they are part of a team that's creating something.

2 Eat together, rather than giving your child separate mealtimes, and show them how much you're enjoying your food.

3 Don't always force your child to clear their plate. Give them positive reinforcement for trying even a mouthful or two of a new food, even if they don't eat all of it.

4 Don't offer 'rewards', in the sense of getting a pudding 'only if you eat your vegetables first'. Children should learn that they can get equal pleasure from both, and that eating healthy foods is not merely a punishment before a treat.

5 Plant a herb garden on a windowsill and let your child help with planting and watering seeds so they can be responsible for creating food.

6 Be patient. You may have to offer a child a new food at least 10 times before they truly grow to accept it.

7 Be a good role model. Don't give your child anything you wouldn't eat yourself – and certainly don't try and make them eat vegetables while you're eating a different, unhealthy meal.

Remember

This article is trying to influence the way that parents treat their children. Look out for persuasive imperative verbs that tell the reader what they should do.

Activity 1: Exploring the article

1 How have these tips for parents been organised? What was the writer's intention when choosing this structure?

2 Identify **two** things parents should and should not do, according to the article on page 200.

| Parents should... | | Parents should not... |

Activity 2: Exploring sentence structures

1 Many of the sentences in the article on page 200 are short. For example:

Cook a meal together.   Don't always force your child to clear their plate.   Be a good role model.

  a) Identify another short sentence in the article.
  b) Sentences in persuasive articles often either tell the reader what to do or explain how or why this is important. What do the short sentences in the article do?
  c) Does using short sentences make these points more or less persuasive? Write **one or two** sentences explaining your ideas.

2 The writer uses longer sentences to give explanations. Look again at paragraph 5 of the text. In this long sentence, there are **two** instructions telling the reader what to do and **one** reason that these things are important.
  a) What is the first instruction?
  b) What is the second instruction?
  c) What is the reason given?
  d) What conjunction does the writer use to link the two instructions?
  e) What conjunction does the writer use to link the reason to the instructions?

3 The writer starts the sentences that tell people what to do with imperative verbs. However, explanation sentences start in a variety of ways.
  a) Identify **one** sentence that starts with a pronoun.
  b) Identify **one** sentence that starts with a noun.

Remember

A sentence can also begin with a noun phrase – a group of words containing a noun and all the other words that add description or information to it. For example:

Parents of picky eaters can do things to help.

A child's diet should be varied.

Activity 3: Experimenting with sentence structures

1 Look at this long sentence from the article on page 200, which tells parents **two** things they should do and **one** thing they should not do:

> Eat together, rather than giving your child separate mealtimes, and show them how much you're enjoying your food.

a) Rewrite the sentence as **three** separate, shorter sentences, with each sentence giving only **one** instruction.

b) Compare your three sentences with the original sentence. Which version is easier to understand? Which version is more persuasive? Write **one or two** sentences explaining your ideas.

2 Look at these two sentences from the article:

> Be patient. You may have to offer a child a new food at least 10 times before they truly grow to accept it.

a) Link these two sentences with a conjunction to form one longer sentence. You could use the Conjunction Bank to help you.

b) Compare your sentence with the original two sentences. Which version is easier to understand? Which version is more persuasive? Write **one or two** sentences explaining your ideas.

Conjunction Bank	
and	but
so	although
as	when
until	before
if	because

Punctuation Boost: Using colons, semi-colons and dashes

Instead of linking clauses with a conjunction, you can link them with a colon, a semi-colon or a dash.

- A semi-colon links two clauses that are related and equally important.
- A colon introduces an explanation or an example.
- A dash can be used instead of a colon or a semi-colon, but only in informal writing.

1 In each of the following sentences, remove the conjunction and replace it with a colon, a semi-colon or a dash.

a) I love tomatoes because they are so tasty.

b) I love cooking but I hate tidying up afterwards.

c) I have never eaten chilli and I never will!

Activity 4: Writing sentences

You are going to write a leaflet that gives parents tips on giving their children delicious food that will keep them happy, healthy and fit.

Plan

1 Think about what you think parents should feed their children. You could use the questions below to help you note down some ideas.

> Should children always be given healthy food?

> Should children be allowed some unhealthy food?

> Should children eat school food, or take their own?

> Should parents let their children have snacks?

> What kinds of snacks would be healthiest for children?

> Should parents insist that children try new foods?

Write

2 Write **five** tips for parents. Remember to:
- use a numbered list to organise your writing
- include at least **one** instruction and **one** explanation in each of your tips
- think about varying your sentence structures.

Review

3 Look at each of your tips. Rewrite each one using different sentence structures. For example:
- If your tip is made up of two or more sentences, you could link them together in one longer sentence using conjunctions or semi-colons.
- If your tip is one longer sentence, you could break it down into two or three shorter sentences.
- You could add variety to the structure of your explanation sentences by starting them in different ways.

4 Compare the two different versions of each tip. Rewrite your tips in the most effective way, using the best parts of your two versions.

This section links to pages 192–195 of the Workbook.

Section 8
Rhetorical devices

In this section, you will explore how writers use language devices to make their ideas more persuasive.

This article is from a website that encourages young people to learn to cook, and adults to help them.

▼ **Read the article and then answer the questions that follow it.**

● ● ●   Search…

Why we must teach our children to look after themselves

1 What are the most important lessons we need to learn in our lives? To be kind? To read and write? To be able to grow and cook our own food? Learning all of these things certainly improves the quality of our
5 lives. But only one of them actually keeps us alive. Yet we are sending our children out into the world with little idea where vegetables come from, and even less idea how to cook them.

The importance of food is unarguable. Food keeps
10 us alive. And the quality of our food improves the quality of our lives. Food is the foundation on which a great education is built. With a balance of essential vitamins, minerals, proteins, fats and carbohydrates, we are preparing our children for success. With a diet of dangerous junk food, we are preparing our
15 children for short lives, with minds and bodies starved of the fuel they need.

If we do not teach our children to cook, we are encouraging them to eat nothing but cheap junk food and microwave ready meals. They will never experience the simple joy of putting three or four or more ingredients in a pan and producing something delicious and nutritious. They will never experience the satisfaction of producing something that everyone
20 sitting together around a table can enjoy. They will never know how much tastier and healthier real food, cooked with real ingredients, and served with real love, can be.

This is why we must teach our children how to grow
25 food, how to keep it fresh, how to cook with real ingredients and how to create real food. This should be the fourth basic skill we teach children in our schools: reading, writing, mathematics and cooking. If your children are being taught anything less than this, they
30 are not and never will be fit for the life ahead of them.

Activity 1: Identifying the writer's argument

The article on page 204 is an argument text: the writer is presenting an opinion and trying to persuade the reader to agree with it.

1 Look at some of the points that the writer makes in the article.

A | Children should be taught to cook.

B | Junk food is dangerous.

C | A poor diet affects our health.

D | Many children do not know how to cook.

E | Home-cooked food tastes better and is better for our health.

F | If we cannot cook, we eat junk food and ready meals.

Answer each of the following questions using **one** of the key points above.
a) What is the problem on which the writer focuses in this article?
b) What is the solution on which the writer focuses in this article?
c) Why, according to the writer, is it important that this problem is solved?

Activity 2: Identifying rhetorical devices

1 The writer uses some language techniques to add impact to the opinions stated. These are known as rhetorical devices. They include:

Rhetorical questions	The writer asks questions without expecting an answer, to draw the reader into the argument.
Direct address	The writer talks directly to the reader, telling them what they should do.
Repetition	The writer repeats a word or phrase to add emphasis to a key idea.
Emotive language	The writer chooses vocabulary that creates an emotional response in the reader.

a) Identify **one** example of a **rhetorical question** from the first paragraph.
   (Look out for a question mark in the article on page 204.)
b) Identify **one** example of direct address from the fourth paragraph.
   (Look out for the pronouns 'you' and 'your', or 'we' and 'our'.)
c) Identify **one** example of repetition from the whole article.
   (Look out for similar or identical words or phrases.)
d) Identify **one** example of emotive language from the second paragraph.
   (Look out for words or phrases that make the situation sound serious and dramatic.)

Punctuation Boost: Using colons

You can use a colon to introduce a list or an explanation. The part of the sentence **before** the colon should be a clause that could be a sentence by itself. The part of the sentence **after** the colon could be a clause that **could** be a sentence by itself, but it doesn't need to be. For example:

There is one good reason to learn to cook: it's fun.

an explanation that is a full sentence

I bought three ingredients: onions, mushrooms and tomatoes.

a list that is not a full sentence

1 Copy the sentences below and add a colon to connect the clauses.
   a) The takeaway comes in three sizes. Small, medium and large.
   b) There is only one way to get enough sleep. Go to bed earlier.
   c) I had four items on my shopping list milk, bread, apples and onions.
   d) I always eat breakfast it helps me to concentrate at school.

2 Complete the sentences below, using a colon to introduce a list or an explanation.
   a) Every night, before I go to bed, I always do three things…
   b) I had some good news this morning…
   c) I've had a great idea…

Activity 3: Using rhetorical devices

Look at this sentence, taken from one student's persuasive writing:

People do not want to eat food that is bad for their health.

1 Rewrite the sentence above, using direct address to talk directly to the reader.

How do I do that?

Underline all the nouns and pronouns in the sentence. Choose which ones could be replaced with the pronouns 'you', 'your', 'we' or 'our'.

2 Rewrite your sentence as a rhetorical question.

How do I do that?

The question could be formed using the sentence starters 'Do you…' or 'Would you…'. Remember to replace the full stop with a question mark.

3 Add some emotive language to your sentence.

How do I do that?

Choose a word in the sentence that could be made more dramatic. Make a list of synonyms for that word. Choose the synonym that is the most emotive and dramatic.

4 Finally, write a second sentence using some repetition.

How do I do that?

Choose a phrase or key word from the sentence. Write another sentence using the same phrase or key word.

Activity 4: Arguing your point

You are going to write **one** paragraph expressing your opinion about the importance of learning to cook.

Plan

1 Think about your opinion: do you think everyone should be able to cook? Choose **one** of the following key points to use as your main argument.

We should all be able to feed ourselves without relying on anyone else.	Cooking takes up a lot of time.	If you cook your own food, you can choose healthier meals with healthier ingredients.	If you cook your own food, you know exactly what you are eating.
Home-cooked food is much nicer than anything you can buy.	Anyone can learn to cook.	Cooking should be done by experts, and not everyone can be an expert.	There are many hazards in the kitchen so it's safer not to cook.

Write

2 Write **one or two** sentences to give your opinion and explain your chosen key point.

3 Write another **one or two** sentences explaining your opinion in more detail. You could include an example from your own experience to help you develop your explanation.

Review

4 Look carefully at the paragraph you have written. Try adding some rhetorical devices such as rhetorical questions, emotive language, direct address and repetition to add impact to your writing.

Section 9
Leaflets

In this section, you will explore the key features of a persuasive leaflet.

Leaflets are often used to advertise services and products. This is a leaflet advertising a business that will deliver pizzas to you.

▼ **Read the leaflet and then answer the questions that follow it.**

FAST, FUN, FILLING AND FANTASTIC FOOD, DELIVERED STRAIGHT TO YOUR DOOR!

1 When you want to eat a freshly cooked pizza, you need to call Build-A-Pizza! We've been building pizzas for years and know exactly how it should be done. Try us once and you'll never eat pizza from anywhere else again. We're just a phone call away!

5 Our pizzas are built on freshly made dough, smothered in tangy tomato sauce, heaped with delicious cheese and loaded with all your favourite toppings – just the way you like it!

Why not make a meal of it with crisp salads, rich coleslaw and crunchy garlic bread? Delicious!

It's easy!
- Choose your pizza
- Order your pizza
- Wait less than 30 minutes for our friendly delivery driver to arrive
- Enjoy your pizza!

Enjoy a massive 10% discount with this leaflet!

Remember

Every word in an advert has been chosen to persuade you to spend your money!

Activity 1: Using an informal register

Advertisements are often written in an informal register. This can help to suggest that the writer is talking to the reader in a friendly, relaxed way.

An informal register often features:
- short, informal sentence structures
- informal vocabulary choices
- contractions such as 'can't', 'you'll' and 'we're'.

1 Which of the sentences in each group below are the most informal? Which are the most formal?

A When you desire a freshly cooked pizza, you should make a telephone call to Build-A-Pizza!

B When you want to eat a freshly cooked pizza, you need to call Build-A-Pizza!

C Want a pizza? Call Build-A-Pizza!

A Delicious!

B That'd be delicious!

C That would be delicious!

A We are just one telephone call away!

B You need to make only one telephone call to order your pizza!

C We're just one phone call away!

2 How formal is the Build-A-Pizza leaflet? Why do you think this is? Use the formality scale below to help you select your answer.

⟵ very informal   quite informal   both formal and informal   formal   very formal ⟶

Activity 2: Identifying the key features of a leaflet

1 Look at the following key features of an advertisement. Write down **one** example of each from the Build-A-Pizza leaflet on page 208.

Organising the text	Language choices
a logo (the name of the business written using a distinctive design)	imperative verbs
a heading	positive vocabulary
a special offer	alliteration
bullet points	rhetorical devices (for example direct address, rhetorical questions, repetition, emotive language)

Punctuation Boost: Bullet points and lists

1 Writers often use bullet points and numbered lists to organise information. For example:

Making an ice-cream sundae

You will need:
- Fruit
- Ice cream
- Chocolate sauce

1 Wash the fruit.
2 Cut the fruit into pieces.
3 Place the fruit in a bowl or tall glass.
4 Add three scoops of ice cream.
5 Pour chocolate sauce over the top.
6 Add any extra toppings of your choosing.

a) Why has the writer of the text above used bullet points?
b) Why has the writer of the text above used a numbered list?

2 Rewrite the text below using bullet points, a numbered list or both.

Treasure hunt
Go to the end of the path. Turn left. Walk for 1 km. Walk around the lake to a wooden bench. Along the way you will need to find: a white stone, a feather, a red flower, a coin.

Activity 3: Gathering ideas

You are going to plan a leaflet advertising a restaurant, café or takeaway.

1 What kind of business will you advertise: a takeaway, a café or a restaurant?

2 What kind of food will your business sell?

3 What is your business called? Give it a name.

4 Which of these features will you include on your leaflet?

| a heading telling the reader why your food is great | a description of some of the kinds of food you sell | a complete menu |
| instructions telling the reader how to place an order | a special offer | a logo |

5 How could you use bullet points or a numbered list to help to organise the information on your leaflet?

Activity 4: Planning key language features

Continue to plan your leaflet advertising a restaurant, café or takeaway.

1 Why should people buy food from your business? Choose **five or six** adjectives that describe your business and the food you will sell. You could choose some of the suggestions below, or use your own ideas.

> delicious | fast | easy | fresh | filling
> good-value | friendly | fun | cheap | healthy
> huge | tasty | varied | quality | satisfying

2 Now think about your menu.
   a) Make a list of **five or six** different dishes that your business will sell.
   b) Note down some words or phrases to describe each of the different dishes as positively as possible.

3 Think about how you could use imperative verbs in your leaflet. Write **two** sentences, using an imperative verb in each one to give instructions to the readers of your leaflet. You could choose some of the suggestions below, or use your own ideas.

> buy | enjoy | visit | try | call

4 Think carefully about your sentence structures.
   - Will you use short sentences and long sentences?
   - How will you structure the long sentences: with dashes, semi-colons, colons or conjunctions?
   - Try to vary the structures you use, to keep your writing interesting.
   - In addition to 'and' and 'but', you could use some of the subordinating conjunctions below.

> so | as | until | if | since
> although | when | before | because | while

5 Look at the vocabulary and sentences you have noted so far. Could you use any of these language features to add impact to them?
   - alliteration
   - direct address
   - rhetorical questions
   - repetition
   - emotive language

Section 10
Reviewing, revising and proofreading

In this section, you will check and improve the accuracy and effectiveness of a student's persuasive leaflet.

This is an example of a persuasive leaflet written by a student.

▼ **Read the leaflet and then answer the questions that follow it.**

THE BEST SANDWICH SHOP IN TOWN

1 Our sandwiches are the best. We carefuly choose the best ingredients. We make the most beautyfull sandwiches.

Our customers choose what type of sandwich they want. We make the sandwich while they wait. Its fresh. It's delicious. It's exactly
5 how they want it.

SANDWICHES

They can choose meat, cheese, vegetables, salad and sauces, they can choose white or brown bread or rolls, they can choose whether to have the sandwich fresh or toasted. The choice is theirs!

Do'nt wait! Try our sandwiches today. Everybody loves them. Youll love them too.

Activity 1: Reviewing vocabulary choices 1

1 Look at the logo above and the name of the business that the leaflet above is advertising ('Sandwiches'). Choose an adjective you could add to the name to make it sound more persuasively positive. You could choose one from the **Adjective Bank** below, or think of your own.

Adjective Bank

tender	succulent	spicy	tasty	crisp
fresh	mouth-watering	juicy	rich	crunchy

2 Look at the different ingredients customers could choose to have in a sandwich.

Copy and complete the list by replacing the **?** in each space. Add at least **one** adjective to each noun to make it more appealing.

tender meat

a) **?** cheese

b) **?** vegetables

c) **?** salad

d) **?** sauces

e) **?** fish

Activity 2: Reviewing vocabulary choices 2

The writer uses the word 'best' several times.

1 The writer could have chosen lots of other different superlatives.
   a) Look at the suggestions below and then write down **two** more superlatives of your own.

freshest | tastiest | most delicious | greatest | loveliest

most appetising | most scrumptious | most amazing | highest-quality | most superb

   b) Rewrite the heading and the first paragraph of the leaflet on page 212, carefully choosing the most persuasive superlatives to replace the word 'best'. You could use **two**, or even **three**, superlatives in a row.

Activity 3: Experimenting with sentence structure

1 Look at the first paragraph of the leaflet on page 212.

Our sandwiches are the best.

We carefuly choose the best ingredients.

We make the most beautyfull sandwiches.

because | as | since

↑

subordinating conjunctions that indicate explanation

in order to | so that | and then

↑

subordinating conjunctions that indicate purpose

   a) Rewrite the three sentences above as **one** longer sentence, linking the clauses together with subordinating conjunctions.
   b) Rewrite the three sentences above as **two** sentences: leave one as it is written now, and link two together.
   c) Which version do you prefer? Write **one or two** sentences to explain your choice.

Activity 4: Adding rhetorical devices

1 Look at the second paragraph of the leaflet on page 212.

> Our customers choose what type of sandwich they want. We make the sandwich while they wait. Its fresh. It's delicious. It's exectely how they want it.

a) Rewrite the paragraph using direct address (using the pronouns 'you' and 'your').
b) Which version is more effective: the original, or your version using direct address?

2 Look at the final paragraph:

> Do'nt wait! Try our sandwiches today. Everybody loves them. Youll love them too.

Which of the following sentences would make the most effective rhetorical question in the final paragraph?

A | Why wait?

B | Why not try our sandwiches today?

C | Will you love them too?

Spelling Boost: Word families

Thinking about how words are formed, and the word families to which they belong, can help you to spell them correctly.

1 Many adjectives are formed by adding a suffix to a noun.

noun	+ suffix	= adjective
use	-ful	useful
delight	-ful	delightful
beauty	-ful	beautiful

Notice that the 'y' becomes an 'i' when the suffix is added.

Write the adjective formed by adding the suffix –ful to these nouns:
a) care **b)** cheer **c)** colour

2 Many adverbs are formed by adding the suffix –ly to an adjective.

adjective	+ suffix	= adverb
beautiful	-ly	beautifully
complete	-ly	completely
happy	-ly	happily

Notice that the 'y' becomes an 'i' when the suffix is added.

Write the adverb formed by adding the suffix –ly to these adjectives:
a) angry **b)** extreme **c)** careful

3 Check the spelling in the student's leaflet on page 212. Can you find the **three** spelling mistakes?

Activity 5: Checking for comma splices

Remember

A comma splice is the incorrect use of a comma to link two separate clauses. Instead, the clauses should be separated by a full stop or linked with a conjunction. For example:

> I needed food, I went to the shop.

One place where commas **should** be used is in a list, to separate items. For example:

> I bought onions, tomatoes, carrots, potatoes and green beans.

Commas can also be used in multi-clause sentences describing a series of events. For example:

> I put the pan on the stove, added the onions and fried them in the oil.

1 Copy out and correct the **one** sentence below that contains a comma splice.

  A Smoke poured out of the oven, filled the kitchen and set off the smoke alarm.

  B I washed up every knife, fork, spoon, plate and cup in the entire house.

  C Mum had made cakes, biscuits, buns and sandwiches, there was so much food!

2 Look closely at every comma in the student's leaflet. Should any of them be a full stop? Note down the sentences around the comma splices and correct the punctuation.

Activity 6: Checking for apostrophes in contractions

Remember

You can use contractions in informal writing. Contractions are shortened forms of two or more words. An apostrophe is used to show where one or more letters have been missed out.

1 Copy out the following contractions, adding apostrophes in the correct positions.

  a) cant   **b)** wont   **c)** Im   **d)** shes   **e)** weve

2 Look closely at the student's leaflet. Can you identify any contractions that are missing an apostrophe, or that contain an apostrophe in the wrong place? Copy them out and correct them.

Section 11
Assessment

In this section, you will create a persuasive leaflet advertising a restaurant, café or takeaway.

HEADING

Special offer!

Activity 1: Writing

 Create a persuasive leaflet advertising a restaurant, café or takeaway, using the layout template on page 216 as a guide.

Plan

Before you write, you will need to plan:
- the name of the business that you are advertising
- the kinds of food that the business sells
- some positive persuasive vocabulary you can use to describe your business and its food.
- the register in which you will write (formal, informal or a mixture of both).

Write

As you write, you will need to think about including:
- imperative verbs to give instructions
- short sentences for emphasis
- different paragraphs that contain different instructions and explanations
- longer sentences linked using a range of conjunctions
- alliteration to highlight key persuasive phrases
- rhetorical devices such as rhetorical questions, direct address, repetition or emotive language.

Activity 2: Reviewing, revising and proofreading

1 When you have completed your writing, you need to review it by looking for improvements you could make.
- Look closely at your vocabulary choices. Could they be more descriptive and persuasive?
- Think about your sentence structures. Would your writing be clearer or more persuasive if you linked some shorter sentences using conjunctions or broke a longer sentence into shorter sentences?
- Consider your use of rhetorical devices. Are they effective? Could you improve them?

2 Finally, check your writing very carefully for errors, in particular:
- spelling errors
- punctuation errors, especially comma splices and missing or misplaced apostrophes.

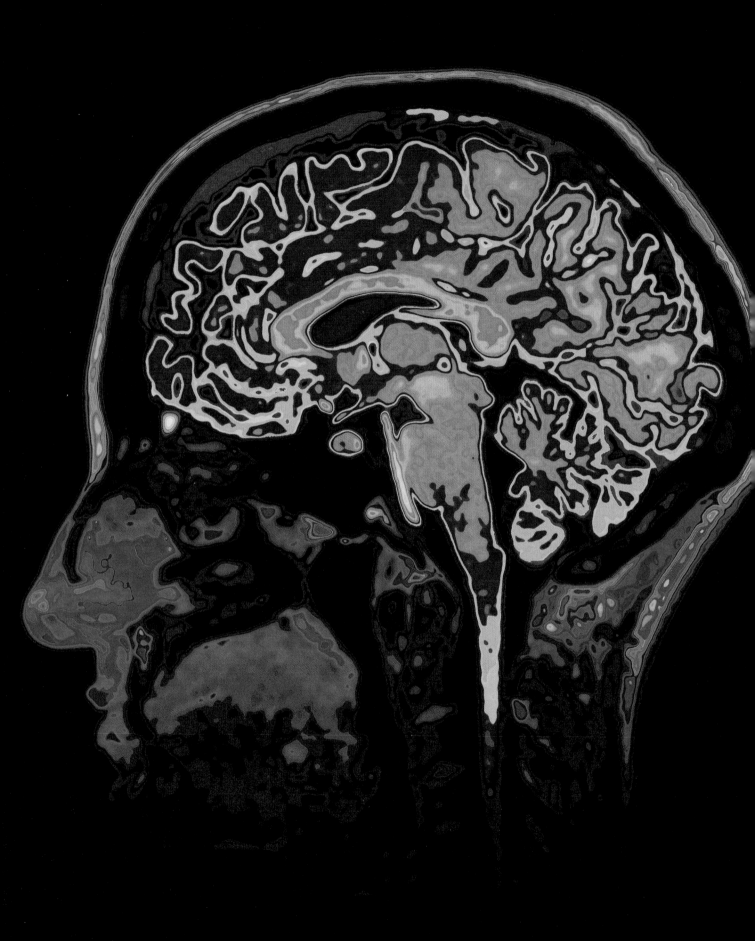

Unit 6
Teach me

This unit focuses on a range of information and explanation texts that instruct and teach. Topics include how to make a bottle rocket, why the dodo became extinct and how the brain works. You will study the structure and contents of texts, considering their purpose and audiences. You will also learn how to plan and write your own speech to teach someone about something important to you.

In this unit you will...

- explore the key features of instruction texts and their purposes.

- explore some of the key features of instruction texts and write your own.

- explore how information can be structured.

- focus on selecting vocabulary to convey information as clearly and precisely as possible.

- focus on structuring sentences to convey information as clearly and precisely as possible.

- answer questions on an informative article and write a short article to assess your progress in the unit so far.

- explore how to structure paragraphs of information.

- explore ways to entertain and engage your reader while you inform them.

- explore ways in which you can begin and end information texts.

- explore ways of planning an informative speech.

- write an informative speech.

By the end of this unit, you will be able to write an effective informative speech teaching your peers how to do or make something, and explain its appeal.

This section links to pages 206–209 of the Workbook.

Section 1
Exploring key features

In this section, you will explore the key features of instruction texts and their purposes.

This information is taken from the European Space Agency's website.

▼ **Read the webpage and then answer the questions that follow it.**

● ● ● Search…

Rocketing into space

The first rockets

1 Everything on Earth – including us – is held down by the force of gravity. Without gravity, we would all float off into space. It is said that Isaac Newton discovered gravity when an apple fell on his head.

In order to reach space, we use a rocket-powered launcher to overcome the pull of Earth's gravity. Other ideas have been put forward from time to time. In 1865, the science fiction writer Jules Verne suggested using
5 a powerful gun to send people to the Moon. More recently, scientists have been studying the use of powerful magnets to send a spacecraft into orbit.

Rockets have been around a long time. They were invented in China, more than 800 years ago. The first rockets were very simple – a cardboard tube packed with gunpowder and attached to a guide stick –
10 similar to the fireworks we use today.

In 1232, the Chinese used these 'fire arrows' to defeat the invading Mongol army. The knowledge of how to make rockets soon spread to the Middle East and Europe, where they were also used as weapons. Later, they also became popular for spectacular firework displays.

How does a rocket work?

15 Have you noticed what happens if you let the air out of a balloon? The air goes one way and the balloon moves in the opposite direction. Rockets work in much the same way. Exhaust gases coming out of the engine nozzle at high speed push the rocket forward.

Most modern launchers, such as Europe's Ariane 5, are very complicated
20 and weigh hundreds of tonnes at lift off. Most of this weight is fuel, such as liquid hydrogen and liquid oxygen.

Rockets need so much fuel in order to overcome Earth's gravity. Only when they reach a speed of 28,000 km/h are they travelling fast enough to enter orbit.

25 Most rockets are made up of two or three stages. When a stage has used up all of its fuel, it is separated to get rid of the dead weight. It then falls back (usually into the ocean and far from populated areas) or burns up in the atmosphere.

Activity 1: Checking your understanding

1 What information does the webpage on page 220 give about each of the following topics? Write down **one** fact or interesting point about each one.

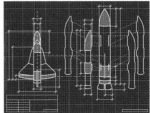

   a) Gravity

   b) How humans can get into space

   c) The invention of rockets

   d) How rockets work

   e) Rocket fuel

Remember

You can choose a key word or phrase from the topic, and then scan the text for it. This should help you find information about it.

Activity 2: Summarising the extract

In order to write a summary, you need to be able to identify key points of information. You are going to write a short summary of one section of the webpage on page 220.

1 Look at the second section of the webpage, under the heading 'How does a rocket work?' This section is written in four paragraphs.

   a) Look at the information below from the first paragraph of this section. Which one piece of information is the most important, and the most relevant to the question in the section title?

   A If you let air out of a balloon, it comes out in one direction and the balloon moves in the opposite direction.

   B Rockets work in the same way as a balloon with the air coming out.

   C Exhaust gases from the rocket engine push the rocket forward.

   b) Now look at each piece of information in the second paragraph of the section. Note down the most important piece of information in that paragraph.

   c) Do the same for the third and fourth paragraphs.

2 Use your answers to question 1 to write a summary of the section headed 'How does a rocket work?' You could use some words from the webpage in your answer – and some of your own.

3 Count how many words there are in your summary. Try to make it only **25** words by selecting information you could omit.

Activity 3: Identifying key features

There are lots of ways in which you can help your readers to understand a topic.

1 Match each key type of information to the quotation in which it appears.

A	Explaining a key idea	(i)	Have you noticed what happens if you let the air out of a balloon? The air goes one way and the balloon moves in the opposite direction.
B	Explaining a purpose	(ii)	In order to reach space, we use a rocket-powered launcher to overcome the pull of Earth's gravity.
C	Giving statistics	(iii)	Rockets have been around a long time. They were invented in China, more than 800 years ago.
D	Explaining the history	(iv)	Rockets need so much fuel in order to overcome Earth's gravity. Only when they reach a speed of 28,000 km/h are they travelling fast enough to enter orbit.
E	Using a familiar example	(v)	Everything on Earth – including us – is held down by the force of gravity. Without gravity, we would all float off into space.

2 Which types of information do you find the most helpful in assisting your understanding? Why is this? Write **one or two** sentences explaining your ideas.

Skills Boost: Textual features of information texts

Two of the key features of information texts are:
- **chronological order**: the order in which something happened, used when writing about events or people's lives
- **subheadings**: smaller headings that appear within a text below its main title, used to signal different topics within a longer piece of writing.

1 Put the following key pieces of information about the playwright William Shakespeare into chronological order.

A	B	C	D
He died in 1616.	While living in London, he wrote his first play.	He married Anne Hathaway.	He was born.

E	F	G	H
He retired from writing plays.	He left his wife and family, and moved to London.	He and his wife had three children.	He wrote his final play, *The Tempest*.

2 Think of **two or three** subheadings you could use if you were writing a **biography** of William Shakespeare.

Activity 4: Planning an information text

You are going to plan an information text about a topic of your choice.

1 Choose a topic. It should be a topic that interests you, and about which you already know some key points of information. You could choose from the suggestions below or use your own ideas.

| football | cricket | gymnastics | stamp-collecting | computer games |

| books | wildlife | music | films | the environment |

2 Think of at least **three** subheadings to organise your information. You could use questions such as the ideas below, changing them to suit your topic, or use your own ideas.

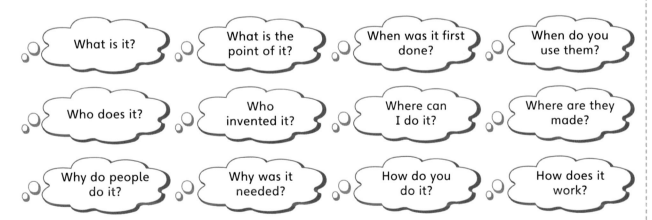

What is it?   What is the point of it?   When was it first done?   When do you use them?

Who does it?   Who invented it?   Where can I do it?   Where are they made?

Why do people do it?   Why was it needed?   How do you do it?   How does it work?

3 Now think about what key types of information you will include.

| Explaining a key idea | Explaining a purpose | Giving statistics | Explaining the history | Using a familiar example |

Remember

This is a planning activity – you do not need to include actual information in your planning, just notes.

Section 2
Exploring an instruction text

In this section, you will explore some of the key features of instruction texts and write your own.

This **instruction text** teaches readers how to make a simple rocket of their own.

▼ **Read the instruction text and then answer the questions that follow it.**

Making a Bottle Rocket

A

1 You can make a rocket with just a plastic bottle and a few other pieces of equipment. By filling the bottle with water and pumping air into it, the pressure inside the bottle builds up. This pressure eventually forces the cork and
5 the water out of the bottle in one direction, which sends the bottle flying off in the opposite direction!

Real space rockets work in the same way: they burn rocket fuel to create a powerful jet of gas. The force of this jet pushes down and pushes the rocket upwards – just like the
10 jet of water that will push your rocket upwards.

B

You will need:
• a cork
• the needle adaptor from a bicycle pump
• stiff card
15 • scissors
• a large plastic drinks bottle
• sticky tape
• water
• a foot pump

C

20 1 Push the needle adaptor through the cork.
2 Cut the card to create four fins and a nose cone. Attach them to the bottle with sticky tape. The card will need to be stiff so the rocket can stand up on the four fins.
3 Pour water into the drinks bottle so it is about a
25 quarter full, and then use the cork to seal it.
4 Take your rocket outside.
5 Stand the rocket up on its fins and attach the foot pump to the needle adaptor. Stand back as you pump! The rocket will soon take off and fly up into the sky.

D

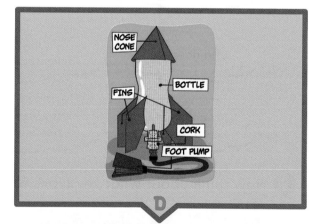

Take care!

30 Make sure you have an adult with you for lift off. The rocket will fly very quickly, and with a great deal of force. It may even burst before it takes off.

Do not go near the rocket once you have started pumping it full of air. It may look like it is not working, but it could lift off at any moment!

E

Activity 1: Exploring key features

An effective instruction text has a number of key features.

1 Look at the five different sections of the instruction text on page 224: A–E. Answer the following questions for each of the sections. Use the **Key Organisational Features Bank** to help you explain your ideas.

> ### Key Organisational Features Bank
> | | |
> |---|---|
> | heading | paragraphs |
> | subheading | bullet points |
> | **diagram** | numbered list |

a) What is the writer's intention in each section? Why has the writer included it in the text?

> In Section A, the writer is explaining

b) What feature or features has the writer used in each section?

> The writer has used

c) How does each feature help the reader to understand the text?

> This helps make the information clear because

Activity 2: Exploring structure

Look closely at the way in which the writer has structured the instruction text on page 224.

1 Look again at section A. Why has the writer positioned this section at the start of the text? Write **one or two** sentences explaining your ideas.

2 Look at sections B and C. Why has the writer positioned section B before section C? Write **one or two** sentences explaining your ideas.

3 Look at section D. Why has the writer positioned section D to the right of section C? Write **one or two** sentences explaining your ideas.

4 Look at section E. Why has the writer positioned this section at the end of the text? Write **one or two** sentences explaining your ideas.

Activity 3: Evaluating an instruction text

1 Which of the following sentences describes an effective instruction text?

    A It explains what the instructions will help you to do.

    B It tells you everything you will need before you start following the instructions.

    C It tells you what to do.

    D It explains everything clearly and is easy to understand.

    E It uses lots of descriptive language to help you imagine the scene.

2 How effective are the instructions on page 224 for making a bottle rocket? Write **one or two** sentences explaining your answer.

3 Look at the following instruction text.

> How to send an SMS text message

> You can use text messages to chat with your friends.

> 1 Decide which friend you want to message

> 2 Write a message.

> 3 Send it.

What advice would you give the writer of this instruction text?

Grammar Boost: Adverbials for sequencing

1 Write a set of numbered instructions telling the reader how to do a simple task. Choose something that is quick and easy! For example:

- making a cup of tea
- making a snack
- brushing your teeth

Adverbials of Sequence Bank

firstly	secondly	then
afterwards	next	later
finally		

2 Now rewrite your instructions without using numbers. Instead, use an adverbial of sequence in each step of your instructions to make the sequence clear. Use the **Adverbials of Sequence Bank** to help you.

Remember

Adverbials of number usually come at the beginning of a sentence. Fronted adverbials are always followed by a comma. For example:

First, take two pieces of bread.

3 Look at both of the sets of instructions you have written. Which do you think is clearer and easier to understand? Write **one or two** sentences explaining your answer.

Activity 4: Writing an instruction text

Look carefully at this map. It shows the location of buried treasure on a remote island, which is marked with a red 'x'.

1 Write a set of instructions telling the reader how to find the treasure on this island. In your instructions, you should include:
- an introduction explaining why someone may want to follow your instructions
- a list of things the reader will need in order to survive the journey and reach the treasure
- instructions for the reader to follow in order to find the treasure
- any warnings that will keep the reader safe on their journey.

This section links to pages 214–217 of the Workbook.

Section 3
Organising information

In this section, you will explore how information can be structured.

▼ **Read the information text below and then answer the questions that follow it.**

The Dodo

1 Near the end of the 16th century, Dutch sailors landed on the island of Mauritius. They found several species of birds and animals that they had never seen before. Perhaps the most famous of these creatures is the dodo – most famous because it was driven to extinction and now remembered in the saying 'as dead as a dodo'.

2 It was thought for a long time that humans hunted the dodo for food – and hunted it to extinction. However, the rubbish pits used by those early settlers in Mauritius were excavated in 2013. Several animal bones were found – but not a single dodo bone. Indeed, accounts from the time describe how unpleasant the meat of the dodo tasted.

3 It is now thought that the dodo was not destroyed by humans, but by the creatures that humans brought to Mauritius. The animals the sailors introduced to the island, along with uninvited rats from their ships, ate the dodo's eggs and destroyed their habitat. Less than 100 years after the arrival of the Dutch sailors, the dodo was extinct.

4 There is little we can say with certainty about the dodo. It was a large, flightless bird related to the pigeon. It was around a metre (3 feet 3 inches) tall with small wings. Other than this, we cannot be sure what the dodo looked like. There are, of course, no photographs from that time and paintings are unreliable as they were almost certainly painted from written descriptions, dead birds that had been inexpertly stuffed or other paintings. European artists were far more interested in making exotic creatures look interesting and colourful than in accuracy!

5 No complete example of the bird's body has survived. There was a stuffed dodo in a museum in Oxford, England, but it was not properly preserved. All but the head and a foot had to be thrown away in the 18th century. The British Museum had a dodo foot, but lost it in the early 20th century. There is a dodo skull in Copenhagen and part of a beak in Prague. Some dodo bones found in the 19th century have been used to create complete skeletons, but the bones are not all from the same bird.

6 This is all that remains of the dodo – the first and most famous extinction known to have been caused by the ignorance of humans.

Activity 1: Finding information

1 Look at the text on page 228 to find information about the Dutch sailors that went to Mauritius.
a) When did they arrive?   b) What did they find?   c) What was with them?

2 Look at the text to find information about the dodo.
a) What is known about the dodo's appearance?
b) What is **not** known about the dodo's appearance?

3 Look at the text to find information about the dodo's extinction.
a) When did it happen?   b) How did it happen?   c) Why did it happen?

Remember

You can scan for key words or phrases in the topics you are researching. For example, you could scan the text for these words:

Dutch | dodo | extinct

Activity 2: Structuring information

Information texts are organised in paragraphs. Each paragraph focuses on one aspect of the topic.

1 Look carefully at each of the six paragraphs in the text on page 228.
a) Which paragraph(s) give the reader a summary to introduce the text?
b) Which paragraph(s) explain theories about extinction?
c) Which paragraph(s) explain what we know about the dodo?
d) Which paragraph(s) explain what is left of the dodo today?

2 Sometimes writers use subheadings to guide the reader. They signal what information you will find in each paragraph or group of paragraphs.

What subheadings could be used to guide the reader through the text about the dodo? You could choose some of the ideas below, or use your own ideas.

Introduction	Finding the dodo	Meet the dodo	Eating dodos	How did the dodo become extinct?
Extinction!	What happened to the dodo?	What we know	All that remains	The dodo's legacy

Activity 3: Information and intention

The writer's main intention in an information text is to give the reader information. However, the writer may also intend to create other responses to increase engagement.

1 Look at the following pieces of information from the text on page 228.

a) Near the end of the 16th century, Dutch sailors landed on the island of Mauritius. They found several species of birds and animals that they had never seen before.

b) The animals the sailors introduced to the island, along with uninvited rats from their ships, ate the dodo's eggs and destroyed their habitat.

c) Less than 100 years after the arrival of the Dutch sailors, the dodo was extinct.

d) This is all that remains of the dodo – the first and most famous extinction known to have been caused by the ignorance of humans.

What is your response to each piece of information? Write **one** sentence for each, explaining your ideas. You could choose from the suggestions below, or use your own ideas.

| **Shock** This piece of information was an unpleasant surprise. | **Anger** This piece of information upsets and annoys me. | **Curiosity** I want to find out more about this topic. | **Interest** This is a surprising fact. |

Skills Boost: Chronological and non-chronological structures

If a text is in chronological order, it describes events in the order they happened. Sometimes writers use a non-chronological structure for effect.

1 Put the following descriptions into chronological order. Some of them may be of things that occurred at the same time.

A A few dodo bones and incomplete skeletons survive today.

B Dodos were extinct by the end of the 17th century.

C Dodos were large, flightless birds found only on Mauritius.

D Mauritius was uninhabited until the end of the 16th century.

E Mauritius was home to a variety of flightless birds and large reptiles.

F Dutch sailors created a settlement on Mauritius at the end of the 16th century.

2 a) Are the events described in the text on page 228 in chronological order?

b) Which is the most effective order? Would a different order be more interesting? Write one or two sentences to explain your ideas.

Activity 4: Writing an information text

Look at the following fact-file about another extinct species.

Fact file: The western black rhino
- It is believed that the last western black rhino died in 2006.
- They were declared officially extinct in 2011.
- Poachers illegally hunted them for their horns.
- Their very poor sense of sight made them vulnerable to hunters.
- They were unable to see anything more than 30 m away.
- They had excellent senses of smell and hearing.
- They could run as fast as 55 km/h.
- They were actually dark grey in colour, not black.
- They could be up to 1.6 m tall at the shoulder.
- They could weigh up to 1.5 tonnes.
- They are believed to have survived for 7–8 million years.
- They lived mainly in Cameroon, in Africa.
- Three other species of black rhino survive, but are critically endangered.
- The estimated population of western black rhinos was:
  - 1 million in 1900
  - 135 in 1980
  - 10 in 1997
  - 0 in 2011.

Plan

1. Think about how you could use the information in the fact-file to write an information text about the western black rhino. Which information could you put under each of these subheadings? Copy the table below and note relevant facts under each heading.

Appearance	Strengths and weaknesses	History	Extinction

2. Look at your notes. In what order could you write these four paragraphs?

Write

3. Use your notes to write **four** paragraphs of information about the western black rhino.

This section links to pages 218–221 of the Workbook.

Section 4
Choosing precise vocabulary

In this section, you will focus on selecting vocabulary to convey information as clearly and precisely as possible.

▼ **Read the instruction text below and then answer the questions that follow it.**

Learn to juggle

Juggling with one ball

1
- Throw the ball from your right hand to your left hand. Try to throw the ball in a smooth arc just above your eye level.
- Throw it back again in the same arc, and catch it in your right hand.
- Repeat. When you can do this ten times without dropping the ball, try moving on to the next step.

Juggling with two balls

5
- Take a ball in each hand. Throw the ball in your right hand to your left hand. Throw the ball in a smooth arc to a height just above your eye-level.
- When the first ball reaches eye-level, throw the ball in your left hand to your right hand in a similar arc.
- Repeat. When you can do this ten times without dropping the ball, try moving
10 onto the next step.

Juggling with three balls

- Hold two balls in your right hand – Ball 1 and Ball 3. Hold one ball in your left hand – Ball 2. Throw Ball 1 from your right hand in an arc to your left hand.
- When Ball 1 reaches eye level, throw Ball 2 from your left hand to your right hand in a similar arc.
15
- When Ball 2 is at eye level, throw Ball 3 from your right hand to your left hand in a similar arc – and catch Ball 1 in your left hand.
- Catch Ball 2 in your right hand and Ball 3 in your left hand.
- Repeat. You're juggling!
- Now all you need to do is practise, practise, practise!

Activity 1: Informing and describing

Writing to inform and to describe are different. Descriptive writing contains lots of descriptive vocabulary, which helps to create a picture in the reader's mind. Information writing should have just enough description to make the information clear for the reader.

1 Write down any adjectives and adverbs that appear in these descriptive sentences:

The young juggler smiled broadly as the small, multi-coloured balls flew quickly around and around in a wild blur before her twinkling blue eyes.

> **Remember**
>
> An **adjective** adds information to a noun:
> *I juggled using <u>small</u> balls.*
> An **adverb** adds information to a verb or adjective: *I <u>gradually</u> improved my skills.*

2 Compare this pair of instructions. The one on the left is taken from the text on page 232.

> Throw the ball from your right hand to your left hand. Try to throw the ball in a smooth arc just above your eye level.

Throw the ball from hand to hand in an arc.

a) Which instruction is clearer?
b) Write down **three** adjectives or adverbs that appear in the instruction from the text.
c) Why do you think the writer chose to use these adjectives or adverbs?
d) Would any of the adjectives or adverbs below help to make the instructions any clearer? Why is this? Write **one or two** sentences to explain your ideas.

carefully | gently | immediately | skilfully | quickly | small | tiny | beautiful | round

Activity 2: Comparing formal and informal registers

Instructions are often written in a formal register. This makes them sound reliable and trustworthy. However, sometimes the writer uses informal sentences to make the text sound friendly and helpful.

1 Compare these pairs of instructions.

A   Repeat. You're juggling!   B Perform all these steps a number of times. This is the first stage in developing juggling skills.

A   Now all you need to do is practise, practise, practise!   B The next stage is to practise frequently in order to improve.

a) Which instructions sound more friendly and helpful?
b) How has a more friendly, helpful tone been created in these instructions?

Grammar Boost: Tense and person

Pronouns and verbs give information about who is doing what, and when it happened.

Different tenses include:

simple past	past continuous	present perfect	simple present	present continuous	future
I ran	I was running	I have run	I run	I am running	I will run

Different persons include:

1st person singular	2nd person singular	3rd person singular	1st person plural	2nd person plural	3rd person plural
I	you	he | she | it	we	you	they

1 In which tense and person are these sentences written?

    a) She was eating her dinner.   *Past continuous, third person singular*

    b) We often walk to school.

    c) They will win the match.

    d) He has slept for hours and hours.

    e) I am learning the piano.

    f) You learned how to juggle.

2 In which tense and person are instructions usually written?

Activity 3: Keeping it clear and simple

Effective instructions are written in short sentences, using clear, simple language.

1 Compare this pair of instructions. The one on the left is taken from the text on page 232.

> Throw the ball from your right hand to your left hand. Try to throw the ball in a smooth arc just above your eye level.

> Use your right hand in order to throw the ball from your right hand into the air, so that the ball travels in a smooth and rounded arc to a height just above your eye level and then, when the ball falls, use your left hand to catch it.

The second instruction contains unnecessary details. Note down **two** of them and explain why each detail is unnecessary.

2 Now look at this instruction from a text about washing your hands.

> Firstly, you should go to the sink and turn on the tap so that water is pouring from it. You must position both your left hand and your right hand under the tap in the running stream of water so that both hands become wet.

Rewrite the instruction, removing as much unnecessary detail as you can.

Activity 4: Writing clearly and precisely

Look at the following set of instructions about washing your hands.

How to wash your hands

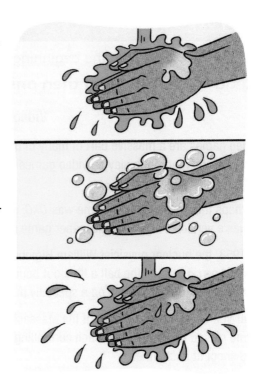

1   Firstly, you should go to the sink and turn on the tap so that water is pouring from it. You must position both your left hand and your right hand under the tap in the running stream of water so that both hands become wet.

2   Next, you need to take a bar of soap in one hand and rub soap on your other hand until you have created a rich, foamy lather.

3   Then, you should rub the rich, foamy lather over your left hand using your right hand. After this, you should rub the rich, foamy lather over your right hand using your left hand. You need to repeat this action until your hands are clean.

4   Next, you should hold both your hands under the tap in the running stream of water, rubbing your hands together until all the rich, foamy lather has been rinsed off.

5   Finally, you need to get a towel and rub it against the skin of both hands until they are dry. Afterwards, you should hang up the towel to dry.

Now you have washed and dried your hands, making them lovely and clean.

1 Which of the following improvements would you make to improve the text above?

   A Add more descriptive vocabulary.

   B Remove some descriptive vocabulary.

   C Add more detail.

   D Remove unnecessary detail.

   E Use imperative verbs to make the instructions shorter, simpler and clearer.

   F Either number each instruction or use adverbs of number (not both).

   G Make the final instruction more informal and friendly.

2 Rewrite the text above, making as many improvements as you can.

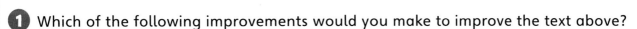

This section links to pages 222–225 of the Workbook.

Section 5
Writing clearly

In this section, you will focus on structuring sentences to convey information as clearly and precisely as possible.

This extract is taken from the beginning of a book about video games.

▼ Read the extract and then answer the questions that follow it.

Video games – The early years

1 Video games are a massive part of many of our lives. Research suggests that young people in some parts of the world spend more time playing video games than watching television or playing sport. But where did our love of video games begin?

Perhaps the first ever video game was *OXO*, created by British professor A S Douglas at the University of Cambridge.
5 It was a version of the pen-and-paper game noughts and crosses, also known as tic-tac-toe.

In 1958, the nuclear physicist William Higinbotham created a game called *Tennis for Two*. The screen was an **oscilloscope** and the ball a little dot bouncing across it. The ball was hit by pressing a button and its angle controlled by turning a knob on a specially built controller.

Four years later, Steve Russell of the Massachusetts Institute of Technology created *Spacewar!* This was a battle
10 game played by two players, each controlling a spaceship circling a planet. The spaceships could turn, accelerate and shoot at each other.

Spacewar! was extremely popular with students at universities around the world but it could only be played on a PDP-1 computer. The PDP-1 was the size of a car and cost hundreds of thousands of dollars. It was, therefore, only available to universities and large companies. By the 1970s, computer technology had advanced. Computers were
15 becoming much smaller and much less expensive.

In 1968, Ralph Baer and a team of developers began working on the first home console system for video games. It was first known as The Brown Box, but was later renamed The Odyssey. It featured 12 built-in games with ten more available on circuit cards that could be plugged into the box. Each game consisted of three dots and one line which behaved in different ways depending on the game being played. For example, in a version of table tennis, two
20 players were represented by two dots which could be used to bat the third dot back and forth across the line.

The Odyssey was not a great success, but it inspired Atari's massively successful home games console which sold in its millions in the late 1970s. This was the first time that many people had played a video game in
25 their home – and it would not be long before Mario the Plumber made his first appearance.

Key vocabulary

oscilloscope: display screen showing electronic signals in the form of lines

Activity 1: Checking understanding

1. Name the **three** earliest computer games that feature in the extract on page 236.

2. Using your own words, write **one or two** sentences explaining what The Odyssey was.

3. Identify **two** similarities between *Tennis for Two* and the games that could be played on The Odyssey.

4. Which of the games described in the extract would you most like to play? Write **one or two** sentences to explain your choice.

Activity 2: Identifying sentence structures

Writers often use shorter single-clause sentences in information texts, to make their meaning as clear as possible. Look at the following sentences from one paragraph of the extract.

A   *Spacewar!* was extremely popular with students at universities around the world but it could only be played on a PDP-1 computer.

B   The PDP-1 was the size of a car and cost hundreds of thousands of dollars.

C   It was, therefore, only available to universities and large companies.

D   By the 1970s, computer technology had advanced.

E   Computers were becoming much smaller and much less expensive.

1. Three of the sentences are single-clause sentences: they each contain only one piece of information, including only one verb.
   a) Which **three** sentences are single-clause sentences?
   b) Which is the verb in each of these sentences?

> **Remember**
>
> A verb can be one word (*I ate a cake*), two words (*I was eating a cake*) or three words (*I have been eating a cake*).

2. Two of the sentences are multi-clause sentences. Each of them contains two pieces of information including two verbs, linked together with a conjunction.
   a) Which **two** sentences are multi-clause sentences?
   b) Which are the verbs in each of these sentences?
   c) Which conjunctions has the writer used to link the clauses in each of these sentences? Use the **Conjunction Bank** to help you.

> **Conjunction Bank**
>
> | and | because | when | although | as |
> | until | during | but | since | before |
> | after | if | where | so | while |

Grammar Boost: Subject-verb sentence openings

Sentences in information texts often begin with a pronoun, noun or noun phrase followed by a verb. This is sometimes called a subject-verb sentence opening.

1 Reorganise each group of words to form sentences with subject-verb openings. Check that each of your answers makes sense and is punctuated correctly.

    a) OXO called was computer game the first

    b) invented in the 1940s was it

    c) set in space computer games old many were

    d) games computer a lot changed have since then

    e) for a long time they popular very will be

Activity 3: Experimenting with sentence structure

1 Look again at the following multi-clause sentences from the text on page 236.

> *Spacewar!* was extremely popular with students at universities around the world but it could only be played on a PDP-1 computer.

> The PDP-1 was the size of a car and cost hundreds of thousands of dollars.

    a) Rewrite each of the multi-clause sentences as **two** separate single-clause sentences. Make sure each one is punctuated correctly.

    b) Is the information in the sentences you have written clearer or less clear than the information in the multi-clause sentences? Why is this? Write **one or two** sentences to explain your ideas.

2 Look again at the following single-clause sentences.

> It was, therefore, only available to universities and large companies.

> By the 1970s, computer technology had advanced.

> Computers were becoming much smaller and much less expensive.

    a) Link all three sentences to create **one** longer sentence using different conjunctions.

    b) Is the information in the sentence you have written clearer or less clear than the information in the three single-clause sentences? Why is this? Write **one or two** sentences to explain your ideas.

3 Look at the following sentences. They all give information about the game *Spacewar!*

It was created in 1962. | It was a two-player game. | Each player controlled
a spaceship. | Each player shot at the other player's spaceship. | It could only
be played on a PDP-1 computer. | It was a very popular game.

Use **all** these pieces of information to write no more than **four** sentences about
Spacewar! You will have to link some pieces of information in multi-clause
sentences using conjunctions. Try to make your writing as clear as possible.

Activity 4: Writing clearly and precisely

You are going to write a short information text about a game or a sport.

Plan
1 Decide which game or sport will be your subject.

Write
2 Write **five** single-clause sentences about your chosen game or sport. They could be about:
- its purpose
- the rules
- the people who play it
- its history.

Experiment
3 Try joining **two** of your sentences using a conjunction, to create a multi-clause sentence. Is the information in this sentence clearer or less clear?

4 Try joining another **two** or all **three** of your remaining sentences using a conjunction, to create a multi-clause sentence. Is the information in this sentence clearer or less clear?

5 Write a final draft of your text, making the information as clear as possible. You could use:
- single-clause sentences
- multi-clause sentences
- a combination of both.

This section links to pages 226–227 of the Workbook.

Section 6
Assessment

In this section, you will answer questions on an informative article and write a short article to assess your progress in the unit so far.

This article is written by George McGavin, a British scientist and television presenter.

▼ **Read the article and then answer the questions that follow it.**

Why I love insects

1 As far back as I can remember, I've been fascinated by the natural world. Indeed, I cannot imagine being that passionate about anything else.

The very first memory I have is of a natural history programme showing two garden spiders. I sat in front of our small black-and-white television set 5 transfixed. I was totally hooked. Ever since, my mind has been drawn to the little lives of tiny creatures.

My degree in **zoology**[1] at Edinburgh University really opened my eyes to the importance of our planet's smaller species. On a field trip to the wilds of Argyllshire, my classmates only got excited about the furry and feathery creatures we encountered and seemed to 10 ignore the millions of wood ants that scurried about gathering food to feed their young.

After a PhD in **entomology**[2] at Imperial College and a quarter of a century in my dream job at the Oxford University Museum of Natural History, where I looked after one of the world's oldest and biggest scientific insect collections, I left for the more risky occupation of being a television presenter.

The last few years have been wonderful. I've been to the ends of the Earth 15 to find and film animals of all kinds. I've witnessed a chimpanzee hunting party in Uganda at very close quarters. I've radio-tagged vampire bats in Chile and come face-to-face with venomous snakes in the Amazon.

But what really excites me still are the much smaller animals, the ones that make all **ecosystems**[3] tick. Crawling into the rotten trunk of a 20 fallen rainforest tree to discover a **dank**[4], hidden world populated by **multitudes**[5] of insects and spiders, and marvelling at the sheer volume and variety of moths attracted to an **ultraviolet light**[6] bulb high up on an extinct volcano in Papua New Guinea are both experiences I'll never forget.

Most of the animal species on Earth eat insects – they are the food of the world. Insects have endured for hundreds of millions of years. They have survived numerous global upheavals and catastrophes and they will continue to be a 25 major part of the Earth's **fauna**[7] for many more **millennia**[8].

Key vocabulary

zoology[1]: the study of animals
entomology[2]: the study of insects
ecosystems[3]: linked systems of animals and plants
dank[4]: damp and dark
multitudes[5]: great numbers

ultraviolet light[6]: light with a short wavelength, not visible to humans
fauna[7]: animal life
millennia[8]: thousands of years

Activity 1: Reading

1 Which of the following sentences best explains the writer's intention in the first paragraph of the article on page 240?
  A to explain how much he loves insects
  B to emphasise how interested he is in the natural world
  C to give background information about his childhood
  D to surprise the reader

2 a) Identify **two** words that clearly convey the writer's love of animals and insects.
  b) Identify a short, single-clause sentence that the writer uses to emphasise his love of insects.

3 The first five paragraphs of the article are structured in chronological order. Identify **three** things in these paragraphs that have happened in the writer's life, in the order they happened.

4 What tone and register has the writer used? What effect does this have? Write **one or two** sentences explaining your ideas.

5 In this article, the writer intends to explain how interesting and important insects are. In your opinion, how effectively has he achieved this? Why is that? Write **one or two** sentences explaining your ideas.

Activity 2: Writing

You have been asked to write an informative article for a school magazine, explaining about something you love. It could be a hobby, an activity, or a topic you find fascinating.

1 Write your article, using the heading 'Why I love _____'.

Before you start writing

- Think about why you love your chosen topic, and how you will explain this to the reader.
- Plan your writing by noting down all the information and ideas you could include.
- Think carefully about how you will organise the information and ideas into paragraphs.
- Consider some subheadings to help you organise your paragraphs and guide your reader.
- Think about what tone and register you will use to convey both your enthusiasm and your information.

As you write

- Use both single-clause and multi-clause sentences, and a variety of conjunctions.
- Check that your vocabulary and sentence structures convey information clearly.

When you have finished writing

- Check your writing for any spelling, grammar or punctuation mistakes.

This section links to pages 228–231 of the Workbook.

Section 7
Paragraphing information

In this section, you will explore how to structure paragraphs of information.

DO NOT READ the extract below! Go straight to Activity 1 and follow the instructions.

Fossils

1 Fossils are the imprints of long-lost creatures, usually the hard parts of them such as bones, shells or teeth. When these creatures die, usually their bodies rot or dissolve. But sometimes, as the mud in the ground or on the sea floor turns hard, the cells that make up their hard parts can be replaced by minerals, turning them to stone. Fossils are
5 wonderful for helping scientists understand what kinds of creatures once lived on the Earth. Expert fossil hunters are called palaeontologists.

Charles Doolittle Walcott was a palaeontologist. He was born in upstate New York, in the United States, in 1850. As a young
10 boy he found school quite boring. It wasn't that he had no interest in things, rather the opposite. He was so curious that he wanted to get outside and explore the world for himself – in particular, he liked to look for minerals, rocks, birds' eggs and fossils.

15 One day in 1909, a freak accident changed the rest of Walcott's life. The way some people tell it, he was walking high up in a remote part of the Canadian Rockies, and his horse slipped and lost a shoe. As the creature stumbled, its foot turned over a glistening rock. Walcott picked it up and saw a row of remarkable silvery fossils. These showed the perfectly preserved shapes of creatures dating back to a time known as the Cambrian period.

Remember how the land is always moving and changing? Well, it turned out that the mountainside Walcott
20 was standing on had been on the sea floor 505 million years ago. Way back then, something – maybe a mudslide – had killed these creatures and preserved them like a time capsule. Walcott's fossils are some of the oldest ever found. The place where he found them is known as the Burgess Shale, named after nearby Mount Burgess. Walcott returned to the site many times and eventually wrote a shelf of books about his finds.

25 And what a bizarre range of creatures they were! There was the strange-looking *Anomalocaris*. Possibly the biggest hunter of its day, it could grow up to a metre long. It used a pair of grasping arms to capture and hold its prey. Another was *Hallucigenia*. This worm-like beast walked on tentacle-like legs. It used the spines on its back to protect itself from being eaten by predators.

But nothing can prepare you for *Opabinia*. This oceanic oddbod had five eyes, a fan-like
30 tail for swimming and a long, grasping nose with a mouth on the end for feeding. There's nothing remotely like it alive today.

Activity 1: Skimming and understanding

The process of 'skim-reading' or 'skimming' involves looking at an extract very quickly to get a general idea of what it is about.

1 One way to **skim** an extract is to look at only the first sentence of each paragraph.
   a) Read only the first sentence of each paragraph in the extract on page 242. Write **one or two** sentences summing up what you think the extract is about.
   b) Again, refer to only the first sentence in each paragraph. Write a subheading for each paragraph, summing up what you believe the paragraph is about.
   c) Now read the whole extract carefully. As you read, check your subheadings. How accurate are they?

2 In information texts, each paragraph often contains a **topic sentence**. This sentence roughly sums up what information appears in the paragraph. It is often the first sentence of the paragraph, but not always. Was the first sentence of each paragraph in the extract its topic sentence? If not, which sentences were the topic sentences?

Activity 2: Responding to the extract

The extract on page 242 gives lots of details about Charles Doolittle Walcott. For example:

A Charles Doolittle Walcott was a palaeontologist.

B He was born in upstate New York, in the United States, in 1850.

C As a young boy he found school quite boring.

D He was so curious that he wanted to get outside and explore the world for himself –

E One day in 1909, a freak accident changed the rest of Walcott's life.

F Walcott returned to the site many times and eventually wrote a shelf of books about his finds.

1 What impression do the details above create of Walcott? Write **one or two** sentences to explain your ideas. You could use one or two of the adjectives below or use your own ideas.

   intelligent | lucky | hard-working | lazy | enthusiastic | inquisitive | adventurous

2 Which **one** of the details above gives you this impression most powerfully, and why? Write **one or two** sentences to explain your ideas.

3 Which **one** of the details above gives you the most important piece of information about Charles Doolittle Walcott, and why? Write **one or two** sentences to explain your ideas.

Grammar Boost: Using pronouns accurately

You can use a pronoun to refer back to a noun or noun phrase. The pronoun must 'agree' with the noun it represents, or the sentence will not make sense. For example:

Although penguins have wings, they cannot fly.

This pronoun refers back to this noun. Because the noun is plural, so is the pronoun that represents it.

1 The pronouns in these sentences do not agree with the nouns they represent. Correct them.

   a) *Anomalocaris* was huge. You could grow up to a metre long.

   b) Walcott found some fossils when they were walking in the Canadian Rockies.

   c) The fossils were the remains of strange-looking creatures. He had been hidden inside the rock for 505 million years.

   d) Fossils are fascinating because you are like time capsules.

   e) Walcott saw a glistening rock. It picked him up.

   f) Walcott loved exploring, but it disliked school because he was boring.

Activity 3: Structuring paragraphs

Remember, the topic sentence in each paragraph of an information text should roughly summarise what information appears in the paragraph. All the other sentences in the paragraph should add interesting detail or useful explanation.

1 Look at all of the sentences in the fourth paragraph of the extract on page 242.

   A   Remember how the land is always moving and changing?

   B   Well, it turned out that the mountainside Walcott was standing on had been on the sea floor 505 million years ago.

   C   Way back then, something — maybe a mudslide — had killed these creatures and preserved them like a time capsule.

   D   Walcott's fossils are some of the oldest ever found.

   E   The place where he found them is known as the Burgess Shale, named after nearby Mount Burgess.

   F   Walcott returned to the site many times and eventually wrote a shelf of books about his finds.

   a) If you had to make this paragraph shorter, which sentence would you remove? Choose the sentence that gives the least-important detail or explanation.

   b) Look at the remaining sentences in the paragraph. Choose another sentence that could be left out.

   c) Repeat this process, removing the least-important remaining sentence each time, until only **one** is left. Does the remaining sentence make an effective topic sentence for the paragraph? Write **one or two** sentences explaining your ideas.

Activity 4: Writing paragraphs

You are going to write two paragraphs about dinosaurs, using the notes below to help you.

Choose **two** topics from A–C.

Dinosaurs

A
- Some dinosaurs ate plants. Some dinosaurs ate meat. Some ate both.
- Fossils of more than 500 types of dinosaur have been found so far.
- The word 'dinosaur' means 'terrible lizard'.
- Dinosaurs lived from 220 million years ago to 65.5 million years ago.

B
- One of the largest dinosaurs was called Argentinosaurus.
- Argentinosaurus was successful because it was too big for other dinosaurs to attack.
- Argentinosaurus could grow up to 30 m in length.
- Argentinosaurus may have weighed 70 tonnes.

C
- Some dinosaurs survived by being able to move quickly.
- The name of one dinosaur, 'Ornithomimus', means 'bird-like'.
- Fossils suggest that Ornithomimus had feathers, and claws that looked like a bird's feet.
- Ornithomimus footprints suggest it could run at the same speed as an ostrich, up to around 40 miles per hour.

1 Write a subheading for each of the two topics you have chosen.

2 Look at the information about the first topic you have chosen.
   a) Choose **one** piece of information to use as a topic sentence.
   b) Choose **two** more details to add to your topic sentence.
   c) Use the information you have selected to write a paragraph about this first topic.

3 Repeat the steps in question 2 to write a paragraph about the second topic you have chosen.

This section links to pages 232–235 of the Workbook.

Section 8
Engaging the reader

In this section, you will explore ways to entertain and engage your reader while you inform them.

This extract is an informative article about the human brain.

▼ **Read the article below and then answer the questions that follow it.**

Look inside your head…

1 If you could look inside your head, the first and largest thing you would notice would be a large grey wrinkled lump about twice the size of your fist. It looks a bit like an old
5 cauliflower or a giant chewed up lump of chewing gum. This is your brain.

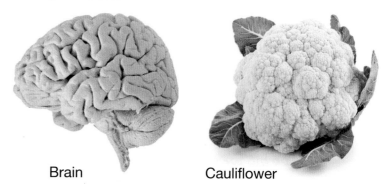

Brain   Cauliflower

All the information and experiences you get from outside your body travel through that lump: everything you see, hear, smell, feel and
10 taste; everything you think, and everything you do. Nerves from your senses deliver information to your brain to let you know what is going on outside your body. These signals travel at around 240 km/h. Your brain sends signals down your nerves to your muscles, telling them to move – so it keeps your heart beating, your lungs breathing and your eyes blinking. These signals move even faster – at around 320 km/h. Every day your brain sends more signals around your body than all the text
15 messages sent from every phone in the world.

Your brain might not look very busy, but it's astonishingly powerful – more powerful than the fastest supercomputer ever created. That's why it takes a lot of energy to keep it thinking and processing. About twenty per cent of your body's energy is used up by your brain.

There are some organs our bodies can survive
20 without. The brain is not one of them. That's why it is protected by your skull. It's also wrapped in three tough layers of tissue called meninges and floats in around 150 ml of liquid. This is called cerebrospinal fluid and it helps to absorb knocks and bumps and
25 stops your brain rattling against the inside of your skull as you move around.

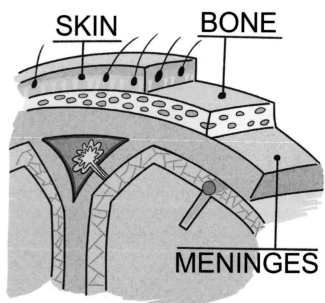

SKIN   BONE

MENINGES

Even with all that protection to keep it safe, your brain can still be damaged. And, unlike bones and skin, it cannot mend itself. That's why you should never
30 dive into water unless you know how deep it is – and always wear a helmet when you are skateboarding or riding a bicycle. Luckily, your brain is very clever and probably knows that already!

Activity 1: Engaging with the extract

Engaging the reader means grabbing and holding the reader's attention, making them want to start and continue reading what you have written.

1 **a)** How informative do you find the article on page 246? Write **one or two** sentences explaining your answer.

  b) Think about the content of the article, rather than how it is written. Identify **two** facts that you found particularly interesting.

2 **a)** How entertaining and engaging do you find the article? Write **one or two** sentences explaining your answer.

  b) Think about the way the article is written. Identify **two** sentences or phrases that you found particularly entertaining.

Activity 2: Exploring techniques for engagement

1 Think about some of the techniques the writer has used to make the article on page 246 informative and engaging:

| statistics | comparison | explanation | advice for readers | humour |

Look at the following sentences from the article.

A It looks a bit like an old cauliflower or a giant chewed up lump of chewing gum.

B These signals move even faster – at around 320 km/h. Every day your brain sends more signals around your body than all the text messages sent from every phone in the world.

C That's why you should never dive into water unless you know how deep it is – and always wear a helmet when you are skateboarding or riding a bicycle.

D Luckily, your brain is very clever and probably knows that already!

Which of the techniques does the writer use in each sentence? In each of your answers, give the name of the technique used and an example from the article. For example:

A   *The writer has engaged the reader with a comparison in this sentence.*
       The human brain is compared to a cauliflower.

2 Look at the structure of the article.
  a) Note down a brief summary of each paragraph.
  b) Note down the way the writer has used the engagement techniques throughout the article. Are they grouped together, or spread out?
  c) In your opinion, what effect does this structure have on the reader's engagement with the article?

Skills Boost: Using synonyms

Synonyms are words with similar meanings. For example:

good | excellent | fine | wonderful | marvellous | pleasant | nice

1 If you wanted to write an engaging information text about the human body, which of the following synonyms would you choose for your opening sentence?

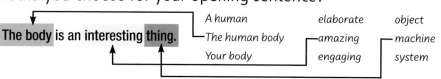

The body is an interesting thing.

A human	elaborate	object
The human body	amazing	machine
Your body	engaging	system

2 Note down as many synonyms as you can for the following words.
   a) big   **b)** scary   **c)** move   **d)** quickly

3 Rewrite the following sentence, using synonyms to make it clearer or more engaging. You could use the synonyms you noted for question 2, or think of others.

> *Tyrannosaurus rex was a big, scary dinosaur but it could not move very quickly.*

Activity 3: Identifying engaging vocabulary

Writers select vocabulary to engage their readers. Look at these sentences taken from the extract on page 246.

A If you could look inside your head, the first and largest thing you would notice would be a large grey wrinkled lump about twice the size of your fist.

B Your brain might not look very busy, but it's astonishingly powerful – more powerful than the fastest supercomputer ever created.

C This is called cerebrospinal fluid and it helps to absorb knocks and bumps and stops your brain rattling against the inside of your skull as you move around.

Remember

If something is 'sensory', it is related to one or more of the senses: sight, sound, taste, smell and touch.

1 Which vocabulary choices in these sentences would you match with the following comments?

   a) *This kind of technical, scientific language makes the information sound reliable and accurate.*

   b) *This kind of sensory language helps to create a vivid description.*

   c) *This language choice creates a funny and surprising image that engages the reader.*

   d) *This powerful language choice emphasises the point the writer wants to make.*

Activity 4: Writing an engaging text

You are going to write two engaging, informative paragraphs of a text about the human heart. Look at the information below.

Adult human beings have:
- one heart
- around 4.5–5 litres of blood in their bodies
- around 60,000 miles of veins and arteries – enough to go twice around the world.

The human heart:
- is about the same size as your fist
- is protected by your rib cage
- has four chambers: the left atrium, right atrium, left ventricle and right ventricle
- beats approximately 100,000 times a day on average
- beats more than 3 billion times in the average lifetime
- is like a big pump made of muscles that pushes blood around the body
- moves approximately 9,000 litres of blood around the body every day
- moves approximately 250 million litres of blood around the body in the average lifetime, which is the equivalent of about 100 Olympic-sized swimming pools
- moves blood through veins and arteries, which are like a huge network of one-way streets
- should be kept healthy, experts say, with 60 minutes of exercise every day.

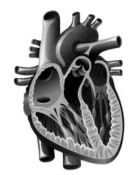

---

1 **a)** Look at the notes above and write down facts for a short paragraph that gives the reader information about **what** and **where** the heart is. You should include the following points:
- **two or three** facts
- **one or two** statistics
- a comparison
- some technical, scientific language.

> **Remember**
> Choose information that will engage the reader.

b) Use the information you have noted to write your first paragraph, thinking carefully about how you will order it to sustain engagement.

2 **a)** Look at the notes above and note down facts for a short paragraph that gives the reader information about what the heart **does**. You should include the following points:
- **two or three** facts
- **one or two** statistics
- a comparison
- some technical, scientific language.

b) Use the information you have noted to write your second paragraph, thinking carefully about how you will order it to sustain engagement.

This section links to pages 236–239 of the Workbook.

Section 9
Reaching conclusions

In this section, you will explore ways in which you can begin and end information texts.

This is an article giving information about the artist, Frida Kahlo.

▼ Read the article below and then answer the questions that follow it.

Frida Kahlo

1 Frida Kahlo was an artist like no other.

2 Frida was born in Mexico in 1907. At the age of six, she contracted a disease called polio, which damaged her right leg. She had to spend nine months in bed. Her father encouraged her to play lots of sport, thinking it would help her to recover. She played football, went swimming and even did some wrestling, which was very unusual for girls at that time!

3 When she was eighteen, Frida was badly hurt in a traffic accident. She had hoped to become a doctor, but the accident ended that dream. Frida spent months in bed recovering from her injuries. She had always loved to paint and draw, and she spent those months painting. Her parents got her a special easel that she could rest on her lap and they hung a mirror over her bed so that she could see and paint herself. Although she was eventually able to walk again, she spent the rest of her life in pain.

4 Frida used her art to show her thoughts and feelings: about the way that society expected women to look and to behave, about her inability to have children and about her disability. In her lifetime, she produced 143 paintings. 55 of them were self-portraits.

5 Inspired by the bright colours and vibrant patterns of traditional Mexican art, Frida painted herself in traditional clothing and jewellery, and surrounded by nature. She wanted to show her heritage, her true feelings and her true self. This is why her heavy eyebrows and facial hair are always exaggerated in her self-portraits.

6 Today, images from Frida's artwork appear on posters, greetings cards, calendars and even dolls. Her house in Mexico is a museum dedicated to her life and work. More than 25,000 people visit it every month.

I PAINT MY OWN REALITY. THE ONLY THING I KNOW IS THAT I PAINT BECAUSE I NEED TO, AND I PAINT WHATEVER PASSES THROUGH MY HEAD.

Punctuation Boost: Proofreading full stops

One of the most important things to check when proofreading is that you have put punctuation at the end of each sentence: a full stop, a question mark or an exclamation mark. It is very difficult to understand writing when these are missing.

1 Look at the following short extract from a biography of Albert Einstein. There are **seven** sentences in it, but all the full stops are missing. Write out the extract, adding full stops and capital letters where needed.

Albert Einstein was one of the greatest scientists and thinkers that has ever lived he was born in Germany in 1879 Albert learned a lot about science and electronics from his father, who ran an electronics company Albert was always very good at maths and physics by the age of 14, he had taught himself algebra, geometry, and calculus when Albert was 15, his family moved to Italy because his father's company had failed Albert did not do well at school in Italy

Activity 1: Exploring the opening of the article

Look carefully at the first two paragraphs of the article on page 250.

1 **a)** In your own words, what is the writer's view of Frida Kahlo?
    b) What sentence or sentences in the article show this view?

2 Why has the writer focused on Frida Kahlo's early life at the beginning of the article?

3 Look at the following suggestions of information the writer could have chosen to include at the beginning of the article.

when and where Frida was born	information about Frida's family	information about Frida's education and qualifications
dramatic events in Frida's life	Frida's successes and failures	Frida's unique and surprising qualities

    a) Which of the suggestions above has the writer chosen to include in the first and second paragraphs?
    b) In your opinion, why has the writer chosen some of these pieces of information, but not others? Write **one or two** sentences explaining your ideas.

4 Paragraph 2 of the article is just 66 words long.
    a) Which information would you include in a 66-word biography of your life so far? Note down **four** ideas.
    b) Write the opening **two or three** sentences of your **autobiography**, ensuring this paragraph is no more than **66** words long.

> **Remember**
>
> An autobiography is simply a biography someone writes about their own life. It is written in the first person.

Activity 2: Exploring the middle and ending of the article

1 Look at paragraphs 3, 4 and 5 of the article on page 250. Which paragraph focuses on each of the following topics?

a) why Frida painted   **b)** what Frida painted   **c)** how Frida became an artist

2 In just **five** words, summarise the focus of paragraphs 3, 4 and 5. Write your answer in the form of a subheading.

3 Look at the final paragraph of the article below, which contains just three sentences. What impression does each sentence create of Frida Kahlo and her work? Write a sentence about each one.

A Today, images from Frida's artwork appear on posters, greeting cards, calendars and even dolls.

B Her house in Mexico is a museum dedicated to her life and work.

C More than 25,000 people visit it every month.

Activity 3: Structuring a biography

1 Complete the sentences below, explaining how the writer has structured the article.

a) At the beginning of the article, the writer gives details of …

b) In the middle, the writer focuses on …

c) At the end of the article, the writer …

2 The following notes are for a student's plan for a biography text about the scientist Marie Curie. How would you sequence the paragraphs?

A a paragraph about her childhood

B a paragraph about how she and her husband discovered two new chemical elements and the concept of radioactivity

C a paragraph about how her discoveries changed the world and are still used today

D a paragraph about how she and her husband won two Nobel prizes for their discoveries

E a paragraph about her pioneering work in the treatment of cancer after her husband's death

Activity 4: Writing an autobiography

You are going to write an autobiographical article about your future self.

Imagine

Imagine yourself at the age of 90. You have lived an amazing life. You have been very successful and are extremely well known for your achievements.

1 What did you become when you finished your education? You could choose one of the suggestions below or use your own ideas.

a superb scientist	an extraordinary explorer	an incredible inventor	a brilliant businessperson
a wonderful writer	an amazing artist	a successful sportsperson	a marvellous musician

Structure

2 Now imagine that you have been asked to write an article about your amazing life.

You will need to include:
- a paragraph or two about your work and greatest achievements
- a paragraph explaining how you changed the world, or how admired and respected you are
- a paragraph about your childhood.

In what order will you structure your paragraphs?

Plan

3 Now start gathering the information you will use in each paragraph of the article.
a) Write down **three or four** key pieces of information you could include in the paragraph about your childhood.
b) Write down **four or five** pieces of information you will include in the paragraph or two about your greatest achievements.
c) In what ways have you changed the world? How can you show the reader that your are admired and respected? Write down **two or three** ideas about the vocabulary you will use.

Write

4 Write the article, using the structure and ideas you have planned. Aim to write around **200** words.

Remember
You are writing about your own life, so you will need to write in the first person.

This section links to pages 240–243 of the Workbook.

Section 10
Planning a lesson

In this section, you will explore ways of planning an informative speech.

Activity 1: Choosing your subject

In the assessment at the end of this unit, you will write a speech in which you teach listeners about either a skill you have or a topic that interests you.

Remember

You need to be interested in the topic or skill you are going to teach – and you need to choose something that you think will interest your audience of learners, too.

1 Look at the suggestions below.

Teaching a skill

How to make something	How to play a sport or a musical instrument	How to learn something new
Knitting Baking a cake Customising clothes	Playing football Practising judo Playing the guitar	Speaking a foreign language Drawing Programming a computer

Teaching a topic

A person	An invention	A scientific subject
A famous actor A famous sports person A figure in history	The internet The printing press The television	The solar system Carnivorous plants Weather

A historical event	An animal	A hobby
The first moon landing The Roman empire The First World War	Penguins Pandas Snakes	Dancing Coin collecting Gardening

a) If you were going to use **one** of these ideas, which would you choose, and why?

b) Which **one or two** would you definitely not choose, and why?

2 Now think about your own ideas.

a) Note down **two or three topics** you might want to teach.

b) Note down **two or three skills** you might want to teach.

Activity 2: Preparing to plan

When you have decided the topic or skill you are going to teach, you need to start gathering the content of your lesson – all the different things you want to include.

Ask yourself:

What will learners need to know?

What will they want to know?

Look at the three model plans below.

How to play the guitar

- The history of the guitar
- How the guitar works
- How a guitar is made
- How to read music
- What the left hand does
- What the right hand does
- Different types of guitar music

Genghis Khan

- Where and when he was born
- His family
- How he came to rule Mongolia
- How he built the great Mongol empire
- The brutality of his army in battle
- How he developed the economy in Mongolia
- How he died

The Black Death

- How many millions of people died
- Where and when it started
- How long it lasted
- How the disease was spread
- How far it spread
- The signs and symptoms of the disease
- The bacteria that caused the disease

1 Choose any **one** of the plans.
   a) Which of the ideas on the plan do you think learners would **need** to know? Write a sentence to explain your choice.
   b) Which of the ideas do you think learners would **want** to know? Write a sentence to explain your choice.
   c) Which of the ideas do you think learners would neither want nor need to know? Write a sentence to explain your choice.

Skills Boost: Ways of planning

There are different ways of noting and organising your ideas before you start writing. You could list them beneath a heading, as shown below. Alternatively, you could arrange them in a spider diagram around a heading, as shown below.

List

Gorillas
- What gorillas are
- Where they live
- What they eat
- Statistics: height and weight
- Intelligence
- Similarities to humans
- Differences from humans
- How endangered they are

Spidergram

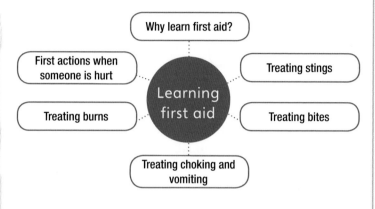

Why learn first aid?

First actions when someone is hurt

Treating stings

Learning first aid

Treating burns

Treating bites

Treating choking and vomiting

1 Look at all the points in the list in the first example.
   a) Use subheadings to organise the points into **three or four** paragraphs.
   b) In what order would you sequence these paragraphs? Number them.

Paragraph 1:
Paragraph 2:
Paragraph 3:

2 Look at all the points on the spidergram in the second example.
   a) Use subheadings to organise the points into **three or four** paragraphs.
   b) In what order would you sequence these paragraphs? Number them.

Paragraph 1:
Paragraph 2:
Paragraph 3:

3 Which did you find easier to organise and sequence – the list or the spidergram?

4 Which will you use when you plan your speech – the list or the spidergram?

Activity 3: Sequencing

How you sequence the information in your speech depends on the subject you have chosen.

1 Look at the possible subjects listed below.

| Climate change | The life of Mahatma Gandhi | Black holes in space | How to create a cartoon | The Olympic Games | chocolate |

Each of these topics should be structured:
- as a series of clear instructions **or**
- in chronological order **or**
- in paragraphs on different aspects of the subject.

a) Which of the subjects would be structured as a series of instructions?

b) Which of the subjects would be structured in chronological order?

c) Which of the subjects would be structured in paragraphs on different aspects?

Remember

Putting information in chronological order means structuring events in the order they happened.

Activity 4: Starting to plan

1 Look at the different ideas for a subject you noted in Activity 1. Choose the subject you think you will be able to make the most informative and engaging for your audience.

2 Write notes to remind you of the things you already know about your subject.

3 a) Identify what things you might want to include in your speech. You could use some of the ideas below to help you.

| How is it done? | Why do they do that? | What is its history? | Where does this happen? |

| What are the reasons behind this? | What ingredients or equipment is needed? | What facts and figures are there? | What makes this so interesting? |

b) What else may learners need or want to know? Note down what new information you could find out.

This section links to pages 244–245 of the Workbook.

Section 11
Assessment

In this section, you will write an informative speech.

Activity 1: Planning

In this assessment, you will write a speech in which you teach listeners about either a skill you have or a topic that interests you.

1 Write down the topic or skill you have chosen as the subject of your speech.

2 Look at all the ideas and information you have gathered. Write **four or five** subheadings you will use to organise your speech.

- These could be the steps your listeners will need to follow as they learn the skill you are teaching them. For example:

| Juggling with one ball | Juggling with two balls | Juggling with three balls |

- Alternatively, they could be the different topics you will cover in each paragraph of your speech. For example:

| Frida's childhood | Frida's accident | Frida's art |

| What is a fossil? | Who was Charles Walcott? |

| How did he find the fossils? |

3 Under each subheading, note all the ideas and information you want to include in that section of your speech.

4 Number the subheadings to show the sequence in which you will use them.

5 Carefully, review your plan. You need to be sure that you have chosen the best information and structured it in the best way. Ask yourself:
- Will my speech be clear and easy to understand?
- Will it be interesting and engaging?

Activity 2: Writing

1 Write your speech. As you write, you will need to think about making your writing as clear and engaging as possible. You can do this by using:

- an appropriate register (formal, informal or a mixture of both), remembering Standard English
- precise, varied and interesting vocabulary
- a variety of sentence lengths, with a variety of conjunctions
- accurate pronouns to reduce repetition
- accurate sentence punctuation.

Activity 3: Reviewing and revising

1 Read through the speech you have written. As you read, ask yourself:

- Is my speech clear and easy to understand?
- Is it interesting and engaging?

Check that:
- the register you have chosen suits your content
- your vocabulary choices make your writing clear and engaging
- you have used a variety of single-clause and multi-clause sentences
- all your pronouns agree with the nouns they represent
- each sentence begins with a capital letter and ends with a full stop, exclamation mark or question mark.

GLOSSARY

abbreviation - shortened **word** or **phrase** (e.g. Doctor becomes Dr; Susan becomes Sue; telephone becomes phone)

abstract noun - **noun** that names ideas you cannot see, hear, smell, taste or touch (e.g. 'happiness'; 'idea')

account - telling or retelling of factual or fictional events (e.g. an account of the football match, or an account of an adventure)

active voice - form in which the thing that is performing the action of a **verb** is the grammatical **subject** of a **sentence**

adjective - **word** that adds information to a **noun**

adverb - single-word **adverbial**

adverbial - **words** (adverbs), **phrases** or **clauses** that add information to a **verb**, **adjective** or other adverbial

alliteration - use of one sound to begin two or more **words**

analyse - examine carefully, to improve understanding

analysis - careful examination that improves understanding

antonyms - **words** with opposite meanings

argument - explanation of an idea with the purpose of changing or guiding someone's **opinions** and/or actions

argument text - text that presents and explains an idea with the purpose of changing or guiding someone's **opinions** and/or actions

article (text type) - usually factual piece of writing about a given topic (e.g. news / magazine / internet article)

autobiography - **biography** someone writes about their own life

biography - **account** of someone's life

bullet point - the symbol '•', used to organise a vertical **list** by introducing each new item

capital letter - upper-case version of a letter, commonly used at the start of **sentences** and for proper **nouns**

character - fictional person in a **story**, play or film

chronological - in a manner showing the order in which events happen or happened

clause - group of more than one **word**, including a **verb**

cliché - **phrase** or idea that is overused and so has lost its impact

climax (in a story) - moment of greatest **conflict**

comma splice - incorrect use of a comma to link two **main clauses**

comparison - looking at similarities and differences between two or more things

conclusion (of a text) - last part, often a result or summary

concrete noun - **noun** that names a physical thing you can see, hear, smell, taste or touch (e.g. 'cat'; 'tree')

conflict (in a story) - challenge or opposition

conjunction - **word** used to connect **clauses**, or before the final item in a **list**

connotation - connected idea

consonant - letter of the alphabet that is not a **vowel**

context - situation or **setting** for a **word** or event that helps to explain it

contraction - shortened form of two or more **words**, using an apostrophe to show where letters have been missed out

coordinating conjunction - conjunction used to link two **clauses** with equal importance

counter-argument - **argument** against a first argument, presenting an objection and/or opposing views

description / descriptive writing - writing that aims to create a vivid image in the reader's mind

determiner - **word** (such as 'the' and 'a') that begins a **noun** or **noun phrase**, indicating whether the noun names something general or specific, and **plural** or **singular**

diagram - simple picture used to illustrate a point or idea, usually in **non-fiction**

dialogue - speech between people or fictional **characters**

direct address - method of speaking directly to the reader or listener

direct speech - **words** exactly as they are spoken, usually given within **speech marks** and with an **identifier**

embedded quotation - quotation positioned inside a **sentence** and that functions as a part of the sentence

emotive language - **words** and **phrases** that stir readers' emotions

emphasis - forcefulness of expression that suggests importance

evidence - supporting **facts** or information

example - something with characteristics typical of its type

explanation text - text that makes information and ideas clear and easy to understand

exposition (in a story) - early part of a **story** that introduces the situation, **characters** and/or **setting**

extract - short passage taken from a text or other source

fact - true and proveable idea

fiction - imagined idea, often a **story**

figurative language - **words** and **phrases** with meanings different from but related to their usual ones, based on their **connotations** (e.g. **similes** and **metaphors**)

finite verb - **verb** that shows **tense** and **person** (e.g. I saw, he made)

first person - storytelling **viewpoint** where the person doing the action is the writer, **speaker** or **narrator**, using the **pronouns** 'I' and 'me'

flashback - scene that shows events from the past

form (of a text) - shape and **structure**

formal (language) - suitable for an audience that is important, in authority or not known

fronted - positioned at the start of a **sentence**

future - verb tense indicating that actions or events will happen but have not happened yet

heading - main title

homophones - words that sound alike but have different spellings and different meanings

identifier - phrase that tells the reader who is speaking (e.g. 'he said'; 'they shouted')

imperative verb - verb that gives a command or instruction (e.g. 'go'; 'come')

impression - idea or **opinion** (about something or someone)

inference - use of clues to work something out

infinitive - root form of a **verb**, preceded by 'to'

informal (language) - casual; suitable for peers

information text - see **explanation text**

instruction text - text that tells readers how to do something

intention - desired effect

introduction (of a text) - beginning, often establishing **context**

key points - most-important ideas in a text

leaflet - sheet or sheets of paper, sometimes folded, including key information on a topic (often used in advertising)

letter (text type) - written way of communicating with a person or organisation, usually sent using a postal service

line (in a play) - single line of text, or one instance of **words** spoken by a **character**

line (in a poem) - sentence or part of a sentence that finishes at the end of a line

list - sequence of connected items written one after another

main body (of a text) - majority of the writing in a text (as opposed to, for example, an **introduction** and/or **conclusion**)

main clause - clause that makes a main point in a **sentence**, and that could stand alone

metaphor - description of something as though it is something else

modal verb - auxiliary **verb** that expresses possibility or importance

modify (a word) - make small alterations to, by adding to or changing meaning (e.g. with an **adjective** or **adverb**)

multi-clause sentence - sentence composed of more than one **clause**

myth - traditional **story**, often about early history or explaining natural events

narration - description by a **story**'s **narrator**

narrative - account of connected events, often **fiction**

narrator - character who is telling the **story**

non-fiction - factual writing; representing truth

non-finite clause - clause that contains a **non-finite verb**

non-finite verb - verb that does not show **tense**, such as an **infinitive verb** or **present participle**, meaning it does not indicate when something happened

noun - word that names a person, place, object or idea

noun phrase - group of **words** containing a **noun** that name a single person, place, object or ideas

object (of a sentence) - thing that is being acted on by a **verb** or **preposition**

onomatopoeia - technique of using a **word** that sounds like its meaning

opinion - personal ideas that may or may not be based on **facts**

paragraph - group of related **sentences** that develop an idea, presented as a block of text

passive voice - form in which the thing that is being acted on by a **verb** or **preposition** is the grammatical **subject**, rather than **object**, of a **sentence**

past continuous - verb tense indicating that events or actions in the past were still happening when something else happened (e.g. The sun was shining when the elephant came out of the jungle)

past participle - verb form indicating completed events or action (e.g. walked)

past perfect - verb tense indicating events or actions in the past that happened before something else (e.g. Jan looked for Ben but he had already left)

past tense - verb tense indicating that events or actions happened in the past

person (of a verb) - manner in which **verb** forms change depending on the person doing the action

personification - metaphor that uses human qualities to describe something non-human

persuasive text - text designed to change or guide someone's **opinions** and/or actions

phrase - group of more than one **word**, without a **verb**

plural - indicating more than one

poetry - stylised text structured by the **rhythm** of language, often used to express ideas or feelings

point of view - opinion, or manner in which events are experienced

preposition - word that expresses how things are connected, for example by place or time (e.g. 'in'; 'with'; 'before')

prepositional phrase - group of **words** that begins with a **preposition**

present continuous - verb tense indicating that events or actions are happening now (e.g. I am walking)

present participle - verb form indicating continuous events or action (e.g. walking)

present perfect - verb tense indicating that events or actions that happened in the past are still having an effect (e.g. I have left: I left in the past, but am still absent)

present tense - verb tense indicating events or actions that are currently happening

presentational features - features used to organise content visually, such as **headings** and **subheadings**

pronoun - word that replaces or stands in for a **noun** or **noun phrase**

proofread - check writing for errors

prose - written or spoken language in its ordinary form - such as in stories or explanations - as opposed to **poetry**

punctuate - give **punctuation** (to)

punctuation - symbols used to assist and alter meaning (e.g. full stops, question marks, exclamation marks, dashes, commas and apostrophes)

quotation - words taken from a text or speech and repeated

quotation marks - see **speech marks**

reasoning - clear, logical explanation or **argument**

register - tone and style of language (see **formal** and **informal**)

relative clause - clause that adds information to a **noun** or **noun phrase**, beginning with a **relative pronoun**

relative pronoun - word that indicates information related to a **noun** or **noun phrase**

repetition - technique of doing or saying something more than once

reported speech - summary or paraphrasing of speech that is included in a writer's or **narrator**'s description

resolution (in a story) - settling and/or explanation of **conflict**

response - reaction; reply

review - evaluate critically

revise - make changes, or recap learning

rhetorical device - language technique that a writer or speaker uses to present ideas persuasively

rhetorical question - question asked when an answer is not expected

rhyme (noun) - similar sounds at the end of two or more **words** or **lines**

rhythm - beat or pulse

scan - look through (a text) for something specific

scene (of a play) - continuous piece of action within a play, often based in a particular **setting**

script - written text of a play or film

second person - storytelling **viewpoint** where the person doing the action is the reader or listener, using the **pronoun** 'you'

sentence - group of **words** that is complete in itself, including a **verb** and a **subject** (sometimes implied): a statement, question, exclamation or command

sequence (verb) - arrange things in a particular order

setting - location

'silent' letters - letters that are not sounded independently when a **word** is spoken aloudsimile - comparison made by using the **words** 'like' or 'as'

simple past - **verb tense** (see **past tense**)

simple present - **verb tense** (see **present tense**)

single-clause sentence - **sentence** composed of only one **clause**

singular - indicating only one

skim-read / skim - look very quickly (at a text) for an idea of its content

slang - informal **words** or **phrases**, often used amongst friends

speaker (in a poem) - see **narrator**

speech marks - **punctuation** marks indicating **direct speech**

stage direction - instruction to people acting in or producing a play, for example about where to stand or what to do

Standard English - English that is grammatically correct

stanza - group of **lines** in a poem (sometimes referred to as a 'verse')

statistic - **fact** relating to numerical information

story - retelling of events, either real or fictional

structure (noun) - manner in which parts of something are organised, arranged and related

subheading - smaller **heading** that appears below a main title, used to signal different topics within a longer piece of writing

subject (of a sentence) - **noun** that is the focus of a **sentence**, usually representing what or who is doing the action described by the **verb**

subordinate clause - clause that adds information to a **main clause** (for example about cause, effect, time, condition or concession)

subordinating conjunction - conjunction used to link a **subordinate clause** to a **main clause**

summary - brief description of the main points

superlative - adjective that shows the highest level of the quality described (e.g. 'biggest'; 'most hungry')

syllable - part of a **word** that makes a single sound

synonyms - words with the same or very similar meanings

synopsis - see **summary**

tense (of a verb) - manner in which **verb** forms change depending on when the action happens

terminology - technical and/or specialised **vocabulary**

theme - overall subject or idea

third person - storytelling **viewpoint** where the person or thing doing the action is not the writer, speaker or **narrator**, using the **pronouns** 'he', 'him', 'she', 'her', 'it', 'they' and 'them'

topic sentence - sentence that clearly states the topic of a **paragraph**

triple structure - persuasive pattern of three ideas

verb - word that names an action or state of being

viewpoint - perspective when telling a **story**

vocabulary - words used

vowel - A, E, I, O or U (letter of the alphabet that is not a **consonant**)

word - arrangement of letters that has one unit of meaning

word class - group of **words** that have similar roles in **sentences**

Published by Pearson Education Limited, 80 Strand, London, WC2R 0RL.

www.pearsonglobalschools.com

Text © Pearson Education Limited 2020
Designed by Pearson Education Limited 2020
Typeset by SPi Global
Edited by Hannah Hirst-Dunton, Liliane Nénot and Judith Shaw
Original illustrations © Pearson Education Limited 2020
Illustrated by David Belmonte at Beehive Illustrations
Cover design © Pearson Education Limited 2020
With thanks to Stephen Cunningham, Sam Hartburn and
Jenny Roberts

Cover images: *Front*: Getty Images/Natthawat

The right of David Grant to be identified as the author of this
work has been asserted by him in accordance with the
Copyright, Designs and Patents Act 1988.

First published 2020

24
10 9

British Library Cataloguing in Publication Data
A catalogue record for this book is available from the British
Library

ISBN 978 0 435 20071 8

Printed in Slovakia by Neografia

Acknowledgements

All Credits

Non-Prominent Text Credit(s):

28, 30 Immediate Media Company Ltd: Bear Grylls: I don't
want to bring up Rambo, Bear Grylls, 12th May 2014 © Radio
Times / Immediate Media; **36 GUARDIAN NEWS AND MEDIA
LIMITED:** Experience: I fell 70ft into a crevasse, John All,
27 Jul 2018, Copyright Guardian News & Media Ltd 2019; **37,
38 GUARDIAN NEWS AND MEDIA LIMITED:** Experience: I
was trapped in a sewer for 12 hours, Jesse Hernandez, 27
Apr 2018, Copyright Guardian News & Media Ltd 2019; **52,
54 U.S. Department of Homeland Security:** Tsunami - Be
Prepared, FEMA; **56 dmg media limited:** How Ning Nong the
elephant saved me from the tsunami: The incredible bond
between a little girl and baby jumbo that inspired Michael
Morpurgo's 'sequel' to War Horse by OLGA CRAIG, 28 May
2016, © dmg media limited; **74, 76, 77 Walker Books:** © 2015
Helen Wang Original text © 2015 Cao Wenxuan BRONZE AND
SUNFLOWER by Cao Wenxuan Published by arrangement with
Phoenix Juvenile and Children's Publishing Ltd, Reproduced by
permission of Walker Books Ltd, London SE11 5HJ www.walker.
co.uk; **82, 84 David Fickling Books:** The Wrong Train by Jeremy
De Quidt, © 2016, David Fickling Books. Reproduced by the
permission of David Fickling Books; **90 Penguin Random House:**
Excerpt(s) from THE NIGHT DIARY by Veera Hiranandani,
copyright © 2018 by Veera Hiranandani. Used by permission
of Dial Books for Young Readers, an imprint of Penguin Young
Readers Group, a division of Penguin Random House LLC.
All rights reserved. **106, 107 Macmillan Publishers:** From THE
GREEN BOOK © 1982 by Jill Paton Walsh, illustrated by Lloyd
Bloom. Reprinted by permission of Farrar, Straus and Giroux
Books for Young Readers. All Rights Reserved; **110 Guardian
News & Media Limited:** Mike Carter, Like nothing else on Earth,
© 2001, Copyright Guardian News & Media Ltd 2019; **152, 153
Elizabeth Jennings:** Friends by Elizabeth Jennings, Reprinted by
permission of David Higham Associates Ltd. All Rights Reserved;
142, 154, 156, 157 Francesca Beard: Grrr by Francesca Beard,
Reproduced with the permission of Francesca Beard; **162, 163
Vernon Scannell:** Nettles by Vernon Scannell, © 1980; **166, 170
Andrew Peters:** Mum by Andrew Peters Reproduced with the
permission of Andrew Fusek Peters; **170 Andrew Peters:** Dad by
Andrew Peters Reproduced with the permission of Andrew Fusek
Peters; **178 Lulu Press, Inc:** Eugene Doyen, A Visit to My Father,
© Lulu.com; **182, 183, 185 Pavilion Books:** Cool Kids Cook by
Jenny Chandler, © 2016, Pavilion Books; **200, 201, 202 Express
Newspapers:** Rob Crosson, Fussy eaters? Here's how to change
your children's eating habits, © Express Newspapers; **220, 222
European Space Agency:** First Rockets + How does a rocket
work, © 2011 European Space Agency; **GUARDIAN NEWS AND
MEDIA LIMITED:** Why I Love… Insects by Dr George McGavin,
26 september, 2014, Copyright Guardian News & Media Ltd 2019;
242, 243 What On Earth Publishing Ltd: Christopher Lloyd,
What on Earth Happened? … In Brief: The Planet, Life and
People from the Big Bang to the Present Day, © 2009, What On
Earth Publishing Ltd

Prominent Image Credit(s):
Cov: Natthawat/Getty Images

Non-Prominent Image Credit(s):
(key: b-bottom; c-centre; l-left; r-right; t-top)

123RF GB LIMITED: Andreykuzmin/123RF 044, Dmytro
Zinkevych/123RF 200tl, Foodandmore/123RF 208, Hemant
Mehta/123RF 204b, Belchonock/123RF 196b, Solarseven/123RF

220t, Samards/123RF 228b, Kostic Dusan/123RF 239r, Corey A Ford/123RF 242b, 245t, Ales Utouka/123RF 092, Victoria Shibut/123RF 176; **SHUTTERSTOCK:** Michael Rosskothen/Shutterstock 26, Sandro Pavlov/Shutterstock 102, John A Davis/Shutterstock 110, Andrey_l/Shutterstock 116, Enik/Shutterstock 117, Muratart/Shutterstock 111, Simia Attentive/Shutterstock 160, Yulia Davidovich/Shutterstock 196t, Africa Studio/Shutterstock 182, 205l, Blue Planet Earth/Shutterstock 186, Larisa Blinova/Shutterstock 188, Someone who cares/Shutterstock 191, Tazzymoto/Shutterstock 194, Morphart Creation/Shutterstock 198, Shutterstock 199b, ESB Professional/Shutterstock 200bl, Olga Miltsova/Shutterstock 200cr, Margouillat photo/Shutterstock 210, HAKINMHAN/Shutterstock 189, Ekaterina Markelova/Shutterstock 203, 199t, 205r, Liv friis-larsen/Shutterstock 213, 3Dsculptor/Shutterstock 220b, Brina L. Bunt/Shutterstock 231, Jesada Sabai/Shutterstock 246l, Egor Rodynchenko/Shutterstock 246r, Pit Stock/Shutterstock 236, BiterBig/Shutterstock 221, Andrey_Popov/Shutterstock 226, Gallimaufry/Shutterstock 228t, Pic4joy/Shutterstock 233,

258t, Taner Muhlis Karaguzel/Shutterstock 237, REDPIXEL.PL/Shutterstock 239l, 257, Salparadis/Shutterstock 240t, Apiguide/Shutterstock 240b, Mark Brandon/Shutterstock 242t, 258b, CHAINFOTO24/Shutterstock 243, Sam Brannan/Shutterstock 245b, Stihii/Shutterstock 248, Sedova Elena/Shutterstock 249, Spatuletail/Shutterstock 252t, 258c, Everett Historical/Shutterstock 252b, Everst/Shutterstock 8, Willyam Bradberry/Shutterstock 50, A3pfamily/Shutterstock 134, SpeedKingz/Shutterstock 218, vkilikov/Shutterstock 223r, 255, RemarkEliza/Shutterstock 255c, Roberto Castillo/Shutterstock 255r, Microgen/Shutterstock 256r, Dotted Yeti/Shutterstock 244, Andresr/Shutterstock 204t.

Kurhan/Shutterstock

iadams/Shutterstock

sirtravelalot/Shutterstock

WoodysPhotos/Shutterstock